GAY MARRIAGE
THE STORY OF A CANADIAN SOCIAL REVOLUTION

GAY MARRIAGE

THE STORY OF A CANADIAN SOCIAL REVOLUTION

SYLVAIN LAROCQUE

TRANSLATED BY ROBERT CHODOS, LOUISA BLAIR, AND
BENJAMIN WATERHOUSE

JAMES LORIMER & COMPANY LTD., PUBLISHERS
TORONTO

James Lorimer & Company Ltd. acknowledges the support of the Ontario Arts Council. We acknowledge the support of the Government of Canada through the Book Publishing Industry Development Program (BPIDP) for our publishing activities. We acknowledge the support of the Canada Council for the Arts for our publishing program.

Cover design: **Meghan Collins**

Archives and Library Canada Cataloguing in Publication

Larocque, Sylvain

    Gay marriage : the story of a Canadian social revolution / Sylvain Larocque; translated by Robert Chodos, Louisa Blair and Benjamin Waterhouse.

Translation of: Mariage gai.

Includes bibliographical references and index.

ISBN10 1-55028-927-6; ISBN13 978-1-55028-927-5

    1. Same-sex marriage--Canada. I. Chodos, Robert, 1947-
II. Blair, Louisa III. Benjamin Waterhouse IV. Title.

HQ1034.C3L3713 2006   306.84'8'0971   C2006-900037-9

Thanks to The Canadian Press for graciously allowing the reproduction of their photographs. Photographers: Ian Barrett (36), Aaron Harris (121), Jonathan Hayward (146, 180, 250)

James Lorimer & Company Ltd.,Publishers
317 Adelaide St. West
Suite 1002
Toronto, Ontario
M5V 1P9
www.lorimer.ca

Printed and bound in Canada.

CONTENTS

Acknowledgements

This book would not have been possible without Dominique's inexhaustible patience, my parents' unconditional support, my brother's ongoing encouragement, my editor's invaluable confidence, my colleagues' kind understanding and the generous cooperation of the participants in this struggle.

In addition to these personal acknowledgements, I would like to pay tribute to all the pioneers who have made it possible for young gays and lesbians to live freer lives.

FOREWORD

When Sylvain Larocque asked me to write a foreword to his book, I first wanted to explore the nature and scope of the project. Since the author was a correspondent on Parliament Hill in Ottawa while I was Minister of Justice and Attorney General of Canada, I knew he had a good knowledge of the issue of same-sex marriage. In fact, from our first meeting, I quickly realized that he had not only extensive knowledge of the issue but also a good understanding of the challenges surrounding it.

His understanding of the issues, combined with the accounts of those involved in the discussions, results in a dynamic and interesting retrospective that allows the reader to understand the foundations of real social debate. It also illustrates the roadblocks those in power face when they seek to assume leadership roles on important social issues. The author highlights the role played by all the stakeholders involved in this debate, particularly by gays and lesbians across the country. In their quest for equality, they managed to set Canada on the path that ultimately led to the recognition of same-sex marriage.

Since the Canadian Charter of Rights and Freedoms was introduced in 1982, it has become one of the cornerstones of our society. Its special character is in part a product of the decision, at the outset, to entrench it in the constitution and elevate it to the status of a fundamental law of our democracy. But its significance goes far beyond its legal status. The Charter also has broad support among Canadians, largely because it embodies many of the fundamental values of our society.

In interpreting the Charter, Canadian courts have helped build a society that is seen as an international leader in human rights. There has been extensive commentary on the role that judges have played — some have even referred to it as "judicial activism." I have always profoundly disagreed with this concept. Furthermore, I do not believe that it could ever be applied to the question of same-sex marriage.

When the government decided in June 2003 that it would not appeal the judgment of the Ontario Court of Appeal, the decision took into account the role of the judiciary, the executive and the legislative power and how they should interact. Our position supported a clear social policy aimed at accepting same-sex marriage and invited Canadians to debate a fundamental question for our society. At the same time, the Supreme Court of Canada was called on to express its opinion — not on our social policy, but on whether that policy was consistent with the Charter. The government's position was, of course, inspired by my own convictions, as I was in favour of the modification of the definition of marriage. I have always believed that the principles of our Charter need to exist on more than just paper. Furthermore, I believe that the more generous and inclusive the institution of marriage is, the more representative of our current society it will be, and the more likely it is to find its place again as a fundamental institution.

Throughout his work, Sylvain Larocque explains, analyzes and teaches and, in effect, contributes to an important debate that will eventually lead one day to true equality — that is, a legal and legislative victory combined with full social acceptance.

Hon. Martin Cauchon
Special Partner
Gowling Lafleur Henderson LLP

INTRODUCTION

Ripe fruit falls by itself,
but it doesn't fall in your mouth.
— *Chinese proverb*

Despite what people might think, same-sex marriage is not a new subject — at least not entirely. In 1968, in the very first televised leaders'
debate in a Canadian federal election campaign, legendary Social
Credit leader Réal Caouette expressed concern at the possibility that
two people of the same sex might be able to get married.

"A man, a mature man, could in the future marry another mature
man," he said, provoking titters in the audience and a smile from the
Liberal leader, Pierre Elliott Trudeau. "This would create problems for
the government for the maintenance of the children born of these
groups."

It was a surprising statement, especially since Caouette made it in
response to a simple question: would the Social Credit leader support
Trudeau's omnibus bill decriminalizing homosexuality? The answer, of
course, was a categorical no.

The event that precipitated Trudeau's famous bill was the arrest in
1965 of George Klippert, a mechanic in the Northwest Territories who
was charged with gross indecency after he admitted to having slept
with four men. Klippert's arrest attracted considerable attention in the

media. In 1967 the Supreme Court of Canada confirmed that he could be held in prison indefinitely, and he would not be released until July 1971, two years after Trudeau's legislation came into force.

In the late 1960s, the persecution of gays was accepted by many Canadians and strongly desired by some. The most tolerant politicians of the era, such as New Democratic Party leader Tommy Douglas (who has since become one of English Canada's heroes), demonstrated their "compassion" by saying that homosexuals suffered from a mental illness and needed to be treated with psychiatry rather than prison.

* * * * *

Throughout Canada, gays and lesbians are still pariahs in some circles. But dramatic progress has been made in recognizing their rights over the last 30 years, and especially in the last decade. Scores of pioneers have come out of the closet and gone to court to fight courageously for a whole range of rights, from the most elementary to the most controversial. On behalf of all gays and lesbians, they have succeed in obtaining a degree of respect, first from governments and then from the private sector as well. Many of these victories have led to financial gains for gays and lesbians, but what they sought above all was social recognition.

At the turn of the twenty-first century, gays and lesbians had won, at least on paper, most of the rights that governments could give them. There was only one last holdout, but it was a formidable one: marriage, the age-old institution that many people believe constitutes the very foundation of humanity. It was the ambition of some same-sex couples to claim access to this institution. What an outrageous idea! The gay and lesbian community itself was divided on whether it was appropriate to make such a demand. But it was a dream that some had entertained for a long time.

Same-sex marriage became the subject of a vigorous debate. The passions unleashed by this issue are all the more striking when contrasted with the near-silence that greeted the extension of adoption rights to same-sex couples and the amendment of rules of filiation to include them. Because Ottawa has no jurisdiction over adoption and filiation, these changes occurred on a province-by-province basis, which probably explains why they took place so quietly. It is worth noting, however, that the concrete ramifications of adoption and filiation are much more significant than those of marriage, although the symbolic importance of marriage cannot be denied.

The intense struggle that gays and lesbians waged for equality in the area of marriage — which, like previous struggles for equality, began in the courts and then ended up in the political arena — is the subject of this book. Some 30 interviews with partisans of both sides in the debate have contributed to its findings. My intention is not to make a case for same-sex marriage. Rather, this is a narrative written by a journalist who was caught in the crossfire of this social revolution. It recounts the development over time of the arguments of both supporters and opponents of same-sex marriage, as well as the tactics used by both sides. My modest hope for this book is that it will contain some inspiration for the activists who will undertake major political campaigns in the future and thus help quicken the pace of change.

1

BLAZING THE TRAIL

Fifty friends and relatives had been invited. The ceremony was to be solemn but relaxed. In spite of the couple's nerves, the unmistakable joy of the occasion made everyone forget that this was an unusual event. No one had rented tails, the church hadn't been decorated, but people read romantic poems and music was played.

"The minister didn't pronounce us man and wife, but as long as love should last," recalled Chris Vogel, a retired civil servant. "We certainly discovered personally the things which are important to other couples: the celebration, the announcement to one's family and friends that one's life has changed significantly, the importance of the other person, the collective participation in the commitment. We observed all those things as we went through the process."

In keeping with the requirements of Manitoba legislation, the marriage was celebrated using the traditional publication of banns. For three Sundays in a row the minister of the Winnipeg Unitarian Church proclaimed the banns to his congregation, and no one opposed the impending union of Richard North and Chris Vogel. In theory, obtaining a marriage licence from the appropriate provincial body, the Vital Statistics Agency, should have been clear sailing.

But the state was not yet ready to sanction their love. After all, this wedding took place on February 11, 1974. When Chris and Rich presented themselves before the Registrar of Marriages, he took one look at them and said, "This is a joke, right?" The two lovebirds replied that they had never been more serious in their lives, but the employee did-n't want to hear any more about it. A few days later they were sent a letter confirming this rejection.

Unwilling to take no for an answer, the couple took the Vital Statistics Agency to court. In Manitoba, as generally in Canada at this time, the laws did not specify that marriages must take place between partners of different sexes. At most they specified that both parties must be consenting. It was simply taken for granted that marriage was a heterosexual affair. It was much later, when gays and lesbians began successfully to assert their civil rights in the early 1980s, that governments finally began to specify in writing that spouses must be of different sexes. In Quebec this occurred in 1994 when the Civil Code of Lower Canada was updated and renamed the Civil Code of Quebec. Until 1994 the Civil Code simply stated that "there can be no marriage without consent." Vogel recalled,

> Our main task at the time was to be able to engender public discussion. This was a topic which people wouldn't talk about. You couldn't say the word *homosexual* without choking. There were very few things that we could do that would attract publicity; the only things that achieved publicity were crimes — you know, murders, rapes and so on — and we needed some positive attention. Marriage was very easily understood. Marriage spoke directly to the issue of homosexual relationships. You didn't have to explain marriage.

Unfortunately for Chris and Rich, the Manitoba tribunal rejected their application after contemplating it for several weeks. Basing their judgment on dictionary definitions and on English law, especially the famous *Hyde* v. *Hyde* judgment by Lord Penzance in 1866 (which dealt with polygamy),[1] the judge concluded that their marriage was invalid and that they could not therefore be registered. Vogel said,

> We realized we had more work to do. Although by that time

we had been dealing with politicians on the matter of the Human Rights Act, we discovered that marriage was the last thing that many of them were prepared to do. Even the sympathetic ones — they were prepared to support us in other things, but not in marriage. Marriage was clearly going to be the last thing that we would be successful in achieving and that turned out to be so. It was too fundamental an institution to the social order, it seems.

Gay and lesbian lobby groups were few and far between in Canada at the time, and none of them were demanding the right to get married. "They felt that marriage was an archaic institution that ought to be destroyed," said Vogel. "They would assume that anyone who got married would behave in a way that hetero couples traditionally behaved — but that, of course, was a foolish assumption."

Other than a couple who held an informal ceremony in a Montreal nightclub in the early 1970s, Chris and Rich were the first same-sex couple to marry in Canada. It was clearly a failure in terms of the law, but not in terms of their love. Nearly 32 years later, the two men still live for each other. They have no children and have a sexually open relationship, but their union is more permanent and meaningful than many heterosexual unions. It appeared they had managed to adapt an ancient institution to their own situation, while keeping the essentials intact: love and mutual support. The state, however, would take a while to recognize this.

Chris and Rich were following in the footsteps of several American same-sex couples who had attempted to get married some years earlier, beginning with Jack Baker and James McConnell in Minnesota in 1971. The movement continued throughout the 1970s. On January 7, 1975, a civil servant from Phoenix, Arizona, granted a marriage licence to two men after realizing that there was nothing in the law that prevented it. The state quickly passed a law restricting marriage to heterosexual couples, and the Supreme Court annulled the marriages. But in March that year, in Boulder, Colorado, a young clerk named Clela Rorex registered five marriages between same-sex couples. The state attorney general declared the unions invalid and forbade any more such homosexual marriages. However, none of the marriages already celebrated were invalidated by the courts and consequently some of these couples are still together to this day, for better or for worse.

* * * * *

With hindsight, it seems that Chris and Rich took the plunge a decade too early. In 1974, the Canadian Charter of Rights and Freedoms was still just a dream. A Canadian Bill of Rights had been adopted in 1960, but as it was not entrenched in the constitution, it had rarely proved to be worth the paper it was written on.

Still, the Winnipeg couple inspired many future advocates of equal rights for gays and lesbians. The first step, taken by the federal government in 1969, had been to decriminalize homosexuality between consenting adults. With its Charter of Human Rights and Freedoms, adopted in 1977, Quebec became the first Canadian province, and one of the first governments in the world, to prohibit discrimination on the basis of sexual orientation. This was a foot in the door, a door that would never close again. By the late 1990s, all the provinces had made discrimination on the grounds of sexual orientation illegal.

It is worth taking a minute to recall the sociopolitical atmosphere of the era. Homosexuality was so taboo that use of the word was an insult in itself. Homophobia, still prevalent in some circles today, was broadly accepted in Canada until the late 1980s. During the federal Liberal leadership campaign in 1968, for example, a political opponent distributed pamphlets accusing Pierre Trudeau of being a homosexual. "Back then, people said the word *homosexual* the way they say *pedophile* today," recalled one observer. "It was a very damaging word." Similar allegations were directed against Sheila Copps in 1982 when she ran for the leadership of the Ontario Liberal Party.

Until the 1980s, in Ottawa, any senior civil servant had to submit to a security check to determine, among other things, if he or she was homosexual. If the answer was yes, the Privy Council Office could advise the minister responsible against hiring the candidate. In the

1950s and 1960s, the Royal Canadian Mounted Police conducted what amounted to a witch-hunt of gays and lesbians in the federal civil service. At least 3,000 files were kept on "suspicious" employees. Many were forced to resign or else simply fired. The Cold War was at its peak and the government feared that homosexuals, especially those in the foreign service, would be vulnerable to blackmail at the hands of the Soviets. Under the influence of McCarthyism in the United States, Canada considered gays and lesbians a threat to national security. The RCMP even developed a curious device called a "fruit machine." It looked like a dentist's chair and was used to measure the dilation of a subject's pupils when presented with pictures of naked men and women. The exercise was eventually declared futile, especially since so few civil servants were willing to undergo the test, and the fruit machine was abandoned in the late 1960s. An American version can still be seen at the War Museum in Ottawa.

Even Trudeau, who decriminalized homosexuality, seemed to hang on to prejudices regarding gays towards the end of his career. In 1981, he said to one MP he was elevating to the cabinet, "Look, if you're homosexual it's none of my business, but if you ever get caught with little boys in a park, I won't be able to stand up for you." Was Trudeau identifying homosexuals with pedophiles, as some people still do today?

Ironically, it was Trudeau who undertook to repatriate the constitution, with the addition of the Charter of Rights and Freedoms, in the early 1980s. It was the Charter that later played a key role in the expansion of homosexual rights in Canada. But things would have progressed even faster if the government had agreed to include sexual orientation in the section that protected the equality of all citizens, as gay activists were demanding at the time. NDP MP Svend Robinson[2] and his Liberal colleague Serge Joyal both tried to convince the then minister of justice, Jean Chrétien, but to no avail.

The Charter was formally enacted in April 1982, but section 15 containing the equality provisions did not take effect until 1985. Although it prohibited all "discrimination," sexual orientation was not mentioned explicitly, unlike discrimination based on race, national or ethnic origin, colour, religion, sex, age and mental or physical disability.

This situation changed in 1995 when the Supreme Court of Canada recognized that sexual orientation, "a deeply personal characteristic," fell "within the ambit of section 15." This was a clear victory for the gay and lesbian community. It confirmed a similar judgment by the Ontario Court of Appeal in 1992 and established a basis for all cases of discrimination based on sexual orientation. "It was an important victory, because it established several principles that have really helped the cause of gays and lesbians ever since," said Cynthia Petersen, one of the lawyers who worked on the case.

In the short term, however, the Supreme Court decision was a defeat. Appellants James Egan and John Norris Nesbit, a couple since 1948, had challenged the exclusion of homosexuals from the definition of the word *spouse* in the Old Age Security Act. The judges who delivered the majority decision justified this discrimination on the grounds that few homosexual couples raise children. In their eyes, it was a reasonable restriction in a free and democratic society.

Undaunted by this reversal, and spurred on by the legal recognition that sexual orientation could be a basis for discrimination, dozens of gays and lesbians continued to challenge numerous provincial and federal statutes before the courts. After years of defeat, in the early 1990s the successes began to accumulate, especially concerning homosexual rights in health care, employment and pension schemes. For gay and lesbian activists who had been struggling since the 1960s, it was none too soon.

In January 1992, Todd Layland and Pierre Beaulne calculated that the time was ripe to claim the right to marry. But in a 1993 judgment, the Ontario Divisional Court put a damper on their hopes by invoking religious arguments — for example, the argument that the central objective of marriage is procreation. "I find that under the common law of Canada applicable to Ontario a valid marriage can take place only between a man and a woman," declared Justice James Southey, "and that persons of the same sex do not have the capacity to marry one another."

After this judgment, Layland and Beaulne separated, but another couple and several activists tried to pick up the pieces and start again. Hopes were raised by the *Egan* case, in which the Supreme Court confirmed that discrimination based on sexual orientation was against the law. Petersen, who was working for the Canada-wide gay rights organization Egale (Equality for Gays and Lesbians Everywhere), recalled,

> We knew that something had been gained with *Egan*, but we thought it would be better to celebrate other victories before pushing any further on the marriage idea. Everyone thought it was a good idea to demand the right to marry, but not in 1996, because we hadn't yet established enough legal precedents. I was afraid not just that we would lose — if that happened we could always try again ten years later — but that we were establishing a negative precedent for other minority groups demanding equal rights.

With the couple's consent, the lawyers eventually abandoned the challenge. But new opportunities arose faster than many expected. In 1999, less than four years after the *Egan* case, gay and lesbian rights were given a major boost by the Supreme Court of Canada, to which several new judges had been appointed. This advance was to lead directly to the expansion of the definition of marriage to include same-sex couples.

The breakthrough was a consequence of a sad situation, however. After living together for ten years, M. and H., a lesbian couple, separated. M. left the conjugal home and applied for partition and sale. Then she sued for alimony, in keeping with the Ontario Family Law Act. To do so, she had to contest the definition of the word *spouse* in the law. Her former partner opposed this, as did the government of Ontario when the case went to appeal.

The highest court in the country, in an 8-1 decision rendered in May 1999, showed a remarkably open spirit towards gay and lesbian marriages. Four years earlier, in *Egan*, judges had concluded that the "ultimate raison d'être" of marriage "transcends all of these and is firmly anchored in the biological and social realities that heterosexual couples have the unique ability to procreate." By extension, the state was

justified in according financial and other privileges only to heterosexual partners. The subject of the litigation in the 1999 case was not the
same as in *Egan*, and therefore the two are not directly comparable.
Nevertheless, the difference in the Supreme Court's tone is striking:

> The exclusion of same-sex partners from the benefits of s. 29
> promotes the view that M., and individuals in same-sex rela-
> tionships generally, are less worthy of recognition and protec-
> tion. It implies that they are judged to be incapable of forming
> intimate relationships of economic interdependence as com-
> pared to opposite-sex couples, without regard to their actual
> circumstances. Such exclusion perpetuates the disadvantages
> suffered by individuals in same-sex relationships and con-
> tributes to the erasure of their existence.

The high court gave the government six months to amend its Family
Law Act to include same-sex couples. The judgment did not target the
federal government and the other provinces, but legislators quickly
grasped that they would do well to modernize their own laws if they
did not want to be dragged before the Supreme Court themselves.

With the *M.* v. *H.* decision, the Supreme Court gave the first concrete
demonstration of a new attitude to homosexual rights. The prohibition
of discrimination on the grounds of sexual orientation no longer
aimed just to protect gays and lesbians themselves, but also their relationships as couples. Until then, Ottawa had always argued that protection of sexual orientation applied only to individuals.

M.'s lawyer, Martha McCarthy, later swore that she didn't take on the
case with the intention of opening up the same-sex marriage option.
The goal was to obtain recognition not only of the rights but, more
importantly, of the obligations of same-sex common-law relationships.
When *M.* v. *H.* came before the courts in the early 1990s, some gay and
lesbian activists were indignant that lawyers were demanding obligations rather than rights. But this was exactly the secret of the success of
this venture: if obligations were imposed on homosexual couples,
rights were sure to follow.

McCarthy said with a smile,

> Throughout the case, for the whole eight years, we would say
> to the media, and to every judge, "This case has nothing to do
> with marriage. This case is about people who aren't married
> and were not asking to engage in mariage." The irony, of
> course, is that the moment the judgment was rendered, we
> thought that the call for equal marriage couldn't be distin-
> guished from *M. v. H.*, which was true. But I didn't write the
> Supreme Court of Canada judgment, you know.

Egale lawyer Cynthia Petersen commented,

> It was also a question of strategy, because it could have been
> dangerous to ask the courts to sanction the right to marriage
> before establishing the rights of same-sex couples. Saying yes
> to marriage would have also been expensive, because it would
> have led to other financial and administrative rights along the
> same lines. The courts would have resisted not just because it
> was a controversial question, but because it was complicated.
> Once most of the other rights were acquired, though, we could
> say to the courts, "We're nearly at the point where spouses of
> the same sex are treated like heterosexuals. All that's left is the
> right to marry."

As far as Petersen and many other gay activists were concerned, all of
the victories of the 1990s were important because they had a real
impact on the life of gays and lesbians: adoption and child custody
(from 1995 in Ontario), workplace rights and others. But the *M. v. H.*
victory in the highest court of the land was a major turning point. It
confirmed that discrimination based on sexual orientation was against
the law and that denying rights and obligations to gay and lesbian couples was against the Charter and unacceptable in a free and democratic society. The way had been cleared to bring up the marriage question.
According to McCarthy,

Unintentionally, it [*M. v. H.*] had became *the* gay rights case in a century of Canadian legal history. It had huge international influence. It was part of a continuum, but it was the big domino that knocked all the other ones down. However, up until the end, we were terrified we would lose it.

* * * * *

In Ottawa, the official opposition quickly figured out that the Supreme Court decision could eventually have an impact on the "traditional" definition of marriage. Less than a month after the judgment, Reform Party MP Eric Lowther moved in the House of Commons that "in the opinion of this House, it is necessary, in light of public debate around recent court decisions, to state that marriage is and should remain the union of one man and one woman to the exclusion of all others, and that Parliament will take all necessary steps to preserve this definition of marriage in Canada." The Calgary MP told reporters that "before the courts tell us what marriage means, we thought it would be prudent to take a leadership role and make it clear to the courts and represent Canadians first. It's a preemptive approach rather than a reactive approach to court rulings."

Government MPs rarely support opposition motions, but on a subject as delicate as the institution of marriage most Liberals felt they had no choice. "The definition of marriage is already clear in law," Justice Minister Anne McLellan said during the debate. "This government has no intention of changing the definition of marriage or legislating same-sex marriage." In March 1998, however, delegates at the Liberal Party biennial convention adopted (by two-thirds) a resolution demanding that Ottawa "recognize same-sex marriages in the allocation of benefits" — yet more evidence that party leaders rarely listen to their own members. A similar resolution was defeated two years later.

McLellan and Lowther denied that excluding gays and lesbians from marriage jeopardized their right to equality. "Under the law, all Canadians are equal," said Lowther. "But the law in Canada says that marriage is a union of a man and a woman. That is supported by tradition and it is supported so far by the courts."

The motion passed easily: 216 in favour, 55 against. Among the early supporters of equal marriage were Bloc Québécois leader Gilles Duceppe, NDP leader Alexa McDonough and many members of their caucuses. The handful of Liberal MPs who opposed the motion included Colleen Beaumier, Mauril Bélanger, Carolyn Bennett and Bill Graham — three of whom later became cabinet ministers.

As is often the case, MPs' conservatism was out of step with public opinion. An Angus Reid poll a few days before the Reform motion was adopted showed that 53 percent of Canadians agreed with homosexuals having the right to marry. Majorities in the three largest provinces were in favour: 61 percent in Quebec, 54 percent in British Columbia and 53 percent in Ontario. Albertans were more hesitant: only 43 percent were in favour and 56 percent against; in the eastern prairies 42 percent were in favour and 53 percent against. In the Maritimes feelings were mixed (48 percent in favour, 53 percent against), according to the survey conducted for the Toronto *Globe and Mail* and CTV.

A parliamentary motion is not binding on the courts, however, and cannot be invoked during legal proceedings. Thus, despite the justice minister's words in 1999, Parliament had never legislated a definition. In late 1990, a law had been passed on the "prohibited degrees" of marriage, but it simply forbade unions between people with close blood ties or ties of adoption. It said nothing about couples of the same sex.

In October 1997, Liberal MP Tom Wappel undertook to correct this omission. His private member's bill declared marriage null and void "unless it is a legal union of one man and one woman as husband and wife and neither the man nor the woman was married immediately prior to that union." Like many backbench bills, this one went nowhere. But in March 1998, NDP MP Svend Robinson struck back with his own bill, which stated that "a marriage between two persons is not invalid by reason only that they are of the same sex." The bill made no more headway than Wappel's. Robinson introduced his bill three more times (October 2000, February 14, 2001, and February 2003), each time in vain. His adversaries responded in kind. Thus, in March 2000 and again in February 2001, Reform MP Jim Pankiw introduced a bill that would have used the notwithstanding clause in the Charter to protect the traditional definition of marriage from section 15, the equality rights clause. Also in March 2000, Liberal Steve Mahoney introduced a bill very similar to Tom Wappel's 1997 bill, and Senator Anne Cools tried again in January 2001.

For years, the federal government had been closely following every court decision with regard to gays and lesbians. In fact, according rights to homosexual couples had been under consideration ever since the *Egan* judgment. Sheila Copps, who was chair of Cabinet's Social Development Committee from 1993 to 1997, remembers examining proposals aimed at giving a kind of legitimacy to same-sex unions. At the time, the federal justice department was toying with the idea of allowing a registry of "domestic partnerships" open to homosexual couples and to two members of the same family living together for the purposes of mutual assistance. The idea was similar to the Pacte Civil de Solidarité (PaCS) established in France in 1999. Although PaCS represented progress of a kind, it still did not satisfy the aspirations of the French gay community, particularly since it does not apply exclusively to people living in conjugal relationships. In principle, even two ordinary roommates could "get pacsed" in France, even though in practice this is rare.

In June 1989, Denmark became the first country to implement the idea of a "registered partnership." This civil union gave same-sex couples all the same rights as marriage, except that of adoption. A person could, however, adopt the child of their "registered partner." Many countries followed suit with some version of this idea: Norway (1993), Sweden (1995), Greenland (1996), Hungary (1996), Iceland (1996), the Netherlands (1998), France (1999), Belgium (2000), Germany (2001), Portugal (2001), Finland (2002), Lichtenstein (2002), Croatia (2003), Luxembourg (2004), New Zealand (2005) and Britain (2005). State or regional governments in Argentina, Australia, Brazil, Spain, the United States, Italy and Switzerland also followed, while civil union legislation was under consideration at a national level in some of these and other countries.

No one in Ottawa dared admit it publicly, but the government was looking closely at "registered partnership" laws if only to forestall claims by gays and lesbians to full access to marriage. "Early on, we said to each other that if we could solve this problem [homosexual claims] by proposing a registered partnerships bill, we wouldn't have to touch the question of same-sex marriage," said Copps. The strategy made sense: in many of the countries where registered partnerships or civil unions were now legal, the population had immediately lumped these unions with marriage, even though they were sometimes far from it. So why risk talking about "real" marriage when they could make do with an ersatz version that caused less controversy?

It must be remembered that until about 1995, the official position of the Canadian government had been to refuse to openly recognize same-sex partners. When a motion on the subject was introduced in the House of Commons by Bloc Québécois MP Réal Ménard, all the ministers made themselves scarce except Sheila Copps. Only some 50 out of 295 MPs voted in favour.

Civil servants and federal politicians continued to reflect on various partnership bills until 2002, but nothing came of these efforts. Finally they concluded that family law — including registered same-sex partnerships or civil unions — was largely a provincial responsibility. Practically the only federal responsibility was the actual definition of marriage. Even the celebration of the marriage was a provincial domain. Although it could not enact registered partnerships, Ottawa was forced to react to *M. v. H.* in 1999. It was already lagging behind numerous private corporations whose pension schemes contained clauses relating to same-sex couples, often as a result of pressure from unions.

In 1997, the NDP-dominated British Columbia legislature had easily passed bills conferring various rights and obligations on same-sex couples, including those related to alimony and pension schemes. Quebec's Parti Québécois government raised the stakes in 1999 when it introduced Bill 32, which gave gays and lesbians the same benefits as common-law heterosexual couples. The National Assembly passed the bill unanimously. The B.C. government followed suit in July of that year.

Ottawa's hesitation can perhaps be traced to the resounding failure of the Ontario NDP government's attempt to expand the rights of same-sex couples in 1994. Bill 167 was defeated by nine votes, largely thanks to an about-face by Liberal leader Lyn McLeod, who gave her support to the bill and then promptly withdrew it. When the votes were made public, gay and lesbian activists virulently denounced McLeod, prompting security guards, some of them wearing rubber gloves, to expel them unceremoniously from Queen's Park.

* * * * *

The tide was quietly turning. In 1998, Ottawa decided not to appeal the *Rosenberg* judgment, in which the Ontario Court of Appeal struck down the definition of "spouse" in an article of the Income Tax Act relating to private pension schemes. Thousands of gays and lesbians could now benefit from surviving spouses' pensions.

In terms of legislation, the goal was to simply extend Canadian pension benefits to gays and lesbians, as the *Rosenberg* case had raised a related issue. But the ministers in the cabinet's Social Development Committee soon felt they needed to go further than this. Sheila Copps said,

> At the time, our thinking was that if it worked for pensions, it should also work for other fiscal instruments. Either you're for gay rights, or you're against. We discussed the fact that there were people who were dying whose partners could not enter the hospital room because the family wouldn't allow it. That wasn't right. We therefore decided that if we could make progress on equality in pensions, we should broaden the discussion to include all areas of the Canadian government's financial responsibilities. Politically, if we could assure the House and the caucus that we weren't touching marriage, we could easily move ahead.

Such a decision was evidently going to imply some costs for the federal government, but these were minimal — between $3 and $12 million a year in lost tax revenues — relative to the budget as a whole for these programs. The Finance Department, which has life-and-death power over any proposed changes in Ottawa, gave the green light without too much fuss. Prime Minister Jean Chrétien and Finance Minister Paul Martin were evidently quickly persuaded that the matter should go forward.

In fact, initial authorization came in January 1999, five months before the Supreme Court judgment in *M. v. H.* Meanwhile the Foundation for Equal Families had just launched a lawsuit forcing Ottawa to adapt 58 federal acts to the needs of same-sex spouses. Worried that it might lose the *M. v. H.* battle, the government suddenly decided to make the first move. Gay activists hoped the reactions would not be too negative: a few weeks earlier Immigration Minister Lucienne Robillard had authorized the joint immigration of same-sex partners without this causing too much uproar. "The government has to deal with this [the rights of same-sex couples] sooner or later," a government source told the *Globe and Mail.* "It's unavoidable."

Sure enough, ministers opposed to what would become the Modernization of Benefits and Obligations Act (Bill C-23) did not seriously rock the boat, even in the more intimate atmosphere of cabinet meetings. "They saw that the people's mood favoured recognizing equality," said Copps. "And politically, it was smarter to get this contentious debate over and done with rather than amending little bits of legislation here and there, which could drag on for years."

* * * * *

The debate on this legislation, which amended 68 federal acts, was far stormier in the House of Commons and the Senate than in cabinet. A number of MPs from the Reform Party, shortly to become the Canadian Alliance, were particularly hostile towards gays and lesbians, as were some Liberal and Bloc Québécois MPs. Eric Lowther of the Reform Party and Gérard Asselin of the Bloc Québécois, among others, deplored the fact that the legislation accorded rights only to couples and not to members of the same family who lived together and supported each other.

An astonished Lowther said on February 15, 2000, a few days after the
bill was introduced in the House of Commons,

> Bill C-23 is a benefits-for-sex bill. It is crazy. Under Bill C-23,
> benefits will be extended to any person who has had, as the
> bill says, a conjugal relationship, regardless of sex. It could be
> male, it could be female, it could be two males or two females.
> Is it not more reasonable to focus on demonstrated interde-
> pendencies and the social contribution of the relationship
> when considering benefits rather than on the private physical
> intimacies of the person being considered?

According to this Reform MP, it opened the door to tax fraud: "Given
that sexual relations seem to be the sole criteria for obtaining benefits,
one wonders how the government will know whether a couple is truly
having a conjugal relationship or simply trying to obtain a benefit." But
Reform members were not the only ones to doubt the seriousness of
relationships between same-sex partners. Liberal MP John McKay said,

> From what I understand, gay and lesbian relationships break
> up at the rate of about 90 percent over the course of one year.
> For public policy purposes one has to question whether they
> should be treated as equivalencies in law. Statistically the rela-
> tionships are clearly not equivalent. My view for public policy
> purposes is that they should not be treated as the same.
> However the bill does precisely that. I will not argue the point
> that common-law relationships, be they homosexual or het-
> erosexual, are not as committed, as loving or as whatever as
> any other relationship, but I do not think that frankly is the
> point.

Réal Ménard, at the time the only openly gay federal MP other than
Svend Robinson, set aside legal arguments and eloquently and pas-
sionately supported the bill:

I would like all the members to ask themselves the following question. Can this House truly maintain, in all decency and fairness, that there is a qualitative difference in the sentiment of love that can exist between two men or two women, and a man and a woman who love each other? There is no difference in terms of how they live as a couple. When you are in love with a man, you go through the same range of emotions. When you are a citizen in a society, you pay the same taxes, you are governed by the same laws, you participate in the same civil society. This is what should be at the heart of our concerns.

Like other supporters of C-23, Ménard urged the separation of religion and state: "Not recognizing same-sex couples is a question of discrimination. It's not a question of religion. As parliamentarians we cannot pronounce on religious issues or on moral issues, which doesn't mean that we are not people of principle."

Later Svend Robinson stated that the intent of the law was simply to "repair" the wrong inflicted on homosexuals over the course of the centuries. His Liberal colleague Hedy Fry was even more enraged, and nearly lost her temper. "Gay and lesbian families are strong families," she insisted. "Gays and lesbians are parents. Gays and lesbians are children. They are sisters and brothers. They are grandparents. I am proud to stand here with my government to put forward a bill that I believe will probably be the single most important bill to come forward in this House in the twenty-first century."

Unfortunately, the debate did not focus only on recognition of same-sex couples, but on homosexuality itself. Reform MP Grant McNally deplored the use of *homophobia* as "a label used to brand those who object to the state's sanctioning of homosexuality." With a curious twist of logic, his colleague Reed Elley blamed the demands of gays and lesbians on the feminist struggle: "A gradual blurring of the sexes occurred that gave young men growing up in many female-dominated, single-parent homes an identity crisis. This led to a rise in militant homosexuality, a coming out of the closet of gay men and women who also demanded equality. The things that had been considered improper went looking for a desperate legitimacy."

In spite of virulent opposition from the Reform Party/Canadian Alliance, Bill C-23 was passed in the House of Commons by 176 votes to 72 on April 11, 2000. It went on to receive Senate approval and, on June 29, royal assent.

Gays and lesbians were generally pleased with the administrative and financial recognition the law gave to couples. But their representatives continued to denounce a "rule of interpretation" that appeared in the preamble to Bill C-23, stipulating that marriage constitutes a union between a man and a woman. This detail was added at the last minute and obviously had nothing to do with the legislation. It was put there to appease those who agreed with legitimizing homosexual common-law partnerships but disagreed with changing the definition of marriage.

Even in the highest circles of the governing party, some were ill at ease. "Many Liberals, including myself, were embarrassed by this use-less addition," confided one of Jean Chrétien's advisers. "I personally thought it was a bad decision, an anti-Liberal decision." The bill's opponents were also indignant and saw it as a very feeble attempt to "protect" traditional marriage. They were not mistaken: the courts would quickly confirm that the definition contained in C-23 was only a nonbinding declaration and therefore did not represent a serious obstacle to the gay and lesbian couples who would appeal to judges to obtain the right to marry. On the other hand, the virulence of the debate over simply recognizing the benefits and obligations of com-mon-law same-sex partnerships offered a glimpse of the controversy that would erupt over the last taboo: homosexual marriage.

2

GAY MARRIAGE GATHERS STRENGTH

Michael Hendricks and René LeBœuf did not fit with the mainstream of society. Sometimes radical, often at odds with prevailing opinion, they've had their share of run-ins with gay leaders. But it is exactly this kind of nonconformism that enabled gays and lesbians of Quebec to obtain the right to marry.

Born in Trenton, New Jersey, Hendricks arrived in Montreal in 1968 to avoid being drafted for the war that the United States had been inflicting on Vietnam for the past three years. For a while, young men could escape the draft by declaring that they were homosexual, but this exemption had been withdrawn because too many were making use of it. Canada, thank goodness, accepted American draft resisters. LeBœuf was living in his native Quebec City at the time and met Hendricks at a New Year's party on January 1, 1973. They clicked immediately, and after three years of travelling back and forth between Quebec City and Montreal, they bought a charming house near the Laurier metro station in Montreal, where they live to this day.

Accepting that he was homosexual had not been easy for Hendricks. He became convinced he was gay at the age of 19, but two years later, as a law student at the University of Virginia, he still felt disturbed about it. He wrote a note for posterity and then tried to take his life. On December 12, 1963, he woke up in a psychiatric hospital. As he regained consciousness, he realized that there was no going back. The faculty had just kicked him out as "mentally unstable," a euphemism for gay. Hendricks decided then and there to live his life to the full, no holds barred, at least for a while. He followed the risky, bohemian gay lifestyle of the era. With time he settled down, but his feeling of being an outcast lingered. Before his mother died in 1993, she said to him, "Find yourself a nice girl, and don't go on living with him [LeBœuf]."

Once he had moved to Montreal in September 1968, Hendricks discovered that the gay life was a little easier than in New York. But it was still a long way from paradise: before homosexuality was decriminalized in 1969, hundreds of gays were imprisoned in Quebec. Police raids on gay bars continued into the early 1990s.

During the AIDS crisis that hit the gay community in the 1980s, LeBœuf and Hendricks became politically active. "Until then we were socialists, not gay activists," said Hendricks. They began to realize the harmful consequences of the legal lack of recognition for same-sex couples, such as the inability of some to participate in medical decisions involving their dying partners, the lack of common property rights and exclusion from employment benefits. Gays were also often subjected to gratuitous violence. In particular, ten murders in the early 1990s attracted public attention to homophobia and the failure of police vigilance around this problem.

In reaction to these events, in November 1993 the Quebec Human Rights Commission held a public consultation on violence and discrimination against gays and lesbians. In 1996, two years after the report was published, the government finally agreed to repeal section 137 of the Quebec Charter of Human Rights and Freedoms, which permitted some forms of discrimination based on sexual orientation, notably in insurance and retirement plans. Without anyone having planned it, the idea of extending marriage to same-sex couples made one of its first appearances in Quebec during these hearings. It surfaced in a brief called *Lesbiennes, mariage et famille* (Lesbians, Marriage and Family), filed by Ann Robinson, a law professor at Laval University.

"In my brief, I analyzed the question of childcare from the perspective of lesbian rights," Robinson explained. "In reflecting on this question, I had the idea of rolling back the borders of discrimination against gays and lesbians as far as humanly possible. That was the context in which I raised the issue of the right of homosexuals to get married." The coming into effect in April 1985 of the Canadian Charter of Rights and Freedoms, which guaranteed equality for all citizens, gave her cause for optimism: "Since that date, the Supreme Court had always ruled in favour of individual rights. The Court pushed the limits of discrimination further and further back. The wave of progress appeared to be unstoppable. And progress, for me, meant that eventually gays and lesbians would be able to get married." Events would vindicate Robinson's confidence, but being a pioneer was certainly not easy at times. "I was the only one who believed that in 1993," she said. René LeBœuf agrees: "She was so avant-garde, it was as if she came from another planet!"

"I don't need to tell you how much they made fun of me, especially in my faculty," recalls Robinson. "They said I was completely mad, the idea was totally farfetched, it went against the whole evolution of Western civilization. But francophone law faculties are not known for their leftist leanings." Indeed, ten years later, many Quebec professors of family law, ethics and anthropology were still vehemently opposed to same-sex marriage.

In spite of Robinson's impassioned brief to the Quebec Human Rights Commission, the final report, entitled De l'illégalité à l'égalité (From Illegal to Equal), did not recommend extending marriage to gays and lesbians, but instead recommended establishing registered partnerships, a concept Ottawa was tossing around at the time. When the report was tabled in May 1994, even Hendricks and LeBœuf were not yet thinking about marriage. "We couldn't even imagine such a thing, we were caught up in other issues, it was the middle of the AIDS crisis," recalled LeBœuf. But three years later, during the gay pride parade in Montreal, they decided to "float the idea." They devised a scenario involving two fake couples — two cousins and "two girls who didn't know each other" — and put up a big white tent. The word *marriage* was never mentioned, but everyone quickly understood the reference.

"Everyone started clapping. It was amazing!" said Hendricks. The

René LeBœuf and Michael Hendricks in Montreal's gay and lesbian pride parade, August 2003. "When Michael and I announced we were getting married, you can't imagine the jokes it caused," said LeBœuf. "It was ridiculous; everyone thought we were mad."

couple then set about trying to convince the Table de Concertation des Lesbiennes et des Gais du Québec (Quebec Lesbian and Gay Roundtable) to support the new claim, but to no avail. They were forced to act on their own and so, like politicians, they consulted the opinion polls. In early 1998, they found to their surprise and joy that for the first time more Quebecers were in favour of homosexual marriage than opposed.

* * * * *

Convinced that civil marriage was the best way to promote the rights of gays and lesbians everywhere in the country, Hendricks decided to be the one to pop the question to LeBœuf in August 1998. Meanwhile, another couple living in Quebec, Martin Dubé and Manuel Gambora, had also unsuccessfully attempted to get married for immigration purposes.

"Why not?" was LeBœuf's halfhearted reply. He was only too aware of the pitfalls that getting married would entail. On September 14, 1998, the couple appeared at Montreal's Palais de Justice and filled out the form for couples wanting to get married. To suit the document to their own situation, they crossed out the word *épouse* (bride) and replaced it with *époux* (spouse). Then they handed it in at the civil marriage office. As they expected, the civil servant at the desk refused their request. "The form isn't right, it has to say bride and groom," she declared. "There has to be a bride!" Witty as always, Hendricks shot back, "Well, René does the dishes and I do the cooking — so I guess he's the groom and I'm the bride!"

The employee was not amused. "It doesn't work like that!" she retorted. The media had been invited and made much of the event, but it caused little more than a mild sensation. In 1998, the priority demand on the gay and lesbian community's agenda was obtaining legal recognition of same-sex partners, which to LeBœuf and Hendricks wasn't nearly enough. As elsewhere in the country, access to marriage was far from a priority, and even less so in Quebec, where even heterosexuals were abandoning this age-old institution. "Marriage, at the time, was a pretty farfetched idea," said LeBœuf. "When Michael and I announced we were getting married, you can't imagine the jokes it caused. It was ridiculous; everyone thought we were mad."

The president of Gai Écoute, Laurent McCutcheon, realized that leading activists in the gay and lesbian community, in Canada as well as in Quebec, were starting to demand that marriage be available to same-sex couples. "I thought they were brave and avant-garde," he said of LeBœuf and Hendricks, "but I was already leading a battle to have common-law couples recognized. I always supported their cause, but I didn't want to abandon my own fight for common-law partnerships and civil unions. I thought that putting all our eggs in the marriage basket would be a strategic error. We had the same goals, but I firmly believed that we were better to take this one step at a time." Work by activists such as McCutcheon led to Quebec recognizing the financial and administrative rights of same-sex couples in June 1999 (Bill 32). The government had been forced to take action as a result of a 1998 court judgment in a case dealing with pensions owed to surviving partners.

Whatever the immediate ramifications of these events for the cause of same-sex marriage, Julie Snyder, the host of the talk show *Le Point J*, inadvertently motivated Hendricks and LeBœuf to continue their fight. She had invited them to appear on her show and had distributed glasses of wine and spoons to the audience. "They tapped their glasses while René and I cut the cake," related Hendricks. "Thanks to Julie, we realized one thing: if you want to promote marriage, you have to play on the clichés for all you're worth, the clothes and the whole bit. In the minds of most people, marriage is a very positive event."

These flamboyant beginnings were followed by many months of equivocation, however. In August 1998, Hendricks and LeBœuf retained the services of a lawyer, Stéphane Gendron, who had plenty of enthusiasm but little idea of how to advance the case. Although he presented a motion in Superior Court, the couple dismissed him a few months later anyway, figuring he was not up to the task. In August 2000, the couple hired two more lawyers, Anne-France Goldwater and Marie-Hélène Dubé, who presented another motion to the court. In the meantime, at the couple's request, Professor Ann Robinson had produced a highly detailed legal study entitled *Le mariage pour les gais et lesbiennes: futur inéluctable* (Same-Sex Marriage: An Inevitability).

* * * * *

Ever since a 1994 amendment to section 365, same-sex marriage had been clearly prohibited under the Quebec Civil Code. But as the definition of marriage was a federal responsibility, the lawyers concluded that the amendment was unconstitutional. "When René and Michael showed up with this file, I thought we had a good chance of winning," Goldwater recalled. "I knew I wouldn't have to bring in expert witnesses: people had long since stopped thinking of homosexuality as a mental illness. All we had to do was to invalidate section 365 of the Civil Code [defining marriage], which violated the constitution in terms of federal and provincial responsibilities. This was not a Charter question — it was going to be as easy as pie!"

On the other hand, no one knew whether the *Hyde* case of 1866, which applied in English Canada, would also apply in Quebec. The only certainty was that the federal Parliament had never legally defined marriage. All hopes were pinned on the fact that the constitution upheld the pre-1867 Civil Code of Lower Canada, in which marriage was not defined either.

But this hope did not take into account Ottawa's dogged vigilance. The couple's lawyers were all ready to plead their case, but federal representatives brought out every delaying tactic in the book — in order, so they claimed, to study the evidence properly. The word *evidence* was a euphemism, said Anne-France Goldwater: "This is the sordid side of the story. I kept asking for a court date, saying it wasn't a complicated case. They kept us waiting — they were consulting the experts. 'What evidence do you need?' I asked. 'What is there to prove?'"

There was nothing to prove, but lots to legislate. On January 31, 2001, the Liberal government introduced Bill S-4 in the Senate. It had a deceptively innocuous title: the Federal Law-Civil Law Harmonization Act, No. 1 — yet another of those technical laws that parliamentarians adopt from time to time to update the statutes. Its goal was to bridge the gap between the new Quebec Civil Code and various federal laws. It was odd, however, that the government first introduced it in the Senate rather than in the House of Commons, contrary to established democratic tradition. What was even more suspicious was that it was passed in the Commons in a week's time, with the consent of all parties, including the Bloc Québécois and the New Democrats. No one raised the question of marriage during the brief debate in the House.

Hendricks and LeBœuf's lawyers quickly saw why the bill was shrouded in mystery. Buried in article 5 was the statement, "Marriage requires the free and enlightened consent of a man and a woman to be the spouse of the other." The distress of gay MPs such as Svend Robinson and Réal Ménard can only be imagined. They supported the bill in good faith, never suspecting that it was sealing the heterosexual definition of marriage for Quebec. A cruel reminder that MPs should read all bills submitted to them before approving them! At the Palais de Justice in Montreal, the news was a slap in the face for Goldwater:

> Nearly a whole year after we had instituted proceedings, they [the federal lawyers] were finally ready to begin the case! At last! It was like a woman who finally has an orgasm! But just before we started, a young federal lawyer asked me tauntingly if I'd seen the new law. I was thunderstruck. I never thought they would adopt a law to obstruct our action. They had slipped a significant social measure into the middle of a highly technical bill! I was exasperated.

The indomitable couple saw it as a dastardly plot, and were convinced that the law had been rushed through Parliament just to wreck their case. "They pulled the wool over our eyes," said Hendricks. The fact is that a bill with identical wording had been introduced in the Senate in May 2000, which makes conspiracy an unlikely explanation. But the earliest version of the bill, introduced in the House in June 1998, stated that marriage "requires that each of the *parties* give free and enlightened consent to be the spouse of the other" (emphasis added), giving a degree of credence to Hendricks and LeBœuf's theory.

John Relton, one of the lawyers who discovered what had been going on, didn't see it in quite the same way: "By pure chance, I noticed this clause just before the bill was adopted by the House. I was stunned." Relton was the head of the Liberal association in Notre-Dame-de-Grâce, a Montreal riding whose MP, Marlene Jennings, alerted both Michael Hendricks and Egale. Relton concluded, however, that it was too late to reverse the situation.

As a gay activist, Relton was disgusted, but he gave the MPs the benefit of the doubt. He recalled that Quebec civil lawyers had been suggesting such a law for years and that the wording of article 5 was the same as that of section 365 of the 1994 version of the Quebec Civil Code. But it is reasonable to conclude that the imminence of Hendricks and LeBœuf's lawsuit encouraged the government to speed up a process of harmonization that had been dragging on for years.

A high-ranking lawyer in the federal department of justice, who prefers to remain anonymous, hotly denies any such interpretation. "Bureaucracy is far too slow for conspiracies!" she chuckled. Goldwater wasn't so sure: "Federal lawyers told me there was absolutely no link between our case and the adoption of the Harmonization Act. They claimed the litigation team had no contact with the legislative team — my reaction to that was *Bullshit!*"

Whether devious machinations occurred or not, the couple's frustration can only be imagined. The legislative change not only slowed down the case, and therefore postponed their marriage, but also complicated the work of the lawyers. Although it was small consolation, this new twist of events qualified LeBœuf and Hendricks for a $55,000 grant from the federal Court Challenges Program, which had already helped Egale in its battle in British Columbia.

* * * * *

The success of *M. v. H.* in the Supreme Court in May 1999 had encouraged lawyers in English Canada to demand marriage rights for same-sex couples. At first, there was even a healthy but unacknowledged competition among them as to who would be the first to launch a legal challenge. They soon began to collaborate, however, to maximize their chances of success. In July 1999, in London, participants in an international conference on gay and lesbian rights began a serious discussion of the challenge. Martha McCarthy, the lawyer who had represented *M.*, attended this conference. But it was not until the fall, at a similar conference at Queen's University in Kingston, Ontario, that the idea genuinely began germinating in her mind.

During the train trip to Kingston, McCarthy and her two colleagues, Douglas Elliott, a lawyer representing Toronto's Metropolitan Community Church, and Evan Wolfson, director of the American organization Freedom to Marry, began to concoct a legal challenge to Ontario's traditional definition of marriage. "We listed all the affidavits that we'd have to prepare," she recalled. "It soon became clear that we had to build a case."

The *M. v. H.* case had not passed unnoticed in the gay and lesbian community. Many couples phoned McCarthy and her colleague, Joanna Radbord, to ask them for help in gaining the right to marry. Activists began to take an interest in the issue. "We wanted to have control over the case," explained McCarthy. "But we thought we couldn't keep saying no to these clients. We have a duty as lawyers with clients who come to us." The lawyers nevertheless tried to select a variety of couples for the case: women and men, young and old, with and without children, and so on.

* * * * *

Around the same time in 1999, Laurie Arron was working hard in the Egale offices in Ottawa to convince his colleagues to embark on the marriage rights venture. Many doubted that the time was ripe. "There were a lot of people on the board of Egale who didn't see marriage as a top priority," he later acknowledged. "Everybody recognized that full equality meant inclusion in civil marriage, but Egale is a small organization with only so many projects on the go."

By January 2003, though, the wind had shifted. Egale contacted

Cynthia Petersen, who had already represented them in several law-suits. "They wanted to find the best place in Canada to launch a suit," she said. "We opted for British Columbia because we knew that the government of the time [led by Ujjal Dosanjh and the NDP] would support the equal right to marriage." For all kinds of reasons, Egale had never seriously considered getting directly involved in the Hendricks-LeBœuf case in Quebec. Among other things, the leaders of the organ-ization were afraid that the couple would not have sufficient media appeal. In addition, Hendricks and LeBœuf didn't want to become "puppets" of Egale, as they put it.

In early May, while Petersen was waiting for a response to her appli-cation to the federal Court Challenges Program for help with the British Columbia case, she read in the papers that two curly-haired men from Ontario, Michael Leshner and Michael Stark, had presented themselves at Toronto City Hall and requested a marriage licence. The clerk denied their request, but refused to justify her decision in writing. Finally, City Hall announced to the couple that it would ask the Ontario Divisional Court to clarify the legality of a marriage between partners of the same sex. Leshner said,

> I was offended. As a lawyer, if someone is going to tell me no, to my face, as a government body, then they sure as hell can give it to me in writing. I'm going to react to that kind of non-sense. So I said, "Okay, I'm coming back in an hour with the media. You will have to explain to them why you can't put in writing and you will confirm to the media that I can't get it because I'm gay."

The flamboyant Leshner, who was working as a substitute crown pros-ecutor in Toronto, was clearly pleased with himself. As a person who had once undergone therapy to rid himself of "internalized homo-phobia," he was not easily put off. He thought back to all the politi-cians whom he had tried to make aware of the issue of homosexuality and who had told him to hold his peace, especially Ian Scott, attorney general of Ontario from 1985 to 1990. Scott had hidden his own homosexuality from the public throughout his career as a lawyer and minister. In 1986, he had agreed to include sexual orientation among the illegal forms of discrimination in the Human Rights Code of Ontario, at the instigation of NDP MPP Evelyn Gigantes. But when Leshner began to claim administrative and fiscal rights for same-sex partners in 1988, Scott refused point blank, saying impact studies were needed. Yet he had been living with a same-sex partner for years. The outspoken Leshner, who finally won this battle in 1992, recalled,

> Ian Scott became everything that I abhorred about the price to pay for being in power. You could be the darling of the legal community, senior partner in a law firm, then attorney general, but there was no way you could come out of the closet. You couldn't set an example. You would be afraid that the premier would take away your portfolio if you were too insistent. My experience taught me that it wasn't only straights who were part of the problem. You have to include gays themselves!

Martha McCarthy, who had been hesitant to include the two Ontario Michaels among the couples involved in her legal challenge, was less than thrilled with the sensation they had caused at Toronto City Hall. "So we said to Leshner, 'You're in if you promise you're going to be well behaved with the media.' It was just naive of me!" McCarthy wanted to keep control over the challenge, which would be impossible if the city itself presented a motion in court. To beat the civil servants to the finish post, she spent all night in the office with Radbord preparing the couples' motion. "We presented our documents to the court 15 minutes before the city did!" she recalled proudly.

Leshner recognizes that his manoeuvre deviated from his well-intentioned lawyer's carefully laid plans: "I didn't ask Martha's permission. I simply called her and said, 'I'm doing this.' It wasn't the first time I had made her angry ... But what's important is that the sensation I caused moved public opinion in favour of the case much faster than Martha could have hoped for. The thing became political overnight." McCarthy's worries with Leshner were not over yet.

Throughout the proceedings, he frequently portrayed the federal government's theory of marriage as depending uniquely on the penis or the vagina of the partner. "How many people did I offend by saying that?" he said sarcastically. "I was simply using vocabulary that everyone could understand."

* * * * *

Less than a week later, on May 26, 2000, the first lesbian couple sponsored by Egale in British Columbia, Cynthia Callahan and Judy Lightwater, copied the two Michaels and attempted to get married in Victoria. "For us, the normally happy event of applying for our marriage licence will be a painful denial of legitimacy, simply because we are the same sex," said Callahan at the time. "It's not right, and it's time for the law to be changed." In the hours that followed their request, Egale's lawyers Cynthia Petersen and Joe Arvay made contact repeatedly with the B.C. attorney general, Andrew Petter, and his advisers. Petersen recalls,

> I spent a holiday weekend at my sister's cottage with a gay couple who were among my best friends. But they got angry with me because I spent the whole time on the telephone with Andrew Petter and his chief of staff, repeating over and over again, "Just issue the licences! Just do it!" They said they would like to, but they thought it wasn't under provincial jurisdiction. I replied, "Everyone knows that the source of the blockage lies with the federal powers, but if that blockage is not valid, you can do it anyway!" If the province had given the licence to that couple, the burden of proof would have fallen on the federal government, who would have had to go to court to say, "You can't do that." It would have been fantastic.

Early the next week, Petter sent out a press release saying that the legal framework for marriage should be clarified for the sake of "dignity" and "human rights." "Clearly, one could let the question of same-sex marriage drag on through the courts for years," declared the Attorney General, "but I think the federal government would be well advised to resolve the issue by clarifying the legislation and offering same-sex couples, along with heterosexual couples, the right to marry."

Several years earlier, Petter had become convinced that full recognition of the rights of gays and lesbians would, sooner or later, involve a redefinition of marriage. When he realized that the issue was coming to a head, he asked the B.C. Ministry of Attorney General for a legal opinion. "I thought that in keeping with the adoption of new laws to protect same-sex couples, court judgments and the evolution of public opinion on the matter, there was a chance common law might have changed to recognize homosexual marriages," he said later.

The lawyers who drew up the legal opinion concluded that although common law[1] had possibly changed to open the doors to marriage between same-sex partners, it was up to the federal government to give the green light. "The legal opinion was one thing," said Petter, "but without a court ruling, you can't really say that the common law has changed. I thought it wasn't appropriate [to issue] the licences without that. I couldn't take half of the legal opinion and ignore the rest."

* * * * *

Cynthia Petersen was imploring Petter to do what the mayor of San Francisco, Gavin Newsom, would do four years later: marry same-sex couples in possible violation of the law. When he heard President George W. Bush recommend a constitutional amendment against gay marriage in his State of the Union address in January 2004, Newsom decided to defy the established order, and on February 12 San Francisco began issuing marriage licences to same-sex couples. He based his argument on article 1 of the California state constitution, which protected the "inalienable rights" of every citizen. Less than a month later, the California Supreme Court nevertheless annulled 3,955 marriages performed in this fashion. In the meantime, Jason West, mayor of the village of New Paltz, New York, took a leaf from San Francisco's book, as did municipalities in Oregon and other states. The courts quickly moved to put a check on their defiance of the law.

Opinion was divided as to the usefulness of initiatives like this. Thanks to Mayor Newsom's efforts, in March 2005, the Superior Court in San Francisco declared the definition of marriage unconstitutional, although this ruling did not become effective immediately. But in Oregon, because of these impromptu ceremonies an amendment entrenching the prohibition of same-sex marriages in the state constitution was adopted by referendum in November 2004. Ten other states followed suit, which prompted some commentators to suggest that the gay issue was a major factor in Bush's reelection, as social conservatives used it effectively to mobilize their forces.

In France, too, the tactic met with limited success. On June 5, 2004, the mayor of Bègles (on the outskirts of Bordeaux), Noël Mamère, decided to celebrate the marriage of Bertrand Charpentier and Stéphane Chapin, in spite of numerous warnings from French authorities. Mamère soon had cause to regret it: he was suspended from his post for a month and the marriage was revoked. The event did stop the government from breaking its promise to pass a law against homophobia, but achieved nothing more.

* * * * *

In July 2000, as the City of Toronto had done earlier, the government of British Columbia asked the courts to pronounce on the legality or illegality of same-sex marriage. Petter told the press,

> This is an action aimed at confirming that the Canadian Charter of Rights and Freedoms actually means something, and more specifically that we can't go on discriminating against same-sex couples. Why would we want to deny same-sex couples the possibility of affirming and reinforcing their relationship? Not just for themselves and their families, but for society as a whole?

"Even though marriage was federal jurisdiction," Petter later explained,

"I realized that the provincial government had a role to play in this by issuing the licences, through our own interpretation of the common law. So I felt we had a responsibility to do the right thing. I couldn't simply maintain the status quo without trying to change it." Until the NDP lost the 2001 election, the British Columbia government made an important contribution to developing the legal expertise needed to promote same-sex marriage. After the Liberals came to power, same-sex couples were on their own again, as the province decided not to take a position in the debate.

With the litigation in process in B.C., three courts in the three largest provinces in the country were now grappling with a key question: did forbidding same-sex marriage violate the Charter, and therefore the constitution?

To add one more complication to their Ontario case, McCarthy and Radbord decided in late 2000 to include two more couples: Kevin Bourassa and Joe Varnell, and Anne and Elaine Vautour, who would all get married a few months later at the Metropolitan Community Church of Toronto (MCCT). At first, the lawyers had selected two other couples (Tom Alworth and Al Pitman, Gail Donnelly and Barb McDowall), but the church's lawyer, Douglas Elliott, pulled them out when he heard that Pitman and McDowall were both divorcees. The lawyers worried that this would prejudice their chances. They had to quickly find replacements, and the two new couples who ended up getting married at MCCT had had very little time to decide to go through with it. At first the Bourassa-Varnells saw little point in getting involved in this adventure. Varnell recalled later,

> We were happy in our sphere, we were in our comfort, we had the recognition — not necessarily the recognition we wanted from our families, but certainly from our friends. And we were enjoying same-sex benefits. It was just one of these situations where you say yes and just hope it's going to work. Everybody said yes having no idea what they were getting into.

As Vogel and North had done in 1974, the MCCT opted for marriage using the publication of banns. McCarthy had studied this approach in detail, and by the fall of 2000, she was convinced that this was the way to go. Her only fear was that Brent Hawkes, the minister of the MCCT, would lose his right to celebrate marriages as a result. They decided to go ahead anyway.

The first proclamation of the banns took place on December 10, 2000, a few days after the editors of the Toronto *Globe and Mail* had given their blessing to same-sex marriages. "I publish the banns of marriage between Elaine Vautour and Anne Vautour," declared Rev. Hawkes to the congregation. "If anyone knows of any lawful impediment to their marriage, they are to declare it now." The two women waited nervously in silence, but no one spoke up to disturb their happiness. The minister repeated the banns for Bourassa and Varnell, and again no one objected, to the great astonishment of the couples. The congregation's applause nearly brought the house down. "Hearing no legal cause raised this day, we will continue to publish the banns the next two Sundays, and we will celebrate that marriage on January the fourteenth," announced Hawkes.

The second reading of the banns was a little more exciting. After they were proclaimed, Ken Campbell, an Evangelical Christian who had led a crusade against homosexuality for many years, stood up to oppose the marriage:

> I find myself constrained by the love of Christ and in the name of Christ and on behalf of His Church, to declare both you and your congregation reprobate and heretic, having rejected the teaching of Christ and removed yourself from Christ and the fellowship of His Church.

Another protester followed suit with similar arguments. Rev. Hawkes attempted to respond to the objections, which only made things worse. Security agents intervened to prevent the protester from approaching the altar. The minister quickly pronounced the objections invalid before inviting the congregation to the last publication of banns on December 24. On that Christmas Eve, two people stood up to protest, but in contrast to the previous week, they made their objections in a calm and orderly fashion. This time there were several politicians in attendance: city councillors Jack Layton (later leader of the NDP) and Olivia Chow, Ontario MPPs Marilyn Churley (NDP) and George Smitherman (later Liberal health minister). The path to marriage was now unobstructed.

Bourassa and Varnell were under no illusions about the likelihood of the government of Ontario agreeing to register their marriage, even though it had been celebrated using the age-old tradition of the publication of banns. But in an attempt to maximize their chances, they added a dash of politics to the event. Bourassa invited Prime Minister Jean Chrétien and Governor General Adrienne Clarkson to their wedding, adding in the invitation, "As a citizen, I am looking for leaders and representatives who will defend our right to marriage and to do so in a public manner ... Will you join us in our pursuit of human rights?"

The couple had no real expectation that some of the most powerful people in the Canadian government would show up at the MCCT that day. At first they were simply curious to see what sort of response they would get to their invitation. The reply astonished them. "Although he cannot be with you for the occasion, the Prime Minister sends his very best wishes for a joyful wedding day and for many years of health and happiness together," read the letter, which was signed by Paul Sparkes, correspondence manager in the Prime Minister's Office. Hardly able to believe his eyes, Bourassa immediately sent off an email thanking Chrétien for his "support" for same-sex marriage.

A little later, Bourassa received a reply from the Governor General: "Their Excellencies regret that, because of previous commitments, it will not be possible for them to accept your invitation. In sending their regrets, Madame Clarkson and Mr. [John Ralston] Saul have asked me to convey to you and to Mr. Varnell their congratulations and best wishes." The couple were overjoyed once more. But did the two men really have Chrétien and Clarkson's support?

Unfortunately, in early 2001 it was still too early for this to be the case. Sure enough, a few days later Bourassa received another letter from the Prime Minister's Office, and this one was a little more sober.

The chief correspondent, Keith Hanash, reminded the couple that the government had extended most of the rights and obligations of heterosexual couples to same-sex couples, but that "nothing in this legislation changed the legal definition of marriage which remains, 'the union of one man and one woman to the exclusion of all others.'"

After her initially encouraging reply had been made public, the Governor General issued a press release that adopted a considerably different tone. It stated that the first letter had been a standard reply that the Governor General's secretary sent to all couples who were getting married, and that a political message from the Queen's representative should not be read into it. "The debate surrounding this ceremony is a public one about a question that touches Canadians' personal beliefs in a very intimate way," read the release. "The Governor General does not wish to be drawn into this debate." Clarkson even felt constrained to reply publicly to the president of the Canadian Conference of Catholic Bishops, Gerald Weisner, who had judged the congratulations emanating from her office to the Bourassa-Varnell couple as "controversial and offensive to most faiths."

Bourassa and Varnell were obviously disappointed with this latest turn or events, which did not prevent them from getting married as planned on January 14, 2001. Unlike Vogel and North's marriage 25 years earlier, the ceremony was held under tight security. Numerous police officers guarded the church both inside and out, and Rev. Hawkes wore a bulletproof vest. There were a few protesters and even a fake bomb threat, but all in all everything went off fairly smoothly. The international media were in attendance: Agence France-Presse, Reuters, *Time* and *Newsweek* magazines and a Japanese TV station. The English-Canadian press kept the debate on the front pages over the next few days. Many of the commentators were favourable to same-sex marriage, a pleasant surprise for Bourassa and Varnell and other gays and lesbians who wanted their partnerships recognized by the state. In the general public, however, many were put out by the photos of Bourassa and Varnell kissing. The papers were inundated with complaints about these pictures.

The visceral public reaction and politicians' nervousness around the question were a foretaste of the scope of the challenge to come. The Ontario minister responsible for the registration of marriages, Bob Runciman, turned down the request to register the same-sex marriages celebrated at the MCCT. "It won't qualify to be registered because of the federal legislation, which clearly defines a marriage as a union between a man and a woman ... to the exclusion of all others," he said. A few months later, the first judge to look into the issue of same-sex marriage since 1993 would confirm that victory was still a long way off.

3

DISCRIMINATORY — BUT DEFENSIBLE?

On October 3, 2001, two months after the end of the hearings, Judge Ian H. Pitfield of the Supreme Court of British Columbia[1] returned his verdict on the motion brought by Egale and the same-sex couples claiming the right to get married. For the first time in Canadian history, a court recognized that the exclusion of gays and lesbians from this institution was discriminatory under the Charter of Rights and Freedoms. The magistrate added a serious proviso to his judgment, however: he considered that such discrimination was justifiable in a free and democratic society. In any case, he added, a new definition of marriage would require a constitutional amendment. And for that to happen, the majority of the provinces would have to agree. "Judges should only change the common law in incremental steps," wrote Judge Pitfield. "A change to define marriage as the legal union of two individuals, regardless of sex, is not incremental. The change would have broad legal ramifications."

At first the couples reacted politely. "This is just the beginning," said Robin Roberts, one of the plaintiffs along with her partner Diana Denny. No one was very surprised at the decision. "Our clients knew when they started that this would be a case that would go on for five years," said one of the lawyers on the case, barbara findlay (who prefers not to use capital letters when writing her name).

Still, the judgment represented one more victory for the recognition of same-sex marriage. "The distinction between opposite-sex and same-sex relationships in the marriage context excludes the latter from a social and legal institution of considerable importance and tends to perpetuate the stereotypical and frequently critical community view of gays and lesbians," wrote Judge Pitfield,

> Notwithstanding the material distinction between opposite-sex and same-sex couples with respect to reproductive capacity, the omission to provide some form of legal status for same-sex couples enhances, rather than diminishes, the stereotypical view that same-sex relationships are less important or valuable than opposite-sex relationships. There is now sufficient practical similarity between the economic and social consequences of opposite-sex and same-sex relationships that affording one but not the other the opportunity to acquire a legal and formal status discriminates in the substantive sense of the word.

This very positive aspect of the decision did not escape the eagle eye of Tess Healy, one of the applicants. "I am very encouraged," she said. "The court has made a groundbreaking decision in finding that it is contrary to the Charter to exclude us from marriage." The executive director of Egale, John Fisher, agreed. "We don't feel we have lost anything," he said. "I think we have gained some advance. But there are still a number of steps ahead of us."

It was inspiring that a judge had characterized the exclusion of homosexuals from the institution of marriage as a violation of equality under section 15 of the Charter. "We knew that this was the crux of the issue," said Laurie Arron, vice-president of Egale at the time. But as has so often happened in the history of the gay and lesbian rights movement, it was a moral victory only and had no impact on everyday life. Judge Pitfield had certainly admitted that the exclusion constituted discrimination, but he had slammed the door on any possibility of correcting the problem — at least for the foreseeable future.

"Marriage, as a federal head of power with legal meaning at Confederation [in the 1867 constitution], is not amenable to Charter [adopted in 1982] scrutiny," he maintained. "One part of the

Constitution may not be used to amend another." This arcane theory, to which even the federal government had not resorted during the hearings, went counter to a well-established principle: the Constitution is a "living tree" adaptable to the way society evolves over time. "We scratched our heads and wondered whether we should take that argument seriously, because it was so ridiculous from a legal perspective," recalled Arron. "We were very disappointed, but we knew that that was not going to fly at a higher court."

Judge Pitfield was cautious, however, and acknowledged further on in his decision that his constitutional analysis "may be incorrect." Probing more deeply, he reflected on the issue in the context of the Charter of Rights and Freedoms, concluding that exclusion may be a violation of section 15. But to open the door to same-sex marriage, it must be proved that this form of discrimination was not justifiable in a free and democratic society, as stipulated in section 1 of the Charter. And there was the rub. "Same-sex and opposite-sex relationships are, at their core, demonstrably different," wrote Pitfield, apparently contradicting what he wrote elsewhere in the judgment:

> They cannot be equated except by changing the deep-rooted social and legal relationship around which Canadian society has evolved and continues to evolve. Because of the importance of marriage in the Canadian context, past and present, the salutary effect associated with the preservation of its opposite-sex core far outweighs the deleterious effect resulting from the refusal to provide legal status to same-sex relationships under the rubric of marriage ... The infringement of the petitioners' equality rights is saved by s. 1 of the Charter.

In any case, legalizing same-sex marriage might cause new social problems, the judge wrote. While a marriage that is not consummated can be voided, he said, "there is no evidence before me as to what would constitute consummation in a gay or lesbian relationship if it should be a factor in the formation of the relationship at all."

findlay was indignant: "The discrimination is recognized, but it's deemed acceptable. The anguish of being told [this] is very difficult to describe. The sense of being people who don't count in the Canadian community is deeply sorrowing." Arron too was dismayed: "I think the decision hit the couples especially hard. Some of them thought they'd be married immediately and they had to delay that, so they were very disappointed about that."

Anne-France Goldwater, one of the Hendricks-LeBœuf lawyers, was another who took Pitfield's verdict very badly. "When he pronounced his verdict, I cried all night," she said later. "I realized that the battle would now be far more complicated and difficult. I even renegotiated my mortgage." Hendricks was even more bitter. "Egale's present to us was to lose B.C.," he lamented. "If they hadn't opened up a front over there, our own issue over here would have been much less work and less trouble."

In hindsight, the Pitfield judgment can look harsh. But courts are in general conservative institutions that advance the law a little at a time. From that moment, progressive forces took hold in a remarkable way: every judge who looked at same-sex marriage after that advanced the cause. Once the discrimination was recognized, it was easier to bring down the last resistance, piece by painstaking piece.

In the fall of 2001, while the world was recovering from the 9/11 attacks on the United States, same-sex marriage was far from making headlines. The gay community paid little attention to the appeal launched by Egale and its couples. It is interesting to note that the federal government took advantage of these new court cases to contest two important but contrary conclusions reached by Judge Pitfield: that excluding homosexuals from marriage was discriminatory and that a simple amendment to the constitution would enable homosexuals to marry.

* * * * *

In November 2001, when the hearings on same-sex marriage in the Ontario Divisional Court and the Quebec Superior Court had just begun, the media paid very little attention. Clearly, the lawyers representing Egale and the couples were a little dispirited by the recent

Pitfield judgment. But they were not completely dejected, as Cynthia Petersen, Egale's representative in B.C. and Ontario, related:

> When we began hearings before Judge Pitfield, one of the federal lawyers told me that her niece of five or six had asked her the question, "Why shouldn't gays get married?" and that she couldn't come up with a decent answer. She jokingly suggested that her niece read her factum! She could present legal arguments, but she had trouble explaining the reasoning in a straightforward way.

As this anecdote illustrates, most of the lawyers representing Egale and the couples felt a kind of superiority towards the arguments of the federal government and religious groups opposed to same-sex marriage. "I've longed for a credible opponent; I've longed for an intelligent thoughtful intellectual response to what we were doing," said Bourassa, one of the Ontario claimants. Sometimes the federal prosecutors gave the impression they were not doing everything within their power to convince the courts of the justice of their position.

"In B.C. we presented completely different evidence than we'd presented in Ontario," recalled Petersen. "But instead of responding directly to the affidavits we presented in B.C., the feds filed documents that they had already presented in Ontario, which didn't even relate to the points that we were raising!" Before the Ontario Divisional Court, however, government lawyers appeared more convinced of their case than their colleagues in B.C. "They personally believed in the federal arguments," recalls Cynthia Petersen. "One of them kept saying to me in the corridor, 'A cat is not a dog and a dog is not a cat.' I didn't quite understand what that had to do with marriage." The lawyer's cryptic remark recalled what a provincial lawyer had said to Michael Hendricks early in the Quebec proceedings: "When are you going to drop this ridiculous suit?"

In support of their position, the government lawyers in Ontario produced no fewer than 20 expert witnesses' reports, from specialists in religious studies, family law, linguistics, statistics and ethics. There was even a conservative Catholic lawyer from the United States and an employee of the Toronto Catholic archdiocese with a degree in anthropology. Joanna Radbord, one of the lawyers for the Ontario couples, was not impressed: "It was like reading the religious right, the federal affidavits!" Some found it especially galling that Ottawa had spent at least $400,000 on these expert witnesses. "In retrospect," said Martha McCarthy, the couple's other lawyer, "they did the best they could when really they had no good arguments to make. Really, they didn't. The writing was on the wall."

Reduced to its essence, the federal government's position was this: not allowing homosexuals to marry is not discriminatory under the Charter of Rights and Freedoms, as only heterosexual couples can procreate. Ottawa did not deny that same-sex "marriages" might have occurred in the course of history. But, they hastened to add, such unions were never "the norm," wherever they had occurred. "Marriage is unique in its essence, that is, its opposite-sex nature," read the federal statement submitted to the Ontario Divisional Court.

* * * * *

It's hard to argue with the observation that marriage has always been almost exclusively reserved for heterosexual couples. But it's fascinating to trace the history of homosexual marriages over time, whether they were given the name *marriages* or not. The ancient Greeks' tolerance towards homosexuality is well known. The historian Xenophon relates that around 378 BCE, in many areas of Greece, "Man and boy live together, like married people." These relations would doubtless be frowned on today, but they were seen at the time as a kind of mentoring and were quite common. Several authors also describe long-term relationships between adult men in ancient Greece, especially among the military. Plato recounted the death of two warriors who were in love with each other during one of the battles that would bring democracy to Athens (514 BCE):

Our own tyrants learned this lesson through bitter experience, when the love between Aristogiton and Harmodius grew so strong that it shattered their power. Wherever, therefore, it has been established that it is shameful to be involved in sexual relationships with men, this is due to evil on the part of the legislators, to despotism on the part of the rulers, and to cowardice on the part of the governed.[2]

Similar phenomena existed in ancient Rome. The eccentric Emperor Nero (who reigned from 54 to 68) was married to Sporus, a eunuch barely out of puberty. "He castrated the boy Sporus and actually tried to make a woman of him," wrote the historian Suetonius, "and he married him with all the usual ceremonies, including a dowry and a bridal veil, took him to his house attended by a great throng, and treated him as his wife." The poet Martial described a wedding between two men in 85 CE:

The bearded Callistratus married the rugged Afer
Under the same law by which a woman takes a husband.
Torches were carried before him, a bridal veil covered his face,
Nor was the hymn to you, O god of marriage, omitted.
A dowry was even agreed on. Does this not, Rome, seem
Enough? Do you expect him also to bear a child?[3]

In 110 CE Juvenal, another poet, made it clear that same-sex unions were not uncommon:

"I have a ceremony to attend," quoth one, "at dawn tomorrow, in the Quirinal valley." "What is the occasion?" "No need to ask: a friend is taking to himself a husband; quite a small affair." Yes, and if we only live long enough, we shall see these things done openly: people will wish to see them reported among the news of the day. Meanwhile these would-be brides have one great trouble: they can bear no children wherewith to keep the affection of their husbands; well has nature done in granting to their desires no power over their bodies.[4]

American historian John Boswell stressed in his seminal work *Same-Sex Unions in Premodern Europe* (1994) that Juvenal not only saw this as an example of the decadence of Roman morals — the main topic of all his work — but was outraged more specifically at the indifference of his fellow citizens towards these unusual practices. In 342, however, a Roman law was passed prohibiting same-sex unions. This is certainly proof that it was a controversial practice but also, more significantly, that it was a common one. The law read:

> When a man marries [a man] as if he were a woman, what can he be seeking, where gender has lost its place? where the sin is something that it is unseemly [even] to know? where Venus is transformed into a different form? where love is sought, but does not appear? We order the laws to arise, justice to be armed with an avenging sword, so that those shameless persons guilty of this either now or in future should be subjected to exquisite punishment.[5]

There is no consensus on exactly what this law meant. In any case, there were fewer homosexual unions as the Roman Empire declined.

Still, with the rise of Christianity in the early centuries of the Common Era, same-sex ceremonies did not disappear immediately, nor was there a stigma attached to them. Boswell notes that *adelphopoiesis*, or religious ceremonies that bound two men together as adoptive "brothers," were without question unions based on love and were probably sexual, although other experts deny this. Documents (all in Greek) testify to the existence of these unions between the eighth and sixteenth centuries, but it is suggested they endured much longer, especially in Greece and the Balkans. In many respects *adelphopoiesis* was similar to a heterosexual marriage, particularly when it comes to the ritual and vocabulary used by the priest. It was celebrated throughout the Christian world, from Italy to Mount Sinai. The official prohibition proclaimed by Rome in the fourth century thus seems to have had little impact. A ninth-century Byzantine legal treatise even describes the practice: "Same-sex unions are of persons, and they [the persons joined through the unions] alone incur impediments to marriage, not the other members of their families."[6]

All this would change in the late Middle Ages, when Christian authorities began to condemn homosexuality more forcefully. Thus in 1306, the Byzantine Emporer Andronicus II Paleologus issued a decree stipulating that "if some wish to enter into ceremonies of same-sex union, we should prohibit them, for they are not recognized by the church."[7] There is a lively contemporary debate as to the significance of these ancient and medieval weddings. It seems clear that in general, European societies did not consider them real marriages, even if in many cases they had similar features, not the least of which was love.

Tolerance towards homosexuality made few strides during the Renaissance. While couples continued to form same-sex unions, they did so at their own risk. In his *Journal de voyage en Italie par la Suisse et l'Allemagne en 1580 et 1581* (A Journal of Travels to Italy via Switzerland and Germany, 1580–1581), the French writer Michel de Montaigne referred to the church of Saint John of the Latin Gate, in which some Portuguese some years before had entered into a strange "brother-hood:"

> Two males married each other at Mass, with the same cere-monies we use for our marriages, taking Communion togeth-er, using the same nuptial Scripture, after which they slept and ate together. Roman experts said that since sex between male and female could be legitimate only within marriage, it had seemed equally fair to them to authorize [these] ceremonies and mysteries of the church.[8]

Montaigne took the trouble to note that "eight or nine Portuguese from this delightful sect were burned at the stake," suggesting that per-secution of homosexuals was on the increase. Even in this climate, however, women disguised themselves as men so that they could marry women. The most famous was the Spaniard Elena de Cespedes (1545–88).[9] The idea eventually spread to the United States, where such "fraudulent" weddings were performed between women from

1780 to about 1920.

In the sixteenth century in the Netherlands, both male and female same-sex couples began demanding the right to civil marriage. In the English county of Cheshire, documents reveal that in 1707 an Anglican minister began to celebrate weddings between female couples. These marriages were registered in the parish records. Such initiatives continued throughout the eighteenth and nineteenth centuries in Britain.

The Western world had no monopoly on homosexual unions. When the Spaniards arrived in America in the fifteenth century, they were amazed to see people of the same sex cohabiting. In 1552, Francisco Lopez de Gomara wrote in his *General History of the Indies*, "Men marry other men who are impotent or castrated, walk like women, do women's work, are used as women are, and cannot carry loads or use a bow." In his 1576 work *Historia da Provincia de Sancta Cruz*, Pedro de Magalhães Gândavo mentions similar "marriages" between women.

The practice was widespread and accepted throughout the New World, particularly among the Aztecs, the Mayas, the Incas and most North American tribes. It was based on the Aboriginal tradition of the *berdache* (from the Old French *bardache*, derived from Italian and Arabic words). "The Native American *berdache* is a person who deviates from his or her traditional gender role, taking on some of the characteristics and perceived responsibilities of the 'opposite' sex," wrote William Eskridge, law professor at Yale University, in an affidavit written in support of the couples before the Ontario Divisional Court. "Many Native American cultures considered *berdaches* to be a third sex," he added, emphasizing that such individuals were revered leaders. He went on to describe marriages between berdaches:

> Often, a male child was consciously raised to be a *berdache*, who
> assumed a special role in the community, mediating between
> the spiritual and physical worlds. Marriages between men and
> male *berdaches* were widespread among Native American cultures. As a general matter, same-sex marriages tended to conform to traditional Native American marriage patterns, in
> which labor was divided between the wife, who kept house, and

husband, who hunted and directed the household. The men who married male *berdaches* were usually attracted to women as well as to men and were not themselves considered *berdaches*. Many such men preferred *berdache* wives for economic advantages, as *berdaches* not only would do the housework, but would help with hunting and other traditionally male activities as well. Other believed that marrying a *berdache* guaranteed greater marital stability, whilst still other conventional men pursued male *berdaches* on the basis of simple sexual attraction.

There were also female berdaches, some of whom married women. As they were thought to possess male attributes, a berdache who married was considered head of the household. The berdache tradition is so far removed from the traditions of the Old World that no one was surprised that Europeans' descriptions of the phenomenon were cast in negative terms. When the berdache tradition was mentioned at all, it was only to demonstrate the savagery of Aboriginals — barbarism, which could only be eradicated by the conquering people.

In China, unions between men during the Yuan and Ming dynasties (1264–1644) were similar to marriages in many respects. During the Tokugawa Dynasty in Japan (1603–1867), samurai went to battle accompanied by their warrior-lovers. In literary accounts, especially in Ihara Saikaku's *The Great Mirror of Male Love* (1687), such relations are depicted as romantic and fiercely faithful. These were not marriages, although they share certain characteristics. As William Eskridge explains,

> The beginning of a relationship between an apprentice (*wakashu*) and a samurai involved a formal exchange of written and spoken vows, giving the relationship a marriage-like status. Each participant promised to love the other in this life and the next — one step beyond our "till death do us part." As in marriage, sex was only one element of the samurai relationship. The samurai was supposed to provide social backing, emotional support, and a model of manliness for the appren-

tice. In exchange, the latter was expected to be worthy of his lover by being a good student of samurai manhood.

Similar unions were celebrated by the Azandes, who live in what is now Sudan. The warrior had to pay a dowry to the parents of the boy he wanted to marry. But even more remarkable in Africa were marriages permitting a woman to become the "wife" of another woman. To do so, she had to pay a dowry to the husband of the woman she desired. Once this was done, she became the "father" of her spouse's children, ensuring a continuation of the family line. These "woman marriages" have been documented in about 30 African groups, including at least nine now living in southern Africa.

This historical summary clearly shows that same-sex marriage is not a new idea, even if it has always been marginalized. And to those unions that have been publicly celebrated and registered must be added the innumerable vows that have been made in private since time immemorial.

* * * * *

As later described by Judge Harry S. LaForme in the Ontario Divisional Court decision (July 2002), the federal government's arguments amounted to this:

> The Attorney General of Canada submits that the institution of marriage is an historical and universal pre-legal concept of an opposite-sex union that was ultimately adopted by law. It contends that there is — and always has been — three basic universal norms, or "Goods and Goals" that constitute marriage. They are (i) procreation, (ii) fidelity, and (iii) sacrament. It argues that — while variables may exist within marriage — the universal norms, namely, the Goods and Goals, always remain. Any relationship, it says, that is outside the universal Goods and Goals does not constitute a marriage.

In the courts Ottawa referred to three normative definitions of marriage established by the fifth-century theologian Augustine of Hippo for the Western (Roman) Church. Augustine was not inventing anything new: Hellenistic Judaism, Stoicism, Alexandrian Neoplatonism, popular Roman prejudice and numerous other traditions had already argued the notion that the purpose of human sexuality should be procreation.

It's worth recalling, however, that for 15 years Augustine had lived with a concubine, who had had a son by him. But as soon as he saw he could marry a rich heiress, he abandoned his lover without further ado. As his relationship with the rich heiress was largely platonic, it's not surprising that he "specifically repudiated procreation as the sole justification for matrimony, insisting that couples who refrained from carnal relations and produced no children were nonetheless properly married."[10] At the time, Christian authorities saw marriage as a sort of compromise with the material world and celibacy as the ideal. But let us not attribute to St. Augustine things that he did not say: in his writings marriage is clearly designed to meet the "natural needs" of "the different sexes for each other's company."

As for the argument that the state cannot modify the definition of marriage as the definition pre-exists the law, it is enough to point out that until the tenth century the Church made little attempt to regulate the institution, leaving the prevailing pagan customs undisturbed. It was not until 1215 that marriage became a sacrament of the Church, and not until the Council of Trent in the sixteenth century that a priest was required to officiate at the ceremony.

* * * * *

Katherine Young was undeterred by any of these historical perspectives. Professor of religion and comparative ethics at McGill University, Young was one of the experts Ottawa had hired to defend its position:

> Same-sex marriage is an oxymoron, because it lacks the universal, or *defining* feature of marriage according to religious, historical, and anthropological evidence. Apart from anything

else, marriage expresses one fundamental and universal need: a setting for reproduction that recognizes the reciprocity between nature (sexual dimorphism) and culture (gender complementarity).

The federal government maintained at the time that this complementarity between the sexes played "a fundamental role in Canadian society."

Young believed that the extension of marriage to gays and lesbians could have "unforeseeable and unfavourable consequences for society," such as the "loss of the cultural norm" of marriage and an "increased polarization between men and women and/or a male identity crisis." Her colleague Edward Shorter, a historian of medicine at the University of Toronto, was concerned about "further destabilization of marriage privately and publicly by breaking the sense of constancy in its mission — the most durable union through which to bear and raise children."

Another expert witness, Douglas W. Allen, Professor of Economics at Simon Fraser University in Burnaby, B.C., also argued that these serious changes to social institutions could have unforeseen consequences. He gave the example of no-fault divorce which, in his view, had negative effects on society. McCarthy recalled,

At one point in [Young's] argument she said that heterosexual-only marriage creates natural incentives for women to be with men, which is good for society and good for procreation, and if there wasn't such incentive in our law then there would be no attraction between men and women. And women would all run into each other's arms like some lesbian science fiction fantasy. And the contribution of men would be reduced to a little more than a teaspoon of sperm. That's your tax dollars at work, in expert evidence.

Early in the hearings McCarthy attempted to bring the debate to a human level. "This case is about ten couples," she said to the court, "real people who love each other and wish to manifest their love through marriage. See these couples as they are. Walk a mile in their shoes." Her associate Joanna Radbord was philosophical about the expert witnesses' evidence and said later that the aggressive tone of Ottawa's arguments made their task easier:

> Our reply factum at the divisional court was excellent, if I may say so, and it was excellent because I was so angry. It was really inspiring. The whole factum of the federal government said, "You are not a human being worthy of respect." And hearing that, it became very easy to write an extremely strong argument. It was totally emotional.

The arguments of expert witnesses recruited by religious groups and given intervener status by the courts went furthest of all. In Ontario they were grouped together under the umbrella of the Interfaith Coalition, which represented conservative Protestants, Catholics, Muslims and Sikhs. According to one coalition expert witness, Daniel Cere of the Newman Institute at McGill University, legalizing same-sex marriage would be an attack on religious rituals. He wrote in his affidavit,

> Catholic religious understanding does not recognize any authority on the part of the state to redefine the nature or the essential properties of marriage ... Same-sex inclusion forces a basic reconfiguration of the nature of civil marriage. In a sense, it de-legitimizes the civil institution as an institution of "marriage" ... The Catholic Church would have to examine this new situation very carefully. It seems to me that canon law would have to consider a number of fundamental questions, including this one: Should the Church continue any form of collaboration with this new civil institution?

In Cere's view, the inevitable outcome would be that "marriage will effectively evaporate from the legal map, to be replaced by the legal recognition of close relationships which involve cohabitation plus some type of sexual relationship."

Abdalla Idris Ali, director of the Center for Islamic Education in North America in Kansas City, spoke in comparable terms in the name of Muslim conservatives. "It will make it harder for Muslims to contribute to Canadian society if the latter insists on unions that our religion considers an affront to Allah," he said. Representatives of conservative Jewish and Protestant congregations also expressed their reservations in regard to the couples' motion, but at least two churches, the United Church and the Metropolitan Community Church of Toronto (MCCT), supported it. "There is no sound reason, morally or theologically, to deny this rite to two persons of the same sex," said Donald Gillies, a retired United Church minister, to the Ontario judges. "Indeed, there is good reason, both theologically and morally, for [sanctioning it]." Brent Hawkes, the minister of MCCT and one of the applicants before the Ontario Divisional Court, argued for a genuine freedom of religion:

> If the common law prohibits marriage between two persons of the same sex, then I believe that this restriction discriminates against MCCT, against me as its senior pastor, and against our congregation on the basis of our religion and our sexual orientation. It also infringes our freedom of religion, for we believe that we are called by God to bless same-sex marriages. It also discriminates against the couples on the basis of sex. We do not believe that the state should refuse to recognize the marriages of any denomination because it disagrees with their religious teachings about marriage. This type of state preference for the marriages of select religions is a relic of past discriminatory times.

Addressing those who claimed that marriage is an immutable institution, he recalled that interracial marriages were no longer illegal in the United States (since the *Loving* case in 1967) and that women now had the same rights as their husbands.

One of the federal government's lawyers, Roslyn Levine, had to concede early on that some heterosexual couples neither could nor wanted to have children. But she urged the court not to get caught up in exceptions and get to the central role of marriage, which was, in her eyes, to unite the two principal halves of humanity: men and women. Keeping the traditional definition of marriage was not discrimination against gays and lesbians, but rather a service rendered to society, she argued. It should not be seen as an attack on the dignity of homosexuals.

* * * * *

Meanwhile, in the Hendricks-LeBœuf case, the federal government rashly tried to blame the Quebec government for subjecting same-sex couples to discrimination in regard to conjugal status, as Quebec's provincial civil union option did not yet exist when the hearings began. It was a desperate but futile move.

The idea of civil unions or registered partnerships open to same-sex couples has been an important issue before the Quebec Superior Court, as it has been before the Ontario and B.C. courts. Judges wondered if these kinds of marriage-substitution arrangements could put an end to the discrimination faced by gays and lesbians. The question was particularly thorny when certain kinds of civil unions were marriages in all but name and involved practically the same benefits and obligations.

On November 9, 2001, the second day of hearings at the Palais de Justice in Montreal, Quebec Justice Minister Paul Bégin announced in the daily paper *Le Devoir* that the government planned to create a new institution, a civil union that would be accessible to same-sex couples. Coincidental — or strategic? Hendricks and LeBœuf saw it as a cunning manoeuvre orchestrated by the Quebec and federal governments to abort their case. According to Hendricks,

> The lawyers asked us, "Do you want to withdraw the case, now that you've achieved civil unions?" Yet all it amounted to was a draft bill! The federal argument was this: "Michael and René want the trappings of marriage, but not marriage itself." In its

first reading, the civil union bill didn't include parental rights,
but why would that matter? It covered all our personal
demands, those of two middle-aged men. We didn't have children and we didn't want any.

Lawyer Anne-France Goldwater was just as skeptical. "The federal
lawyers were stunned," she said later. "They were so pleased with the
civil union bill." But after hearing Bégin say that he would have legislated same-sex marriage in Quebec if he had the power, she became
convinced of the PQ government's good faith. "Civil union was a
band-aid solution," she said. "They weren't trying to derail our cause."

The president of Gai Écoute, Laurent McCutcheon, was another who
didn't believe the Quebec government was trying to harm the
Hendricks-LeBœuf case with the civil union bill. But he recalled the hul-
laballoo that greeted the bill when it was introduced. As he had been
demanding legal recognition for same-sex partners for years, he could
hardly be opposed to the idea. "We were in the mindset of the French
PaCS philosophy, which wasn't marriage, but which went further than
simple recognition of common-law partnerships," he recalled.

The bill nearly went off the rails when other gay and lesbian representatives denounced it publicly, attacking Bégin for leaving out parentage rights for homosexuals. "I had a call from the minister's office,"
McCutcheon said later. "We were going to lose the whole thing. They
gave us 48 hours to convince the [gay and lesbian] community to support the bill or the government would abandon it. Everyone finally
agreed to support it and fight to improve it when it was sent to a parliamentary committee." Passed in June 2002, the legislation finally
opened up civil unions to homosexual as well as heterosexual partners
and extended adoption rights to same-sex spouses. It also abolished the
requirement of heterosexuality in the Civil Code section on marriage
(365), which in any case had been unconstitutional. Some found it
strange that parentage regulations had been changed in such a casual
manner, when for many it was an issue that was as fundamental as marriage. Certainly, if the debate on parentage rights had been as far-reaching as that on marriage, the discussion could easily have degenerated.

During the hearings in November 2001, Judge Louise Lemelin did not take Quebec's intention to introduce civil unions seriously. But when Bégin released his draft legislation in December she agreed to hold an additional day of hearings, in March 2002, to study the potential impact of civil unions on the same-sex marriage demand. But the judge ultimately concluded, as others had done before her, that to accord civil union status to same-sex couples would limit them to an institution that was "separate but equal." This was the principle the U.S. Supreme Court had rejected in its famous racial segregation case, *Brown* v. *Board of Education*, in 1954.

* * * * *

On July 12, 2002, two months before Judge Lemelin issued her judgment, the Ontario Divisional Court released its decision on that province's same-sex marriage cases. Unlike Judge Pitfield of the British Columbia Supreme Court, the Ontario magistrates had no qualms about refuting the key argument made by the federal government and the conservative religious groups: that procreation was an essential element of marriage.

"Even if it is still true, at least for the time being, that a same-sex couple needs a third person in order to conceive a child, heterosexual procreation ... is becoming ever narrower and unsteadier as basis for marriage," declared one of the judges, Robert A. Blair, citing such common alternative reproductive technologies as artificial insemination, in vitro fertilization and surrogate motherhood. "As a social institution, marriage represents far more, in my view, than simply a heterosexual relationship leading to the birth of children." Many heterosexual marriages do not produce offspring, he noted, deducing that "if heterosexual procreation is not necessary to the nature of the institution, then the only difference regarding access to marriage between a same-sex couple and a heterosexual one is sexual orientation." Blair concluded that this constituted discrimination.

His colleague Harry LaForme rejected the argument that extending marriage to same-sex partners would be damaging to heterosexual unions. "There simply is no evidentiary basis to support the proposition that granting same-sex couples the freedom to marry would either diminish the number of children conceived by heterosexual couples, or reduce the quality of care with which heterosexual couples raise their children," he said. In fact, he asserted, opening marriage to homosexuals is in the best interests of children. "Excluding gays and lesbians from marriage disregards the needs, capacities, and circumstances of same-sex spouses and their children. It declares an entire class of persons unworthy of the recognition and support of state sanction for their marriages." In proposing simple "legal recognition" of gay and lesbian unions, Judge LaForme concluded, the federal government is only showing "tolerance" and not "full acceptance" of this fact.

All three of the Ontario Divisional Court judges agreed on the diagnosis after examining the motion brought by the couples, Egale and the MCCT: the exclusion of gays and lesbians from the institution of marriage was discriminatory and could not be justified in a free and democratic society. The next step was to declare the traditional definition of marriage, defined in Canadian common law, invalid and unconstitutional. "I'm convinced that in the end, the law must recognize this," said Judge Blair. The judges now had to agree to the right moment to administer the remedy, which was easier said than done.

Blair suggested giving the federal government two years to amend the law. In the eventuality that Parliament (or another court) had done nothing in that time, gays and lesbians would be able to get married as of July 12, 2004. Judge Heather Smith recommended a similar solution but without explicit details as to what would happen if the government hadn't acted after two years. Judge LaForme suggested a more forceful approach: if it had been up to him, gays and lesbians would have been able to get married as of July 12, 2002, the day the judgment was released.

Arriving at such a radical solution was not easy for Judge LaForme. "My worries do not come from not knowing what the correct remedy is — I know full well what that is. Rather, they flow from the question of who is, or ought to be, responsible for providing the remedy." He decided to take the plunge anyway. The courts generally have to show a certain deference towards legislators, but not always, he said. He recalled that the federal Parliament had never legislated to prohibit same-sex marriages and that the classic definition in the *Hyde* case had been shredded by decades of jurisprudence (for example, who talks of "eternal unions" any more?). In any event, he insisted, discrimination against homosexuals had gone on long enough. He even cited Martin Luther King, Jr.'s *Letter from the Birmingham Jail*, written in April 1963: "We must use time creatively, in the knowledge that the time is always ripe to do right ... Now is the time to lift our national policy from the quicksand of injustice to the solid rock of human dignity."

And so, for the first time in Canadian history, a judge decreed that marriage should be "the lawful union of *two persons* to the exclusion of all others." As his was a minority opinion in the Divisional Court, homosexuals could not get married that very day, but the door had been opened wider than ever before. "Judge LaForme is the hero of all the judges who studied the matter," said Kevin +Bourassa later.

"We were weeping, hugging, screaming," recalled McCarthy. Although it was a clear victory, the moment when it would come into effect was less so. "Privately, we told ourselves: what does it mean? What is the remedy? We still went out to the media 45 minutes later and said *victory*. I mean it was a massive victory, and it was the first win. Finally, somebody had won a case in Canada." Still, the three judges had to append a related order clarifying precisely how the decision would apply. They confirmed that if the government had not acted two years later, on July 12, 2004, common law would change and same-sex couples would be free to marry in Ontario.

"I'm kind of demanding, I suppose," said Radbord. "I was disappointed, yeah: there was no equal marriage! And that's very typical in gay and lesbian cases: there's a lot of statements about 'you're right!', but there's no actual remedy. So to me, the remedy was essentially meaningless: I wanted to get married!"

Radbord is now married to another woman.

4

FIRST STIRRINGS IN OTTAWA

The Ontario Divisional Court ruling caused a commotion in Ottawa. It was the second court in the country to declare that the traditional definition of marriage was discriminatory and the first to suggest that same-sex marriage might one day be a reality. The instigators of this modest social revolution felt that they were nearing the finish line, but its opponents were just getting the bit between their teeth. For politicians, this was a hot potato, deposited on their plate by the Ontario judges, who were quickly labelled "activists."

On the day the Ontario ruling was released, no federal minister was available to present the government's arguments. In all fairness it *was* July 12, the middle of summer, and Prime Minister Jean Chrétien was on holiday at Lac des Piles, his property in the St. Maurice Valley.

Justice Minister Martin Cauchon made himself equally scarce. On that cloudy July day, the Canadian Press wire carried an article in which Cauchon declared his intentions on another hot topic, the decriminalization of marijuana. The article appeared the next morning in papers across the country. Same-sex marriage was not yet among the minister's top priorities, but it soon would be.

Although the ruling had been impatiently anticipated for several months, Ottawa had taken its time preparing for it. On April 30, 2002, a civil servant in the justice department wrote to his colleagues, "The decisions from Ontario and Quebec will soon be released, Quebec has just introduced a same-sex union bill, and we haven't even decided how we are going to respond to the Law Commission of Canada [which recommended the legalization of same-sex marriage]. Very soon we could find ourselves in panic mode on the issue."

In the days following the release of the Ontario decision, politicians and activist groups pressured the federal government not to appeal it. "We'll just be urging the federal government to get on with what the court has decided and to do something about the issue," said Ontario Premier Ernie Eves after a special cabinet meeting in Belleville. "If two people decide that they want to call themselves spouses, [it's] not for me to interfere [with] that." Eves was echoing the Quebec government, which had just created civil union status, a marriage in all but name that was open to both heterosexuals and homosexuals. The two openly gay members of the House, Svend Robinson of the NDP and Réal Ménard of the Bloc Québécois, begged Cauchon and Chrétien to "do the right thing" and refrain from appealing the judgment.

Those opposed to same-sex marriage rights also began to agitate in public. Bishop Jacques Berthelet of Saint-Jean–Longueuil wrote to Cauchon as a political spokesperson for the Catholic Church of Canada:

> The Canadian Conference of Catholic Bishops is greatly troubled by the recent decision of the Ontario Divisional Court that the definition of marriage be changed to include same-sex partnerships. Please take whatever measures are necessary to respect the deeply held convictions of the majority of Canadians that marriage between a man and a woman is a unique institution that is deeply rooted in our history, culture and religious traditions.

Alberta's Premier Ralph Klein, like Eves a Conservative, fervently opposed to same-sex marriage, immediately made clear his own particularly extreme position, from which he has never budged. He favoured applying the notwithstanding clause, a rarely used provision that makes it possible to delay the application of a Charter ruling for up to five years. Robert Bourassa's government in Quebec had used the clause to nullify a Supreme Court ruling on the language on signs in the late 1980s. The government of Saskatchewan had also used the notwithstanding clause. As the definition of marriage is a federal and not a provincial domain, Klein could not go it alone, which did not deter him. A week after the Ontario ruling was released, he said,

> [same sex marriage] simply will not happen in this province, because the sanctity of marriage and the solemnization of marriage, under the Marriage Act, is written law, that it is between a man and a woman ... That's not to say we won't do our part to protect gay rights. But marriage is where we draw the line.

To counteract negative messages about same-sex marriage, Kevin Bourassa and Joe Varnell, applicant couples in the Ontario case, went on a cross-Canada tour. "We knew the finish line was now in sight," said Bourassa. "We had real hope, so we doubled our efforts, mortgaged our house, toured the country, put more resources into the battle."

While politicians and lobbyists tried to get Ottawa to lean one way or the other, the Leshner-Stark couple decided to test the waters. The day the Divisional Court ruling was announced, the two Michaels presented themselves at Toronto City Hall once again to ask for a marriage licence. The city clerk, Ulli Watkiss, said she wanted to take time to read the decision and obtain a legal opinion before making a move. She promised to meet the couple a week later to inform them of the city's decision. Before this meeting took place, the couple's lawyer, Martha McCarthy, received a letter from the city's litigation department that confirmed everyone's worst suspicions: homosexuals would have to wait until the end of the suspension period — two years — before they could get married. "It is our position that until the expiration of that period, the city clerk may not issue marriage licences to same-sex couples," said the city's lawyer, Leslie Mendelson. "The court has asked you to be patient," added Watkiss politely.

Michael Leshner did not take kindly to this. "I'm saddened and distressed. It's wrong morally, it's wrong legally, it's wrong politically.

They're saying they're impotent, and that's just a lie," he said. He was particularly frustrated at not being able to get married even though Premier Eves had spoken in favour of same-sex marriage. "If Ontario wants this to happen, why can't gays and lesbians in Ontario marry?" demanded Leshner. He went on to blame the federal government: "The problem is in Ottawa. Ontario has basically spoken. This is a love story. This is a Jean Chrétien–Aline love story. It's no different, and if he says it's different, he's wrong and he doesn't deserve to be prime minister."

As predicted, the federal government appealed the ruling. Martin Cauchon announced this as casually as possible. "At present, there is no consensus, either from the courts or among Canadians, on whether or how the laws require change," he wrote in a press release dated July 29, 2002, the deadline for launching an appeal. "The Government believes it is the responsible course to seek further clarity on these issues." In the absence of the Minister of Justice in person, journalists and other observers could only grasp at straws in trying to understand Ottawa's reasoning faced with a ruling that was itself so reasonable. Cauchon had written,

> In today's society, the existence of a committed relationship is of great importance to our lives, whether for opposite-sex couples or same-sex couples. At the same time, there are important reasons why we as a society must consider carefully the issues around changing the fundamental nature of marriage and what the implications of such a change might be.

The declaration mentioned that the Netherlands was the only country currently permitting same-sex marriages.

Documents obtained under the Access to Information Act have since revealed that civil servants in the justice department saw recognition of same-sex marriage as an "extreme" last resort, as extreme as using the notwithstanding clause to maintain the traditional definition of marriage. They nevertheless pointed out that the "symbolic value" that many Canadians attached to heterosexual marriage was based more on "an idealized past" than on historical fact. Whatever the case, the legalization of same-sex marriage looked as though it might provoke "undesirable reactions" among Canadians.

* * * * *

In a motion brought before the Ontario Court of Appeal on July 29, the federal justice minister submitted that extending marriage to gays and lesbians constituted a "significant rather than a slight legal change." In other words, it was not a decision the courts should make. Egale immediately denounced the "waste" of millions of dollars of taxpayers' money that an appeal would entail. "What today's announcement means is that these costly and time-consuming proceedings must continue," said Executive Director John Fisher. He added,

> We, and all the couples, are in this for the long haul if need be. But sometimes we get tired of going to court in case after case after case, to fight for every little scrap of human dignity. Just once, it would be nice to see the government show some leadership; just once it would be nice for them to demonstrate a commitment to treating all Canadians equally, to do the right thing because it's the right thing, and not because they were forced to by the courts. It's a sad reflection on Canada's human rights record that not once has the government taken the lead in treating lesbian, gay, bisexual or transgendered Canadians equally. Whether the issue was ending the ban on gays in the military, prohibiting sexual orientation discrimination or providing same-sex benefits, the government has consistently abdicated responsibility, and asked the courts to tell them what to do.

An end to the proceedings was imperative on financial grounds alone. The Ontario Divisional Court had ordered Ottawa to reimburse a large part of the honoraria paid to the lawyers defending the "victorious" couples, which amounted to several hundred thousand dollars. To this amount would be added costs incurred in other provinces and in courts of appeal.

"We stand for all gays and lesbians in this country who will not give up, who will stand together and say our love will persist and you must recognize it," said Alison Kemper of Toronto, who with her partner Joyce Barnett was one of the applicant couples. "The government should stop fighting and introduce a bill in Parliament immediately," said Martha McCarthy at a press conference.

A month after Ottawa presented a motion to the Court of Appeal, McCarthy and her colleague Joanna Radbord responded with their cross-appeal, in which they demanded that the Ontario Court of Appeal immediately authorize same-sex marriages. Giving the government two years to change common law was an "excessive" delay that would perpetuate a "grave injustice," they claimed. In their motion arguing for the applicant same-sex couples they wrote,

> There is no need for deference to Parliament when the impugned provision relates to the common law, as opposed to legislation. If the government wishes to receive the court's guidance, it should not be permitted to obtain it at the applicants' personal cost. In all of the circumstances, it would be unjust if the court allowed the Attorney General of Canada leave to appeal without making leave conditional on the payment of the applicants' personal costs.

Svend Robinson accused Ottawa of hiding behind the courts, while Réal Ménard called the government's reaction "cowardly" and demanded a debate in the House. Two days after Ottawa's decision was announced, Toronto City Council pressed the government to reverse its decision and pull out all the stops to open marriage to homosexuals right away.

In July 2002, a slight majority of the Canadian population supported the Ontario Divisional Court's ruling, according to a survey of 1,200 respondents by the Pollara polling firm. About 48 percent said they were in favour of legislating same-sex marriage, while 43 percent opposed it. Slightly more than half of women (51 percent) recommended the change, while men were divided (46 percent in each camp). Among young people there was a broader consensus: 61 percent of 18- to 34-year-olds were in agreement with entitlement to marriage rights. On the other hand, only 28 percent of those over 65 were in agreement. Pollara president Michael Marzolini concluded that same-sex marriage would not be long in coming. "The writing is on the wall for this issue," he said in an interview with the *National Post*. "It will become more popular. It will become more and more acceptable. Government can lead public opinion or it can follow it and this is an opportunity to lead it rather than follow it."

* * * * *

Martin Cauchon maintained later that he took the case to the highest Ontario court against his better judgment:

> When the Divisional Court ruling was announced, I had to appeal it because the government position was against same-sex marriage. This had been reiterated in 1999 when it voted on a Reform motion. I was uneasy with the traditional definition of marriage. When this file landed on my desk I realized I was uncomfortable with the *status quo*.

Considering his age and education, it's not surprising that Cauchon became a supporter of same-sex marriage fairly early on. As with many people of his generation (he was born in 1962), he had gay friends and saw no problem with relationships between people of the same sex. In fact several years ago he had come to the conclusion that gay and lesbian couples would eventually acquire legal equality. One event had particularly affected him in this respect. Early in his professional life, Cauchon met a gay man who was determined to hide his sexual orientation in spite of a very successful career. Cauchon even remembers a party at the man's house where everything had been rearranged to hide the fact that his partner lived with him: "I remember thinking, 'This is ridiculous!'"

Cauchon's internal conflict was acute. On one side were his personal convictions; on the other was ranged the vast machinery of government, the majority of politicians, a large segment of public opinion and, most significantly, Jean Chrétien. A Liberal Party resolution in favour of same-sex marriage adopted during a 1998 party conference (but overturned in 2000) didn't appear to carry much weight. No one in government seemed even to remember it. "I decided that if I had to confront this question as minister of justice, I wanted to be true to my convictions," he recalled. "For that to happen, I had no choice but to try to steer the party in a new direction."

Cauchon called a meeting with Chrétien's advisers and Alex Himelfarb, clerk of the Privy Council, to look for a way to launch the debate in the government and the population at large. "I said, 'Listen, I'm not comfortable with appealing the decision, I'm going to ask for a parliamentary committee to hold public hearings we'll produce a working paper that presents various possible solutions,'" said Cauchon.

The idea caught on. During the week after the government appealed the Ontario decision, federal ministers held teleconferences to fine-tune their position on a file that was looking more and more controversial. Cauchon defended his idea of public hearings, but other ministers were starting to say simply that perhaps the time had come to entitle same-sex couples to marriage. Very few cabinet members were, in fact, deeply opposed to the change. Some feared that by prolonging legal proceedings Ottawa would give the impression that it was unwilling to fulfil its responsibilities. However, the cabinet was aware that opponents were still in the majority within the Liberal caucus.

Social conservatives in the Liberal Party, such as Ontario MPs Tom Wappel, Roger Gallaway, Pat O'Brien, Dan McTeague and Paul Szabo, promised to campaign against any deviation from the government's stated position. Behind the scenes there were complaints that despite its appeal of the Divisional Court's decision, the cabinet wasn't being nearly strenuous enough in defending the traditional definition of marriage.

The same-sex marriage debate landed on Parliament Hill just as another struggle, much more important in Liberal eyes, was reaching a climax: the mortal combat between Prime Minister Jean Chrétien and Finance Minister Paul Martin. In June 2002, after months of tension, the Prime Minister had forced Martin out of cabinet. Chrétien himself had not yet announced his retirement from politics. Throughout that summer of 2002, intense backroom manoeuvring was going on in the two camps, as both vied to win public opinion and more especially the favour of the Liberal caucus. Right-leaning MPs favoured Martin, while the progressive wing of the party closed ranks behind Chrétien. For months on end the same-sex marriage file suffered collateral damage from the battle royal going on between the two groups. Still, Martin supported the decision made by Chrétien's cabinet to refer the case to the Ontario Court of Appeal. "There are conflicting court cases and I think that what we've now got to do is wait for the higher court and take guidance from them," he said in an interview with the *Toronto Star*.

Opponents of same-sex marriage were right to be worried. In August 2002, soon after the cabinet held its teleconferences, some ministers began to speak out publicly in favour of the change. Heritage Minister Sheila Copps took the first step. "I don't think that from the point of view of equality we should be prohibiting anybody from entering into a legal contract if they choose to be together," she said. Three other ministers, Allan Rock (Industry), Bill Graham (Foreign Affairs) and Stephen Owen (State), all decided to take a stand by participating in the Vancouver gay and lesbian pride parade. "The option that I'll be asking my colleagues to favour is recognition of same-sex marriages," said Rock to a *Toronto Star* reporter. "It's an important step along the road to equality." A few hours later Graham had his say, also to the *Star*:

> I respect those who believe in the integrity of marriage. That is a very important institution for us as Canadians, and for society. I think it is equally important that gay and lesbian people who are in an affectionate relationship over time want to commit themselves to that relationship. That is also good for society; allowing those people to engage in that societal act is, in the end, going to reinforce the institution of marriage. It won't weaken it. It reinforces it.

Bill Graham later offered an astonishing explanation for his sudden support. "One of the reasons I became a supporter of same-sex marriage," he acknowledged, "is that it differentiates us from the Americans. Sooner or later, perhaps in 15 years or so, the Americans will come to the same conclusion after much conflict. But as minister of foreign affairs I thought same-sex marriages would give Canada the trump card." Worldwide public opinion remained strongly opposed to redefining marriage, but there was no question that such a revolutionary move would focus a lot of media attention on Canada.

Other federal politicians, such as Bloc Québécois leader Gilles Duceppe and future NDP leader Jack Layton, had long been in favour of redefining marriage. Their Progressive Conservative counterpart, Joe Clark, followed suit in September. As one might expect, ministers who were open to homosexual rights were soon under attack from other MPs. Dan McTeague accused Allan Rock of breaking cabinet solidarity, putting himself in a delicate position vis-à-vis the Liberal caucus and going back on the commitment to the status quo he had made earlier as minister of justice. "Mr. Rock's position breaks caucus solidarity which is forged by consensus, so perhaps he should consider a career as a backbencher," McTeague said.

Meanwhile Egale was circulating the names of other ministers they believed were favourable to same-sex marriage: Jane Stewart, Paul deVilliers and Jean Augustine. All cabinet members in favour of changing the definition of marriage were Chrétien supporters. Their attempts to bring their colleagues into line were beginning to bear fruit: on August 7, 2002, a week after it appealed the Ontario Divisional Court's ruling, the government announced that a parliamentary committee would hold public hearings on the recognition of same-sex marriage. It was undoubtedly a personal victory for Martin Cauchon and other believers in entitlement to marriage rights, even if many gay and lesbian activists regarded it as just another tactic for wearing down the government's opponents.

Cauchon presented the hearings as the government's way of "taking leadership, opening a discussion on the question and listening to the people." After all, said Chrétien, same-sex marriage is "a very complex problem that needs careful study." Speaking to reporters, however, Chrétien and Cauchon refused to reveal their personal opinions, which were, in fact, diametrically opposed. "If we are going to go down that path [same-sex marriage], it's much too early at this point in time," said Cauchon. "I have views," said Chrétien. "But my views are one thing. I am the prime minister of Canada and I have to decide after a committee will have studied the problem. I could decide tomorrow, but that's not the process."

"We welcome the news that government is open to reviewing its options to put an end to the discriminatory exclusion of same-sex couples from marriage," wrote John Fisher, executive director of Egale, in a press release. "At the same time, human rights should not be subject to a popularity contest. There comes a time when government needs to stop talking, and take action to ensure that Canadians in same-sex relationships are treated equally. The time for leadership is now. Same-sex marriage is inevitable — Canadians know it, the courts know it, and government knows it."

In the Prime Minister's Office everyone was aware of the objections of the gay rights lobby, but what they feared more was a revolt in the Liberal caucus, which was largely behind Paul Martin at the time. One of Chrétien's advisers, who preferred to remain anonymous, explained:

> The gay and lesbian rights groups were saying, "Okay, you should just publicly declare you're going in the direction in favour of it." But I think our feeling was that that would have been too hasty a decision. Because of the dynamic in the Liberal caucus, it would just have preempted the process. We would have had a big mess on our hands and a very big internal fight, so we said, "Let the process unfold, let's create an opportunity for discussion on it."

The justice minister was looking at three possible scenarios for avoiding the extension of marriage to same-sex partners. The first was to legalize registered civil unions for homosexuals and heterosexuals, with the same features as marriage in all but name. The second was more radical: that the state eliminate civil marriage altogether and hand over the institution to religious authorities. In other words, it would withdraw marriage from heterosexuals to avoid giving it to homosexuals! The idea had been suggested by Justice Robert Blair in his Ontario Divisional Court ruling, in spite of his support for same-sex marriage. The third scenario was maintaining the status quo, keeping marriage for heterosexual couples.

Before releasing the working paper to be used by the parliamentary committee convened to study the marriage question, Cauchon decided to meet members of the gay and lesbian community in Montreal. "They told me very clearly," he said, "that they had been battling for equality for quite long enough — don't show up with something midway like civil unions. That didn't interest them at all; in fact they found it insulting. I could understand that." Laurent McCutcheon, president of Gai Écoute, was at the same meeting. He felt it cemented a favourable view of Cauchon among gays and lesbians. "A couple of women who were there said it was important for them to be able to marry, as one of them was pregnant," he recalled. "This was the real thing. I think these arguments had an emotional impact on him."

This was mid-August 2002, and by now the promised working paper was nearly ready. Cauchon took an unusual step for a cabinet minister: he intervened to make sure that the debate didn't diverge from the objective at hand, which was to permit same-sex marriage. But publication of the document, due in September, was delayed by the Chrétien-Martin duel and an unexpected speech from the throne. It finally came out in early November.

* * * * *

Meanwhile Ottawa was being shaken by a political earthquake whose epicentre was Chicoutimi. Jean Chrétien, to everyone's astonishment, took advantage of a Liberal caucus meeting on August 21, 2002, to announce that he was retiring as prime minister — but not until February 2004! Frenzied activity aimed at ensuring Chrétien's "legacy" to Canada consumed Ottawa over the next few months. Some of the gifts bequeathed by the "little guy from Shawinigan" were ratifying the Kyoto accord on greenhouse gas reduction and passing a law limiting donations to federal political parties — but not same-sex marriage. At least not yet.

Not surprisingly, then, the courts once again jumped the gun on the government. On September 6, 2002, Justice Louise Lemelin issued her judgment on the Hendricks-LeBœuf case in the Quebec Superior Court. Like the Ontario Divisional Court, she declared discrimination against gays and lesbians in the domain of marriage to be unjustifiable. But she dared not go as far as Justice LaForme had gone and refrained from changing the law on the spot. Her decision was nevertheless a solid backing for granting marriage to same-sex couples, especially as she categorically rejected civil union as a substitute:

> The historic disadvantage suffered by homosexuals is recognized and well documented. They have attempted for many years to gain recognition as full citizens due the same respect and the same rights as others. Gays and lesbians have suffered isolation, harassment and violence. Homosexual relations were only decriminalized in 1969. Homosexuality was considered an illness. In spite of progress, they are still subject to ridicule and, in certain circles, stereotyping ... A legal provision that excludes them from a civil institution as important as marriage will be taken as a negative sign. Being treated yet again as different will only serve to perpetuate their special status.

After this reminder, Justice Lemelin turned her attention to the federal government's principal argument: that procreation is the central purpose of marriage. "Respect for the social and historic values of traditional marriage does not mean we should not examine the institution in the light of the Charter," she said, "without which no preexisting discrimination can be corrected. The novelty of the applicants' demands raises the following question: is procreation the sole reason for getting married today? The Court does not think so." In justifying this position, the judge stressed that in Quebec civil law, it had been many years since impotence had been considered an adequate reason to annul a marriage: "Marriage is not necessarily defined by the children born of the union. Marriage is an exclusive, intimate and lasting union between two people who commit themselves to life in common and mutual support."

The magistrate concluded that excluding homosexuals from marriage created "a discriminatory distinction" that "undermines human dignity and denies the applicants equality rights under section 15 of the Charter." All that was needed now was to determine whether such discrimination was justifiable in a free and democratic society, as required by section 1 of the Charter. And for this another of Ottawa's arguments had to be dealt with: that the state did not create marriage, but was simply following an ancient religious tradition based on the complementarity of opposite sexes:

> No one would deny that religions have played an important role in marriage — indeed, their beliefs and their rites have framed the institution. The secularization of marriage, however, requires government to recognize that the institution is a civil one, and cannot be defined exclusively by religion. We are no longer living in the homogeneous society of a century ago. Multiculturalism, diverse religious beliefs, and the secularization of many societal institutions all testify to the openness of Canadian society. The state must ensure respect for each citizen, but no group has the right to impose its values on others or define a civil institution.

Justice Lemelin's trickiest problem was how to resolve the discrimination issue, the same issue the judges in the Divisional Court of Ontario had struggled with. She first noted that the federal lawyers had not established "real and urgent concerns" that would justify violating the rights of the Hendricks-LeBœuf couple. Nor had Ottawa established that redefining marriage would threaten "peace or public order." Finally, the judge rejected the government's position that "all rights pertinent to the flourishing of homosexuals as full participants in society" had already been recognized. But unlike the courageous Justice LaForme from Ontario, Justice Lemelin refrained from writing a new definition of marriage herself. "It is the responsibility of elected representatives to take the first steps towards reform and to take stock of all the ramifications," she declared. "The courts should show restraint."

The judge therefore declared inoperative section 5 of the Federal Law-Civil Law Harmonization Act, No. 1, along with the Modernization of Benefits and Obligations Act, both of which restricted homosexuals' access to marriage. The same applied to the first paragraph of section 365 of the Quebec Civil Code, which had been repealed anyway three months earlier when the *Loi instituant l'union civile* had been passed. But like most of the judges in the Ontario Divisional Court, Lemelin suspended the application of her ruling for two years. If the Ontario and Quebec courts of appeal had not subsequently intervened, the Lemelin ruling would have had no impact at all on parliamentary decisions, as the judge refused to declare that her decision would be enforceable when the two-year period expired.

Nonetheless, Hendricks and LeBœuf welcomed the decision with joy. "It's been four years since we filed our first motion, and we've been wondering when this decision would come and what it would be," said Hendricks to a Montreal *Gazette* reporter. "We're absolutely floored, we're so pleased." The couple were disappointed, of course, to have to wait two years before celebrating their wedding: "We didn't think we'd win all the points, but everything was right except the time. We'd like it to be sooner; at my age, two years is a lifetime."

One of their lawyers, Anne-France Goldwater, was particularly pleased at Justice Lemelin's analysis of civil union, which had just become legal in Quebec. "What makes the Quebec victory important for all of Canada is that [Lemelin] had the chance to look at a civil union law and to comment herself as to whether that would be enough of a solution for gay and lesbian couples," Goldwater said. "But Justice Lemelin said in very strong terms that a civil union, as wonderful as it is because of all the economic rights that it gives, is still not marriage."

The day after the ruling was made public, the couple had already decided to appeal it in the hope of reducing their waiting time. Right on cue, Ottawa decided to appeal a few days later, but for different reasons. Hendricks and LeBœuf were overjoyed. "We're delighted they appealed," said Hendricks. "We won, and we want to make sure that Quebec civil law is considered in any decision at a higher level ... We want to have a Supreme Court decision for the simple reason that it is carved in stone."

In September 2002, the bill for the Hendricks-LeBœuf legal battle topped $180,000. While the lawyers assumed $100,000 of the costs and $60,000 was obtained through the federal Court Challenges Program, the couple had to extend the mortgage on their house to come up with the remaining $20,000.

5

PARLIAMENT GETS INVOLVED

The Standing Committee on Justice and Human Rights finally began to meet to discuss same-sex marriage on November 27, 2002 — a few months late. As is often the case with parliamentarians, they ended up talking about lots of other things too, including some extra issues that were not on the agenda.

From the start, Vic Toews of the Canadian Alliance was indignant that Justice Minister Cauchon had excluded a discussion of legal recognition of dependent family relationships from the debate:

> I think this is a wonderful opportunity to talk about relationships and legal relationships between family members, be it the rather common example of a mother and a daughter living together. The daughter is a retired teacher and has a pension. If that daughter dies, what happens to the mother? Isn't there some kind of concern that the state should express in respect of how that mother will cope in the future?

Lisa Hitch, justice department senior counsel, answered Toews: "[Minister Cauchon's] preference would be, given the timelines that have been given to us by the court with regard to the issue of marriage and same-sex unions, that if that broader issue of dependency is of interest to the committee, the committee could possibly consider it separately." Anyway, she added, dependents and their informal care-givers already qualified for tax exemptions. Benefits for couples are more generous, she acknowledged, but they go with obligations such as child support payments that don't apply to caregivers and their dependents.

The backgrounder that Cauchon had submitted to the committee was clear on the issue. The three possible scenarios that MPs were invit-ed to consider were recognition of same-sex marriage, state withdraw-al from involvement in marriage and keeping the status quo. The doc-ument leaned heavily in favour of the first option, even though Cauchon had not yet abandoned the idea of a Canada-wide registry of civil unions that granted the same rights as marriage.

At first the chair of the standing committee, Liberal MP Andy Scott, was opposed to same-sex marriage. He had even declared that a legal "firewall" ought to be constructed around the traditional definition of marriage. The other MPs on the committee were almost evenly divided for and against, so that an interesting debate — to say the least — was assured.

Liberal MP Ivan Grose asked pertinently what the point of this com-mittee was, since in the end it was the courts that would have the last word on the subject. This was not the first time this sentiment had been expressed: ever since the Canadian Charter of Rights and Freedoms had been adopted in 1982, elected representatives had real-ized that legislation they passed could be declared invalid by the courts, and there was nothing they could do about it. Vic Toews and his colleagues John McKay and Derek Lee also found it deplorable that the courts had not taken into account the Reform Party motion of 1999, which defined marriage as a union between a man and a woman, or a similar clause contained in the Modernization of Benefits and Obligations Act of 2000. Hitch replied that judges gave more weight to duly constituted laws than to motions.

The work of the committee thus began with a legal discussion, but when meetings resumed after the holidays the virulent attacks began. Peter MacKay wondered what the point was of debating same-sex mar-riage when a 2001 survey showed there were 68,000 people living in same-sex common-law relationships in the country — only 0.5 percent of all couples. There are far more homeless people than that, he noted. "In my mind, it comes down to a simple matter of priorities," MacKay said in an interview with the *Globe and Mail* on January 28, 2003. "I would suggest that homelessness is a bigger issue, as one example. I walked by four people in subzero temperatures on my way here this morning ... In the minds of Canadians, when it comes down to priorities, there are issues that must register higher. I don't think this stuff even ranks in the top ten."

The Bloc Québécois and the executive director of Egale, John Fisher, criticized this attempt to relativize the importance of gay rights. "It's as if because only 34,000 couples define themselves as homosexual, it's not an important issue," said Bloc Québécois MP Richard Marceau. "When you're talking about a fundamental right, whether there's only one couple or 34,000 couples or a million couples, the importance is the same, in my opinion." Fisher stressed that no one questioned the rights of people with disabilities, even if they are also a minority. "We are concerned that some MPs are using numbers to minimize the issue," he said.

* * * * *

The following week, gay and lesbian activists began to fight back. "I think you have to ask whether anyone, anywhere, can give you a rational reason for excluding us," said Laurie Arron, head of Egale's marriage committee, on February 4. "We submit that the answer is, no, there is no rational reason for excluding us. The only reason to exclude us is to condemn being gay or lesbian. That's it."

Two days later, an Ottawa Catholic named Richard Hudon, representing the Association of Christian Families, made some of the most offensive suggestions heard during the whole six months of the committee hearings. Far from apologizing for being homophobic, he accused some of the MPs of "heterophobia." Expanding marriage rights to include gays and lesbians, he said, was "insanity" and would be "[conniving] with the destruction of our civilization." It would be a corruption of the institution for the sake of a "relatively minuscule number of active homosexuals," he said. "Two men buggering and fellating each other cannot beget any progeny out of their aberrant sexual practices." He insisted that discrimination was a necessity in our society: "Will we put a murderer in jail or will we let him go free? We need to exercise discrimination."

NDP MP Svend Robinson pointed out the contrast between the message of love the church claimed to present and this "hateful diatribe" by Hudon, who replied that Robinson was showing a lack of Christian charity "by dragging me into your circle of homosexuality, which I abhor."

Liberal MP John McKay didn't go quite this far, but he did suggest that the legalization of same-sex marriage would be a pyrrhic victory. "You will have destroyed, if you will, the symbolism that you craved," he said, "while having gained nothing." The same day, Monica Perazzo and Gabriel Pinkstone of the Quebec Lesbian Mothers Association were bombarded with questions from Liberal and Alliance MPs, who wanted to know in what way marriage would reduce discrimination against the children they wanted to have. Unsatisfied with the answers, one MP criticized them for talking too much, while another looked away while they gave their explanations. This odious lack of courtesy elicited a reminder from committee chair Andy Scott to his colleagues that the witnesses were there to inform the MPs, and not the reverse. The MPs should feel free to ask witnesses questions and express opinions, "but I don't think we're here to inform them, particularly."

As they left the meeting room, the two women could not help commenting on the difference in tone between the hearings in Ottawa and those in Quebec a year earlier on the subject of civil union. "I feel that there were people who had already made up their minds and they're just here to prove their point," said Pinkstone. "Their questions are not actual questions. Their questions are ways of stating their already decided opinions. There was a badgering of the witness, not letting people finish their sentences, etc."

But reporters covering the deliberations had not yet seen the worst. On February 11, it was the turn of Rita Curley, a member of the

Catholic Women's League and Christian family life convenor of the league's St. Ignatius Martyr Council in Ottawa, to have her say. She began by quoting Jesus in the Gospel according to St. Matthew: "For this reason a man will leave his father and mother and be joined to his wife, and the two shall become one, so they are no longer two but one." To equate homosexual unions with marriage, Curley continued, "is just as logical as to equate anarchy with government." In passing she also condemned contraception, divorce, abortion, extramarital sex, pornography, euthanasia and, of course, homosexuality. And for her final *coup de grâce*:

> To redefine marriage to be more inclusive of homosexuality is to create a new morality in which homosexuality is not merely tolerated but is normalized and would branch out into sexual activity with babies, children of both sexes, and with animals.

"Active homosexual behaviour," she added, was "the main way that AIDS is spread." In conclusion, she declared, "We've had enough of unholy alliances and unholy relationships. They are nothing but a dead end and an end to society … Let us restore Christianity to its rightful place." Rita Curley ended by reassuring her listeners that God loved them anyway. On the recommendation of Senator Anne Cools, another fervent opponent of same-sex marriage, Rita Curley was award-ed a Queen Elizabeth II Golden Jubilee Medal in 2002.

Robinson, who had heard quite enough by now, denounced Curley's testimony as venomous:

> I've been silent, but I will not be silent any longer. As a gay man, to hear a witness equating me with pedophiles, with those who would have sex with babies, with those who would engage in bestiality, is not acceptable from any witness, and I won't accept it. It's not acceptable. Frankly, I'm disappointed that no other member of this committee has spoken out. If this kind of hatred and venom were directed at blacks or Aboriginal people, does anyone think that members around

this committee would be silent and just listen as this kind of hatred is spewed? I don't think so.

Kevin Sorenson did not agree, however. "I certainly didn't take your remarks as being hateful," he said to Curley. But perhaps her subsequent remarks gave him pause. "The people who are homosexuals — I find from my experience of other people that these people have been molested in their childhood," she said, "and that's what gave them the habit. It started them off on the wrong foot. But they can change."

The next witness, Pierre Pariseau, continued in the same vein. He suggested that as only a tiny minority of homosexuals, probably a few hundred, "value faithfulness and are capable of some stability," marriage should not be expanded to include same-sex couples. "The powerful homosexual lobby has managed to force the gay marriage issue to the top of this government's agenda," he said, "while ignoring far more important health issues related to the gay lifestyle and their consequences on public health." David Corbett from the Foundation for Equal Families responded to this argument:

> As for the actual sexual practices of gay men, which is a matter of great, almost prurient interest, there has been a social history to that, and it flows from the secrecy and lack of legitimacy of those relationships. If you're outside the rules to begin with, then you start to wonder whether you shouldn't throw out all the rules. Those relationships will be stabilized by the public promises that come from marriage, which will strengthen those domestic institutions for those and the couples who are in them. That's the whole point of that kind of public commitment. You will see the effect of it in the stabilizing of those relationships 10, 15, 20 years down the line.

His colleague Michelle Douglas from the same organization added that "the foundation believes that equal marriage will in fact strengthen the institution of marriage by expanding the range of loving couples who subscribe to its tenets." It was Douglas's court challenge over the exclusion of gays and lesbians from the military that had led to their being admitted to the Canadian Armed Forces in 1992.

René LeBœuf pushed the point home before the committee: "Once [same-sex marriage] happens, we will be able to get beyond the social marginalization that has historically been our fate. Never again will young Canadian gays and lesbians have to face the bleak future that lay before us when we were adolescents. Gays and lesbians will no longer be treated by the law and by society as social pariahs — a marginal group that can be gotten rid of."

These words had little effect on Liberal MP John McKay, who quoted an American study claiming that many homosexuals intend to marry "not only as a way of securing benefits but as part of a self-conscious attempt to subvert the institution of marriage from within."

* * * * *

The next day, February 12, committee chair Andy Scott saw fit to issue a warning to his colleagues. "The issue is an emotional one," he said, "and feelings are strong on either side — even strong in the middle. I think we all have to be a little measured in the language we use, because the people sitting with you as witnesses, and around this table, have different views as well." His appeal was at best partially effective.

The first witness of the day's hearings was Daniel Cere, director of the Institute for the Study of Marriage, Law and Culture at McGill University. He repeated more or less the same arguments he had made previously in an affidavit, but this time highlighted certain points. He was worried about the impact of same-sex marriage on children. "The same-sex marriage project in a certain sense signals a society no longer confident to promote a form of life that specifically affirms the importance of this connection between children and their natural parents," said Cere. He went on to speak of the broader consequences of such a change:

The proposal to delete heterosexuality from the definition of marriage will change the internal meaning of this institution, no doubt about it. It will inevitably affect the identity of those who are shaped and sustained by this institution. Thoughtful gay and lesbian theorists readily admit this.

To support his point, he cited a passage from *Bodies and Pleasures: Foucault and the Politics of Sexual Normalization*, a 1999 book by philosophy professor Ladelle McWhorter of the University of Richmond in Virginia. If homosexuals, she wrote, are

> allowed to participate as gay people in communities and institutions [that heterosexuals] claim as theirs, our presence will change those institutions and practices enough to undermine their preferred version of heterosexuality and, in turn, they themselves will not be the same. [Heterosexuals] are right, for example, that if same-sex couples get legally married, the institution of marriage will change, and since marriage is one of the institutions that supports heterosexuality and heterosexual identities, heterosexuality and heterosexuals will change as well.[1]

Reached by email, McWhorter clarified her position: although she is not a champion of same-sex marriage, she is not against it. She was simply predicting the effects it might have on the institution — effects she does not necessarily see as negative. Cere insisted on his point, however. "We can press on with the project, but our generation won't be the ones who will have to bear the costs and risks. These will be borne by our future generations." Cere added that his comments were not intended to denigrate same-sex relationships.

The president of Gai Écoute, Laurent McCutcheon, was next up at the microphone. Studies have shown, he said, that young gays and lesbians are much more likely to commit suicide than the rest of the population:

> Why is that? Because there are still people like [Daniel Cere], like others in society, who reject homosexuality and do not

wish to allow homosexuals to live their lives to the full … The call line that I represent receives at least 20,000 calls a year from young people in difficulty or in distress. The great hardship for homosexuals is rejection, and I hope that the results of this committee's efforts will not yet again constitute rejection.

Gwendolyn Landolt, vice-president of Real Women, a right-wing group whose offices, ironically, are in the same building as those of Egale, presented several reasons why same-sex marriage should not be recognized. She dwelt particularly on the dangers for children. All the literature on homosexual parenting has been reviewed, she said, "and the evidence from several studies does not establish that homosexual parenting is equivalent to heterosexual parenting. The unreliability of current studies on same-sex parenting was determined in a number of studies."

Liberal MP Hedy Fry, who practised family medicine for over 20 years in a Vancouver neighbourhood where many of her patients were gay and lesbian, pointedly refuted Landolt's testimony about the short-lived nature of same-sex unions: "I would like to correct Ms. Landolt, from my own small experience, that not only were most of these relationships, far more than the heterosexual relationships I saw, sexually faithful; many of them were long-lasting. They lasted 20 years, 30 years, 35 years. The couples died together."

Later the committee asked Bill Ryan, of the Centre for Applied Family Studies at McGill University's School of Social Work, to respond to the arguments of the Real Women representative on the parenting abilities of gays and lesbians. "Let us simply state," he said, "that 25 years of research into this area by peer-reviewed scientists in both North America and Europe has clearly concluded that children and their social, psychological, emotional and sexual development are not negatively affected by being raised in same-sex households."

Katherine Young, professor of religion and comparative ethics at McGill, again advanced her theory that same-sex marriage was a threat not only to the family but also to men. Because of reproductive technologies, she said, "Men are already on the marginal side of family life in the sense that you can get a new generation with a teaspoon of sperm." Instead society should be encouraging men to commit themselves to family life to ensure the survival of the human race. Same-sex marriage, whose main objective is obviously not reproduction, should therefore be avoided:

> I don't know what kind of society we'd get if we took the majority of men, the heterosexual men, and got them out of this life process altogether. What does that group then do? They're no longer looking toward the future. Do they become the death-oriented group? Do they become a separate, polarized group? Do they become antagonistic to women and children? There are all sorts of things that could happen if we go down [the same-sex marriage] route ... Something very serious can happen with children.

In other words, expanding marriage to include same-sex couples would mean that heterosexuality was no longer the norm. "Take that away and you no longer have something that supports heterosexual identity and that reproductive process," said Young. Other witnesses were concerned that changing the definition of marriage might encourage teenagers to identify as gay or lesbian — which they regarded as a negative thing.

One of the most interesting presentations came from a colleague of Young's, Paul Nathanson, a Jewish homosexual who was strongly opposed to same-sex marriage. He used an analogy to challenge one of the arguments in its favour:

> Jews have lived as minority communities for centuries and yet managed to maintain their collective self-esteem, often despite prejudice or persecution far more severe and far more pervasive than anything gay people endure in Canada. Why? Because self-esteem originates within both the individual and the community. In other words, it can be neither conferred nor denied by the state or any other external source.

Single heterosexuals, he argued, can also lack confidence because their status as single counters the social norm of being in a couple. Nathanson recognized that gays and lesbians suffer more from lack of self-esteem than heterosexuals, but suggested that not being able to marry was not the necessarily the reason: "Speaking as both a Jew and a gay man, therefore, I disagree profoundly with this claim for the necessity of gay marriage." Anyway, he added, there's nothing obliging people who love each other to get married.

Margaret Somerville, director of the McGill Centre for Medicine, Ethics and the Law, would speak along similar lines when the committee heard testimony in Montreal in late April: "Those in the gay community who want same-sex marriage are right to seek meaning in their relationships and to want to have that meaning publicly recognized. They are wrong, however, to try to do it by co-opting the institution of marriage. It cannot function in that way without being deformed and destroyed."

On a personal note, Bill Hawke, father of a heterosexual daughter and a gay son, attempted to raise MPs' awareness of the unequal way society treated his children's relationships:

> When our son told us he was gay, we had to educate ourselves as to what impact that had on his life. We found that he was still the son we understood before, but his sexual orientation was different from what we'd envisioned. He was still the son we loved, and would continue to love, so much. He was not different as a person.

> As he grew up, we were concerned about the opportunities that would be denied him because of his sexual orientation, and we were astounded to learn that the government was part of the restricting groups. Our two children, who in our eyes were born equally, are not treated equally by our government. Change has come a long way since we started on the road to adulthood with our son and daughter, but there remains a significant obstacle in our son's path.

Our daughter lived in a common-law relationship for five
years, and she and her partner were married last year. She had
a private ceremony of her choosing, with a few friends, with a
representative of the government officiating. Our son will not
have that opportunity as the law currently stands. You are not
allowing him to marry. Why?

Would our marriage be diminished in any way because our
son is recognized as an equal and allowed to marry? We see no
effect. In fact, we'd be proud to stand with our son in the same
ceremony that we celebrated 35 years ago when we pledged
our lives together.

The next day, February 13, the committee heard from Archbishop
André Gaumond of Sherbrooke, representing the Canadian
Conference of Catholic Bishops, who suggested that opening civil mar-
riage to homosexuals would mean wiping out God's role in society:

Marriage is the recognition of a structure that stems from
nature. We have no control over nature. It is given to us and we
have to accept it. We believe that nature was bestowed upon us
and that we can discern God's will through it. Recognizing
marriage means recognizing God's role in the organization of
society.

Earlier, Jean Ferrari of the Canadian Christian Women's Organization
for Life had been even less subtle. "In Canada, in a great display of
magnanimity, we have granted rights to accommodate vocal, affluent
minorities, not on the basis of common sense, but in a show of tolerance," she said, adding that homosexuals were responsible for the
AIDS epidemic.

On February 18, Pastor William Oosterman of Westboro Baptist
Church said he feared that legalizing same-sex marriage would make
Canada "the laughingstock of present and future generations." He
went on to take issue with the Charter of Rights and Freedoms: "The

charter is there to protect us from intrusive government, not to impose. It is now being used by the homosexual community to demand that we condone their sin as marriage."

That day a representative of another religion, Joanne Cohen, coordinator of the Coalition of Canadian Liberal Rabbis, responded to the idea that same-sex marriage would annihilate the institution altogether:

> The extension of recognition to Jewish marriages in Ontario's Marriage Act in 1857 did nothing to diminish the status of Anglican marriages at that time, so any discussion of the diminished status of marriage as a result of same-sex marriage is a zero-sum game and, I believe members of our coalition would agree, a zero-sum argument that is specious at this time.

The next day comparisons between same-sex marriage and polygamy took off again and didn't die down for several days. Responding to endless questioning by Vic Toews, Brent Hawkes of the Metropolitan Community Church in Toronto offered a little history lesson:

> Consistently, whenever we've talked about human rights legislation, human rights codes and relationship recognition down through the years for gays and lesbians, people have raised the issue of polygamy. I don't recall any cases before the courts about human rights legislation that once gays and lesbians were given the right to have jobs, all of a sudden people who were involved in polygamy wanted the right to have jobs. Giving gays and lesbians the right to marry is no more opening that door than giving heterosexuals the right to marry.

A week later, Jackie Harper, representative of the Interfaith Coalition for Same-Sex Marriages, came to the same conclusion based on her own experience:

> Certainly within the United Church of Canada's history, in 1988, when we made the decision as a church that hetero-

sexual and homosexual people would be considered equally to be called to the order of ministry, we heard every kind
of concern about pedophilia, and so on, an increase in
child abuse, that we would be setting churches up for legal
challenges based on sexual impropriety, and out of our
experience that did not happen.

That day, the continuing debate on polygamy began to exasperate
Claudine Ouellet, executive director of the Coalition Gaie et Lesbienne
du Québec (Quebec Gay and Lesbian Coalition). She said to the MPs:

Honestly, I find that this insults the intelligence of a lawyer to
suggest that if we adopt an inclusive definition of marriage, we
are opening the door to virtually any type of perversion or illegality, since we are indeed talking about unlawful acts here.

* * * * *

Inadvertently, Nathalie Des Rosiers, president of the Law Commission
of Canada, an independent research institute financed by Ottawa, provided ammunition for the opposition. During her earlier appearance
before the committee on January 30, she had said,

In our view, what's interesting is that there is no reason for
why [polygamy] should be excluded. It's not in the interests of
the people in a polygamous marriage — even what I would
call the victims — to have their union not recognized, because
they cannot benefit from the protection that marriage gives.

Des Rosiers admitted that the lack of consent in many polygamous
unions was a problem, but that the prohibition in the Criminal Code
was enough of a deterrent. The snag was that for years the authorities
had been aware of a polygamous community in Bountiful, B.C., where
the police had not dared intervene. Governments were apparently
unwilling to prosecute for fear that the accused would challenge the

constitutionality of the clauses banning polygamy. If the government lost the case in the courts, politicians would find themselves with an even thornier issue on their hands.

MPs who were opposed to same-sex marriage leapt on the testimony of Des Rosiers, now dean of the civil law section of the University of Ottawa's Law Faculty. Vic Toews demanded of numerous witnesses that they prove that legalizing same-sex marriage would not lead to legalization of polygamy, which is legal in many countries and in which, as in same-sex couples, love can be genuinely present. In addition, he noted, Canada has taken a Judeo-Christian rather than a Muslim position with regard to polygamy, so why not do the same with regard to same-sex marriage, even if this goes against the practices of some progressive churches? The question was not unreasonable — that is, not if polygamy and homosexuality are placed on the same footing.

During the committee hearings in Vancouver, on April 1, Hedy Fry responded that polygamy poses too great a risk of exploitation, especially to women, for it to be legal in Canada. "But I have yet to hear a good reason from a rational point of view as to why we cannot support same-sex relationships," she added. During the Montreal hearings in late April, however, two women recommended the legalization of group marriage. Myriam Brunel and Nancy Leclerc claimed that such marriages did not necessarily involve subservience. "The way I'm defining group marriages here," explained Leclerc, a bisexual mother with a son, "is group marriage based on polyamory — being the capacity to love more than one person."

* * * * *

The parliamentary committee visited ten cities, in which MPs met many opponents of same-sex marriage as well as many gays and lesbians who gave personal testimonies. The cost of these hearings, including travel and other services attached to the study, was nearly half a million dollars, and no fewer than 475 witnesses were heard. In Sussex, New Brunswick, Bloc Québécois MP Richard Marceau expressed his sympathy for the witnesses:

> I cannot help beginning by saying how uncomfortable I feel in
> seeing you here before us and hearing you try to convince us
> that your relationships are just as valid as the one I have with
> my spouse. I think it is rather strange that you should have to
> convince other people that your family is just as loving, just as
> devoted, just as valid as mine. Because you are of the same sex,
> you have to convince us, because most of the people around
> this table are in heterosexual relationships. My first comment
> is that I wished that you did not have to do this.

This was one of the few times that Marceau showed emotion. Most of
the time he kept his arguments strictly within the bounds of legal reasoning. "I guessed there were more people in favour of minority rights
than there were in favour of same-sex marriage," he said later. He and
Réal Ménard had agreed to divide up the tasks between them. "I left the
legal arguments to Richard," said Ménard. "Richard can't talk about
how it feels to be homosexual, because he isn't homosexual and has-
n't had the experience of stigmatization that we've lived with."

The increasingly hostile remarks directed towards gays and lesbians
were nevertheless an indication that there was still a lot of work to be
done. Thus the vice-president of the Alberta Federation of Women
United for Families, Corry Morcos, declared that "homophobia does
not exist. Speaking out against a very small vocal minority should be
considered free speech. We encourage open, reasoned debate.
Changing natural laws that have withstood history and civilizations
needs democratic and majority consent." During the same session, Ted
Morton, political scientist at the University of Calgary, Alberta "sena-
tor-elect" and Stockwell Day's former guru, attacked "gay culture":

> I suggest that the gay community cannot have it both ways
> when it comes to sex. They cannot ask us to believe they are
> simultaneously straight and kinky, responsible parents and
> sexual libertines. Sexual promiscuity is simply incompatible
> with stable families.

As an ardent defender of liberty and privacy, he said, "I'm willing to tolerate lots of things that I don't personally care for, or even that I disapprove of. But I think there's a difference between tolerating something and enshrining it in law."

The tone was a little less strident in Iqaluit, the capital of Nunavut — the committee's last port of call. Elders told MPs that they had never heard of homosexuality before sustained contact with non-Aboriginals a few decades earlier. A few courageous homosexuals nevertheless made an appearance, mentioning that they were not the only ones but that most preferred to keep quiet for fear of rejection by other members of their isolated communities.

The Standing Committee on Justice and Human Rights hearings did finally permit a real debate on the question of marriage, even if it would be overtaken by the courts. But before we move to the court rulings and the political reactions they unleashed, let us end with one of the most touching moments in the committee's tour. At one point the Raging Grannies, a group of completely outrageous old women who denounce injustice through song, burst into the Vancouver hearings to provide a bit of comic relief and make a serious point at the same time. They sang the following lyrics to the tune of "When I was a Lad" from Gilbert and Sullivan's *HMS Pinafore*:

When I was a lad of twenty-three
I said Ma, I'm gay, and I gotta be me.
I said, son, you're the apple of my eye —
Gay or straight, you're my kind of guy.
It wasn't easy — gay bias is rough,
But he conquered life's hurdles, 'cause he was tough.
He conquered life's hurdles, and now you see
He's a VIP in th' community.
He conquered life's hurdles so perfectly
That he's taught us all a lesson in liberty!
He was first in his troop to be Eagle Scout —
Now the BSA said, "Sorry, you're out!"
The Army beckoned. "Don't ask, don't tell."

That wasn't his dish — and that's just as well.
He found his way to his own career —
And he's famous now, even if he's queer.
He conquered life's hurdles, and now you see
He's a VIP in th' community.
He conquered life's hurdles so perfectly
That he's taught us all a lesson in liberty!
When you judge a person on the basis of sex
You use a very narrow and warped index.
Lesbians and gays are in every field
And their human rights can never be repealed.
If you look with empathy you will find
Our diff'rences enrich all humankind.
If you look with empathy you will find
Our diff'rences enrich all humankind.

6

THE TURNING POINT

Judges often pick their moments, for better or for worse. The judges of the British Columbia Court of Appeal chose to release their decision on same-sex marriage on May 1, 2003 — the day after the standing committee hearings ended.

After two rulings in Ontario and Quebec in favour of redefining marriage, a rejection of the applicant couples' motion by B.C.'s highest court would have been astonishing. Far from repudiating the opinions of their eastern colleagues, the B.C. judges made frequent reference to them, as if the case was already closed. In her decision, Justice Jo-Ann Prowse quoted a historical analysis by American law professor John Witte, which had been also quoted by the Divisional Court in Ontario:

> The state eclipsed the church as the principal external authority governing marriage and family life. The Catholic sacramental concept of the family governed principally by the church and the Protestant concepts of the family governed by the church and broader Christian community began to give way to a new privatist concept of the family whereby the wills of the marital parties became primary. Neither the church, nor the local community, nor the paterfamilias could override the reasonable expressions of will of the marital parties themselves.

The B.C. Court of Appeal quickly dispensed with the most controversial of the conclusions reached by the trial judge, Ian Pitfield: that the constitution needed to be changed to permit same-sex marriages. The three high court judges went on to confirm that it was discriminatory to forbid same-sex marriage and that this discrimination was unacceptable in "contemporary Canadian society."

Judge Prowse cited a Law Commission of Canada report entitled *Beyond Conjugality* (2001), which condemned the concept of civil union and described it as a way to perpetuate gays and lesbians' second-class status. It also pointed out that the state must set an example when it comes to human rights:

> There is no justification for maintaining the current distinctions between same-sex and heterosexual conjugal unions in light of current understandings of the state's interests in marriage. The secular purpose of marriage is to provide an orderly framework in which people can express their commitment to each other, receive public recognition and support, and voluntarily assume a range of legal rights and obligations. The current law does not reflect the social facts: as the Supreme Court of Canada has recognized, the capacity to form conjugal relationships characterized by emotional and economic interdependence has nothing to do with sexual orientation. Furthermore, whether or not denial of same-sex marriage infringes the Charter, adherence to the fundamental values of equality, choice and freedom of conscience and religion requires that restrictions on same-sex marriage be removed; the status quo reinforces the stigmatization felt by same-sex couples.

Judge Kenneth Mackenzie said that, in general, the public had welcomed the progressive expansion of gay rights since the 1970s. "Civil marriage should adapt to contemporary notions of marriage as an institution in a society which recognizes the rights of homosexual persons to non-discriminatory treatment," he wrote. However, the B.C.

judges were not prepared to go as far as Judge LaForme and order an immediate redefinition of marriage. They sided with the other judges of the Ontario Divisional Court and ordered a stay of application until July 12, 2004. Curiously, though, in their decision they observed that gays and lesbians had waited long enough and that same-sex marriage was ultimately inevitable. "Further consultation will not change the fact that there are those in favour of same-sex marriage and those against it," wrote Judge Prowse.

In general, the applicant couples were pleased with the judgment, even if they would have preferred to be able to get married right away. Some, such as 29-year-old Tanya Chambers and her 34-year-old partner Melinda Roy, even circled the judges' deadline in their datebooks. "July 12, 2004. That will be the day," said Chambers. "The second it's legal, we're going to do it." She had no idea that a month later a legal volcano would erupt in Ontario, enabling them to move their wedding date even closer.

Meanwhile, conservative groups were upset at the judgment. "Marriage is a social institution," said Michael Martens, a spokesperson for the American-based organization Focus on the Family. "Institutions are not about rights, they're about serving society, and marriage does a very good job of that."

* * * * *

In Ottawa, Justice Minister Martin Cauchon caused a stir when he let his feelings be known for the first time in public. Calling the B.C. Court of Appeal's decision an "important judgment," he said, "The three decisions are all going in the same direction. So I have to take that into consideration." Cauchon carefully refrained from announcing immediately whether the government would appeal the new decision, as it had earlier done with the Ontario and Quebec decisions. "It's an important social issue for Canada," he said. "When you look at the situation in Canada, people are divided." Many journalists suspected, however, that he did not want to appeal it. "My personal position is irrelevant," he said to them. "It's a government decision." He nonetheless took the opportunity to send a message to the members of the standing committee. "I just hope they will table their report pretty soon, and when I receive the report I'll have to come up with a government position," he said.

Cauchon was not the only one to detect a change in the air. The day after the judgment was issued, it emerged that the Liberal Party's research department had produced a report wholeheartedly endorsing the legalization of same-sex marriages. The authors explicitly criticized the idea of offering same-sex unions rather than marriage. "Should the federal government institute a civil registry as Quebec has done? No. The creation of such a registry would not solve the fundamental problems of equality and justice that are at the heart of this question," read the document, which had been confidentially distributed to the Liberal members of the standing committee.

The Liberal analysts added that the creation of a Canada-wide civil registry would require discussions with all the provinces, which would inevitably cause friction. "Given provincial and territorial jurisdiction over the matter," they wrote, "some of them will claim that the federal government has no business creating a civil registry." As for the idea of the state withdrawing from the institution of marriage and leaving it to religious bodies, the Liberal Party analysts dismissed it out of hand. "Religious institutions cannot act alone in this matter; marriages they authorize might not carry the weight of law unless registered." Furthermore, "In Canada, according to the division of powers, it is the provinces that register marriages. Thus, some provinces might decide not to register same-sex marriages."

The authors of the document were prescient about the changes on the horizon. "It's very plausible that the highest court in the country [the Supreme Court] will conclude that a definition of marriage based on heterosexuality is unconstitutional," they predicted. Responding to the document, Richard Marceau of the Bloc Québécois concluded that "recognizing same-sex marriage is the only just way forward."

That hot spring even Paul Martin, in the midst of his bid to succeed Jean Chrétien, seemed prepared to make concessions. He still recommended the establishment of a civil union registry for gays and lesbians, but he was beginning to hint that marriage might be a possibility. "The government cannot discriminate on the basis of rights, regardless of which way you go in this area," Martin told the *Edmonton Journal* on May 2. "Given the B.C. case that was decided yesterday, and we'll see what happens to the Ontario and Quebec cases, if this is an issue of rights then I think the Canadian government simply cannot discriminate."

Long before Jean Chrétien had his say, Martin dismissed the idea of appealing the case to the Supreme Court. "My own view is, if you've got ... three courts deciding across the country [about same-sex marriage], that ends it," Martin said. "I don't think we should be dragging this out." If only! Martin admitted more than once, however, that the issue was not an easy one for him. "There's a long tradition. On the other side these are loving couples," he said. "The emotions run very deep. So I'm wrestling with this. But the one thing I'm not wrestling with is if it's a question of rights."

MPs opposed to same-sex marriage did not regard the new decree from the B.C. Court of Appeal the way Martin did. Alliance MP Vic Toews said,

> As a former constitutional lawyer, a director of constitutional law in Manitoba, I've seen the court take its own political agenda and put a wrap of legal statements around it. I don't agree with that approach to the interpretation of our Charter of Rights. I think it's a blatant misuse of our Charter of Rights.

* * * * *

On May 8, 2003, the House of Commons debated a motion sponsored by Toews demanding that the government "bring in measures to protect and reassert the will of Parliament against certain court decisions," which, according to him, were threatening the institution of marriage.

As if to demonstrate that reasserting the will of Parliament may not always be a good idea, MP Elsie Wayne, Progressive Conservative deputy leader under Joe Clark, made an inflammatory remark about gays and lesbians' demands to be included in the institution of marriage. "If they are going to live together, they can go live together and shut up about it. There is no need for this nonsense whatsoever and we should not have to tolerate it in Canada," she said, alluding to gay and lesbian pride parades. Outside the House later, Wayne said that she considered the homosexual lifestyle "unfortunate" and that most people see it as "not natural."

PC MP Scott Brison, an openly gay man who was in the running to succeed Clark, demanded Wayne's resignation, which she refused to submit. "I regret that some have been offended by my remarks," she added, "because this was certainly not my intention." Joe Clark refused to remove her from office, but sent out a press release dissociating himself from his MP's questionable remarks.

* * * * *

The appeal hearings had taken place in B.C. in February and in Ontario in April, while the parliamentary Standing Committee was in full swing. The arguments in the appeal courts were quite different from the ones advanced in the lower courts in 2001. "The important shift was that at the appeal level, there was no longer an argument about the case," said Kevin Bourassa, one of the Ontario applicants. "The appeal was largely focused on the remedy; they [Ottawa] had already almost agreed that the case was lost. It was more what should we do about it; that's where the argument was."

An intervention by Cauchon early in the case may have helped shift the tone. "I remember meeting with a lawyer in Toronto who was working on a document we were preparing, and asking her to change some of the content because there were things in there that were unacceptable," he said. Federal prosecutors had not yet given up their arguments based on the importance of procreation in marriage, however. Joanna Radbord, one of the lawyers for the Ontario couples, recalled,

> By the time we were in the Court of Appeal, I was very pregnant and very emotional. So the suggestion that we don't procreate — you know, I was suffering morning sickness and I was

reading their offensive arguments. That was just too much! I was like eight months pregnant, I was huge and they were talking about how we don't procreate. And I was standing there as the living example of the lesbian procreator!

Luckily for Radbord, the judges would ultimately give short shrift to the government's arguments along these lines, and the lawyers quickly sensed as much. "Very early on," said Martha McCarthy, "Chief Justice [Roy] McMurtry said this to a federal lawyer: 'There is a shameful history of treatment of gays and lesbians in this country, dear colleague.' So we had a moment of thinking: wooh! That was our first sort of clue that maybe there was sympathy for our argument."

* * * * *

As the B.C. Court of Appeal's judgment was the third in favour of expanding marriage to include same-sex couples, pressure on the standing committee was mounting, and Cauchon was expecting its report as soon as possible. But the MPs were still deeply divided. The witnesses they had heard, who were also split down the middle on the issue, had not tipped the balance one way or another.

Supporters of same-sex marriage on the committee produced their own preliminary report in which they made the somewhat farfetched claim that "most of the committee members support this choice." To shore up their position, they stressed that the traditional definition of marriage had been changed a few months after it was entrenched in the famous *Hyde* case in 1866. "In 1867, the Fathers of Confederation assigned responsibility for divorce to [the federal] Parliament," read their report, which has never been published. "Less than a year after the *Hyde* decision which defined marriage as heterosexual, the 'for life' part of the equation was no longer applicable in Canada. The 1866 definition was and never has been cast in stone." The MPs' first recommendation was clear:

The committee believes that the time has come to change the

definition of marriage so as to permit same-sex marriage. Marriage thus becomes the union of two people, to the exclusion of all others. By virtue of this statement, whoever is already in a civil union or in a domestic partnership arrangement cannot marry a third party. This allows the celebration of same-sex marriages without affecting heterosexual couples who wish to participate in this social institution.

MPs in favour of redefining marriage were not convinced by the argument that this change would open the door to other more controversial kinds of marriage: "The committee does not believe that this proposal would compromise any future ability to prevent polygamy or other similar practices. The Criminal Code already deals with such eventualities." Nor were they persuaded by fears about the future of society:

> Neither do we believe that the motion would have a negative impact on marriage and families as we know them. If social institutions have changed in recent years, this is due to the social tensions inherent in modern life and to changing gender roles. All in all, the committee was impressed by the number of gay and lesbian couples they heard from who are living in stable, long-term relationships, and many of whom are raising children.

The MPs were careful to take the concerns of religious groups seriously. As the celebration of marriage is under provincial jurisdiction, however, all they could recommend was that an interpretive clause be added to the preamble of any future law to make it clear that religious groups were not obliged to celebrate marriages that were not consistent with their beliefs. They also raised two other possibilities: negotiations could be undertaken with the provinces to ensure respect for religious freedom (which is guaranteed under the Canadian Charter, in any case), or else this specific question could be referred to the Supreme Court.

The report was supportive of same-sex marriage, but it was not the definitive view of the committee. In late May 2003, a number of MPs were still trying to pressure their colleagues into being satisfied with a final report that recommended establishing civil unions. If they couldn't convince the other MPs, they would issue their own dissident report. But it was too late.

* * * * *

The revolution occurred on June 10, 2003, and it started in the Ontario Court of Appeal, which has a reputation for being progressive. Amazingly, the people behind this historic day in the history of gays and lesbians everywhere in the world were simply going about their usual business as if nothing was happening on that sunny Tuesday. At least, that was what the *Globe and Mail* informed us several months later.

As the decision was making its way to the lawyers for the applicant couples, at 9:30 a.m., Chief Justice McMurtry was in his office, editing documents or reading his mail. Just before 10:30, he put on his black robes and strode into room 10 in Osgoode Hall in Toronto, where Ontario high court sessions are held, to hear a criminal proceeding. His colleague Justice Eileen Gillese was at home in London, two hours from Toronto. After eating breakfast and driving three of her children to school, she was settling down to edit a judgment, dressed casually in jeans. Her computer suddenly beeped: it was a brief email to confirm that the envelopes had been delivered. She went back to her work. Justice James MacPherson was in the middle of his daily one-kilometre swim. Later he went for his annual medical checkup before watching the news on TV, which raised a smile. "Wow," he chuckled to himself, "they moved fast!" On the screen were the two homosexuals who had forced him to study the thorny issue of marriage.

Many thought the ones who really moved fast were the judges of the Ontario Court of Appeal. For the first time in the world, a court ordered that gays and lesbians be permitted to marry, immediately. The Netherlands (April 2001) and Belgium (June 2003) had legalized same-sex marriage, by parliamentary legislation, not court decisions.

In contrast to Canada, the legalization of same-sex marriage had caused very little controversy in the Netherlands. The media had hardly mentioned the passage of the new law by the two chambers of the Dutch parliament in 2000. The question had been debated since the early 1990s, however, so the Dutch were already familiar with the issues (in September 2000, 62 percent were in favour of the change). In February 1990, an Amsterdam court had refused to decide on the issue and tossed the ball back into the politicians' court. In 1996, the parliament passed motions demanding that the government study expanding adoption and marriage rights to include gays and lesbians. An independent body (the Kortmann Commission) was established, which in 1997 recommended permitting same-sex couples to marry and to adopt Dutch children. After several years of dithering, the government finally introduced a bill, which became law on April 1, 2001.

The day after the first same-sex marriages were celebrated in Holland, neighbouring Belgium announced that it would follow suit. But Belgium didn't go as far as the Netherlands. It did not entitle homosexuals to adoption rights: the coalition in power (made up of liberal, socialist and green parties) had studied the question in depth, concluding that the population was not yet ready. In January 2003, however, a large majority in the Belgian Chamber of Deputies passed a bill expanding marriage rights to include same-sex couples. The bill was supported by 92 members and opposed by 22, with nine abstentions.

* * * * *

Like the Ontario Divisional Court, the Quebec Superior Court and the B.C. Court of Appeal, the highest court in Ontario concluded that excluding homosexuals from marriage was discriminatory under section 15 of the Charter and that this discrimination was unjustifiable in a free and democratic society: "Heterosexual married couples will not stop having or raising children because same-sex couples are permitted to marry. Moreover, an increasing percentage of children are being born to and raised by same-sex couples." This unanimous judgment was the product of lengthy discussions and at least 20 drafts.

Obviously the crucial part of the case was how best to redress the injustice. In a few paragraphs the judges rejected the federal lawyers' argument that an eventual redefinition of marriage was the responsibility of Parliament. "These considerations do not arise where the genesis of the Charter breach is found in the common law and there is no legislation to be altered," decreed the judges, noting that any additional delay would perpetuate the injustice:

> There is no evidence before this court that a declaration of invalidity without a period of suspension will pose any harm to the public, threaten the rule of law, or deny anyone the benefit of legal recognition of their marriage. We observe that there was no evidence before us that the reformulated definition of marriage will require the volume of legislative reform that followed the release of the Supreme Court of Canada's decision in *M*. v. *H*. In our view, an immediate declaration will simply ensure that opposite-sex couples and same-sex couples immediately receive equal treatment in law in accordance with s. 15(1) of the *Charter*.

To make themselves quite clear, the judges issued an order to the city clerk of Toronto to deliver marriage licences immediately to the applicant couples and another requiring the Office of the Registrar General of Ontario to register the marriage certificates of Elaine and Anne Vautour as well as those of Kevin Bourassa and Joe Varnell, who had been married at the Metropolitan Community Church in Toronto on January 14, 2001. If the Court of Appeal judgment is thought of as having retroactive force, these two same-sex couples were the first in the world to be officially married, beating the Netherlands by just over two months.

* * * * *

Standing together on the red carpet at the Registrar's Office on the main floor of Osgoode Hall, the couples and lawyers waited nervously for the judgment to come down. It was not yet 9:30. Martha McCarthy, one of the lawyers for the couples, was wearing a white suit that she had bought in case she was asked to a wedding that day. If not, she would deliver the concession speech that she had been working on for half the night. Her pockets contained enough tissues to provide for either eventuality.

When the envelope finally arrived, McCarthy and her colleagues flipped straight to the last page of the 60-page judgment. "We did it!" she shouted, and the crowd began hugging, weeping and making phone calls. "I started singing 'We're Getting Married in the Morning' from *My Fair Lady* to the media," recalled Michael Leshner, one of the applicants with his partner Michael Stark. From Leshner's point of view, time was short: they had to make the most of this reprieve before the federal lawyers demanded a stay of judgment: "I expected the federal government to appeal and I wanted the genie out of the bottle. I just thought that if there was one gay marriage out there, you couldn't reconstruct Humpty Dumpty."

McCarthy, though, was hesitant: "I said to my clients, 'There will be no weddings if there is a motion to stay that comes across our fax machine,' if the feds wanted to stop it. They could have had a motion to stay waiting just in case, right? They could have sent it over to our fax machine five minutes after the judgment came. But they never did it."

Preparations for the first civil marriages between same-sex partners in North America could now begin. Leshner had asked not one but three judges to stand by to celebrate the marriages that very day — "just in case the first two get knocked over by a bus on the way," he joked. Leshner saw it as a done deal. His forthcoming marriage would happen partly thanks to Roy McMurtry, formerly Ontario's attorney general, to whom Leshner had come out more than 20 years before. The occasion was a Christmas party for the employees of the Ontario Ministry of the Attorney General held in the tony neighbourhood where McMurtry lived.

The ceremony took place in exactly the same way that thousands of heterosexuals, over the years, had celebrated their unions in courthouses all over the country. "By the power vested in me by the Marriage Act, I pronounce you Michael, and you Michael — affectionately

Lawyer Martha McCarthy on June 10, 2003, a few minutes after the Ontario Appeal Court's historic judgment that legalized same-sex marriage, with the judgment to take effect immediately. "We never ever thought [the judges] would do it," she said. "Never."

known as 'the Michaels' — to be lawfully wedded spouses," intoned Mr. Justice John Hamilton, judge of the Ontario Superior Court. The two men looked at each other tenderly and then gave each other a long and loving kiss.

While they were posing for photos, Leshner and Stark were beat out by Joanna Radbord and her partner, who got married only minutes before the Michaels. Radbord recalled,

> In my wildest imagination, I thought that we could get an immediate remedy, so I told my spouse, "Bring our passports, just in case." As we were driving to the courthouse, we were listening to Céline Dion — "A New Day Has Come" — and I was feeling that this could be the brand new day. It was very

thrilling to be married that day, being so pregnant and feeling the baby was kicking as we were getting married. It just felt nice being acknowledged and legitimated as a family. It was a very special moment.

Radbord married for personal reasons, but also for ideological and even sociological ones:

We don't have to participate in this institution in the same way as they [heterosexuals] do. We can transform the institution from the inside out and by our participation in it, we do transform it, we challenge its historical patriarchal meaning. So as a feminist, I've never had any issue about participation in marriage at all. As a feminist, I completely believed it was absolutely necessary for gays and lesbians to have access to marriage.

Laurie Arron of Egale was also bowled over:

We were surprised. We were expecting a suspension, shorter than the one imposed by the other courts, but a suspension anyway. We were convinced that it was the only reasonable thing to do, but we were nonetheless stunned because we just didn't think that the judges had that sort of courage. And that really had always been the issue in the marriage cases: how much courage did the judges have? Were they going to do what they really perceive to be what the law requires or were they going to compromise in the name of political concerns?

Kevin Bourassa and Joe Varnell are eternal optimists, so they were less surprised, although clearly thrilled with the verdict. "We were always ... hoping for the better side of humanity to shine through," said Bourassa. "Throughout this entire process, we've always been hopeful, maybe unrealistically, but our optimism has rarely disappointed us." By contrast, Martha McCarthy has never quite grasped — even in hindsight — what got into the three judges of the Ontario Court of Appeal to make them go so far so fast:

> We were stunned, completely shocked. I mean we had debates right up to the moment that we were doing the appeal about how hard how we should argue for no suspension of the judgment, because it was a pie in the sky argument. Nobody ever anticipated that the feds would not appeal at that point. They were fighting us tooth and nail with some quite aggressive arguments. So we had this ongoing debate, Joanna and I, about how hard we should sell it, because you lose credibility if you ask for unrealistic things. In the end, we sold it hard, we asked in the most aggressive possible terms: you must not suspend. This was not a constitutional emergency of a nature that required a suspension. A couple of marriages weren't going to change anything for anybody. It didn't meet the test. We never ever thought they would do it. Never. The day we went to pick it up [the judgment], we never thought they wouldn't suspend it. We sold it hard, but privately, we thought it was a loser. We thought they would never be so outrageous.

In the firmness of the ruling and its concrete impact, Egale lawyer Cynthia Petersen saw a victory for all minority groups seeking to uphold their rights before governments. "It's a great precedent, not just for gays and lesbians, but for human rights in general," she said.

* * * * *

True to their duty to be discreet, the Ontario Court of Appeal judges have never commented directly on their same-sex marriage judgment. The most that Chief Justice McMurtry said, in an interview with the *Globe and Mail*, was that "we cannot be concerned with whether a decision is going to be popular." But he added, "We obviously think we got it right." In a speech to the Canadian Bar Association in Regina in February 2004, McMurtry tried to answer critics who had accused him of indulging in "judicial activism," especially on social questions:

> as elected representatives, [Politicians] have the practical obli-
> gation to advance the interests of the majority. When this
> obligation conflicts with the rights of groups or individuals in
> society, it is not necessarily the duty of elected representatives
> to protect the minority. In stark contrast, it can be said that
> the judicial function may well be anti-majoritarian in the
> sense it is often charged with the responsibility to protect the
> minority.

McMurtry pointed out that it wasn't the courts' role to represent private
interests either:

> They are impartial bodies that must reflect the basic values of
> our society. Courts are not necessarily democratic institutions,
> as they are not bound by the majority of public opinion.
> However, I believe that when the majority takes away the rights
> of a minority, that is not a democracy. Democracy is, therefore,
> a delicate balance between majority rule and individual rights.
> The values that should direct a judge are basic and fundamen-
> tal values rather than the outcomes of public opinion surveys.
> They cannot be transient and revolving fashions of the day.
> They are not headlines. They reflect history rather than hysteria
> ... When a society is not faithful to its basic values, a judge may
> be required to intervene.

This does not mean that judges' discretion is absolute: if it were, that
would signify "the beginning of the end for democracy," McMurtry
said. But that constraint shouldn't stop judges from using their personal experience as a guide to help interpret society's values — and
adapting the law in consequence. "While a judge should often be guided by public consensus, there are times when the court should lead the
way and be the crusader for a new consensus," he concluded, citing the
famous *Brown* v. *Board of Education* case in which the U.S. Supreme

Court declared school segregation unconstitutional.

Ironically enough, it was Roy McMurtry who as attorney general (from 1975 to 1985) had always refused to include homosexuality among the prohibited forms of discrimination under the Ontario Human Rights Code. He finally came around to seeing that he had been wrong. "I would be the first person to say it should have been amended," he conceded. One can safely say that he granted himself an unconditional pardon.

7

THE NEW POWER BALANCE

The July 2002 decision of the Ontario Divisional Court may have taken the Ottawa establishment by surprise, but the ruling by the Ontario Court of Appeal in June 2003 came as a real shock for MPs and ministers. Before they even had time to read the decision, gays and lesbians had begun to marry in Toronto. In the space of a single day, June 10, no fewer than 21 couples (15 gay and six lesbian) took advantage of the new right, unthinkable only a year earlier.

One of the first people in Ottawa to react was, of course, Martin Cauchon, who had been a covert supporter of same-sex marriages for some time and who had just been given substantial leverage by the courts. "The effects of this morning's decision are immediate, and we are fully aware of that," he told the press. "That's why we have to act quickly." He admitted that the same-sex marriages taking place at that time were "legally effective," but was careful to add that this was "for the time being, because I can't predict the future."

For the previous month, the House of Commons Standing Committee on Justice and Human Rights had been considering the same issue. Even though the committee staff had already drafted a preliminary report supporting equal marriage rights, the truth of the matter was that MPs could not reach an agreement. Cauchon, who wanted to settle the debate quickly, made it known to MPs that they should pick up the pace.

The committee met behind closed doors on the same day, in a

marathon session aimed at finding a compromise if possible. To increase the pressure, the MPs in favour of same-sex marriage organized a press conference where only the Canadian Alliance was not represented. Like many others, Bloc Québécois MP Richard Marceau was afraid the opponents of same-sex marriage would force the committee to recommend use of the notwithstanding clause in the Canadian Charter of Rights to suspend execution of the court decision. "We strongly recommend that there be no appeal and that use of the notwithstanding clause be disregarded," he said. Liberal MP Marlene Jennings, representing the Montreal riding of Notre-Dame-de-Grâce–Lachine, explained, "We will encourage, and press our government to improve the definition ... and make the necessary changes to the legislation." Even more conservative-minded MPs rallied round the court decision. "We're all Liberals, after all, and I sincerely believe that the redefinition of marriage sends the right message, in keeping with Liberal values," said Nick Discepola, Liberal MP for Vaudreuil–Soulanges.

Alliance MP Vic Toews was adamant: the government should appeal the decision to the Supreme Court right away. "The definition of marriage is an exclusive responsibility of the elected Parliament," he pleaded, repeating that it was not up to the courts to dictate laws. It was, of course, ironic that he should have to rely on the courts to return legislative power to the elected representatives. The openly gay Bloc Québécois MP Réal Ménard pointed out that such a convoluted situation would not have occurred if MPs had taken responsibility sooner:

> From a parliamentary point of view, it's a pity we didn't take control over the marriage debate, that we didn't take the initiative. Of course, speaking as an activist, I'm glad the courts ruled the way they did. But if you asked me if I consider it legitimate and democratic that Parliament should not have taken the lead in a decision of this importance, then I'd have to say I find it deplorable. We, as parliamentarians, should have exercised our leadership.

* * * * *

While the politicians hesitated, some same-sex couples did just the opposite. "The phone's been ringing off the hook," an employee at Toronto City Hall told reporters, adding that calls were coming in from across the country, and even from the United States. After a few hours, other municipalities in Ontario followed Toronto's lead.

"At Ottawa City Hall, like in most other municipalities in Ontario, people didn't know what to do and the provincial — Conservative — government was not clear about its intentions," recalled Alex Munter, then an Ottawa city councillor. Openly gay, he went on to coordinate the Canadians for Equal Marriage coalition:

> There was a 24-hour period of indecision at City Hall. I spoke to the Mayor [Bob Chiarelli], the City Manager and the City's lawyers. Some of them wanted to do nothing until things became clearer and I told them, "It's the law now. If there's an appeal and another court decision, then the law will change again. But for now, the law has changed and the city must comply with it." I had to explain the situation to people, but in under 24 hours the city started issuing marriage licences.

Astonishingly, Ernie Eves's Conservative government did nothing to stop gay couples from marrying in Ontario. "What two people do in a relationship with each other is really none of anybody else's business," declared Eves, who later, in the runup to the 2003 provincial election, withdrew his support for the redefinition of marriage. "If the decision says that two people of the same sex can get married, that is the law of the land, then we will register," added Ontario Attorney General Norm Sterling, who refused to reveal what he personally thought about the question of same-sex marriage.

* * * * *

Behind the closed doors of the weekly Liberal caucus meetings, things were beginning to change. Respect for democracy required giving MPs and senators a chance to express their views at each meeting on what had clearly become the main focus of interest in Ottawa. Supporters and opponents of same-sex marriage spoke out forcefully, and sometimes aggressively, in the hope of influencing the prime minister, to whom all the speeches were primarily directed. "The debate became extremely tense," recalled Liberal Senator Serge Joyal. "At one point I felt I had to speak out, because the opponents were making so much noise."

Joyal feels that he made an impression on Jean Chrétien that day. He alluded to an episode from his own experience 20 years earlier, when he was the MP for Hochelaga-Maisonneuve and cochair of the Special Joint Committee on the Constitution of the Senate and the House of Commons (1980–81). During the debate on the Charter of Rights and Freedoms, he personally asked Chrétien, as minister of justice, to include sexual orientation as one of the prohibited grounds for discrimination listed in section 15, which already included ethnic origin, religion and sex: "Mr. Chrétien replied, 'The section is not exhaustive, so people will be able to plead [sexual orientation] in the courts when the time comes.' In other words, it was not excluded in principle, but would be judged on a case-by-case basis." Chrétien also suggested that adding sexual orientation to the Charter would require the consent of at least Ontario and New Brunswick, the only two provinces that initially supported repatriation. At the June 11, 2003, caucus meeting, Joyal felt he had no choice but to speak out:

I said to Mr. Chrétien, "Prime Minister, do you remember 20 years ago, when we passed the Charter?" You could have heard a pin drop in the room. "Twenty years ago, I asked you for an amendment, and you replied that it would be best not to amend section 15, that the situation in the courts would change, and that one day we would have to recognize that people have equal legal rights regardless of their sexual orientation." Then I said, "Prime Minister, I think that day has come. It's time to grant recognition. The courts have made their decision." I saw Mr. Chrétien's face change; he was looking at me. We have always had a tense relationship, for all kinds of reasons. But this time,

he gave me a signal that meant "Yes, I remember, you're right."
And I'm certain it had an effect on him.

At the same Liberal caucus meeting, Foreign Affairs Minister Bill Graham made a stirring plea. "It's about time we go in the same direction as the Charter, and act like we live in the twenty-first century," he said. Graham had long been convinced of the need to expand marriage rights to include gays and lesbians, but to ensure that he used his influence within the government, lawyer Martha McCarthy contacted him several times in the days following the Ontario Court of Appeal decision.

Egale focused its lobbying on the MPs on the parliamentary committee looking at the question. "It's hard to lobby the Justice Minister or the PM directly," noted Laurie Arron, Egale's marriage specialist at the time. "I mean, Egale has never had a meeting with Jean Chrétien or even Martin Cauchon." This is quite a contrast with the representatives of multinational corporations, who can meet with some federal ministers several times a year.

* * * * *

In the provincial capitals, few politicians spoke out on the issue, preferring to leave this contentious question to the federal government, which in any case was responsible for defining marriage. In Quebec City, a spokesperson for the justice minister of the time, Marc Bellemare, pointed out that the National Assembly had gone as far as it could when, a year earlier, it had introduced civil unions for both heterosexual and same-sex couples. In Alberta, however, the Conservative government of Ralph Klein predictably took a stand and wrote to Martin Cauchon asking him not only to appeal the Ontario judgment but also to apply for a suspension of its application. Many religious groups, including the Canadian Conference of Catholic Bishops, followed his lead. Klein even threatened to invoke the notwithstanding clause in Alberta to prevent same-sex marriages, but was quickly told by legal experts that only Ottawa could take this step.

The political debate continued the next day, June 12, at the first pub-

lic meeting of the standing committee following the release of the
Ontario Court of Appeal decision. NDP member Svend Robinson pre-
sented a motion asking the government not to appeal either the
Ontario decision or the decision of the British Columbia Court of
Appeal. "I think the time has come for this committee ... to take a stand
on this issue of fundamental justice and equality," he explained.
Robinson also responded to the criticism that Parliament was caving in
to "judicial activism" by refusing to take the case to the Supreme Court:

> I think every member on this committee has to clearly under-
> stand that isn't the case; that life changed for us as parliamen-
> tarians on April 17, 1985. That was the date the equality rights
> provisions of the Charter of Rights came into force. At the
> heart of those equality rights provisions is a recognition that if
> elected representatives, whether federal or provincial, take
> action or don't take action to ensure the equality of the citi-
> zens we represent, the courts will in fact do so. We as elected
> representatives asked the courts to take on that task when we
> adopted the Constitution of Canada.

Robinson then made a more personal comment: "Along with other gay
and lesbian people in this country, I am tired of being treated as a second-class citizen in my own country. I'm tired of seeing taxpayer dollars being used to fight against basic equality for gay and lesbian people." Coming from someone who, at the age of 20, had married a
woman in the hope of eradicating his own homosexuality, this was a
powerful message.

Robinson's arguments did not, however, convince his Liberal colleague Pat O'Brien, who indignantly denounced the "incredible judicial arrogance" of the three Ontario judges. He gave the judges' position his own ironic twist: "Zap, we have just redefined marriage and
you, Parliament of Canada, elected representatives of Canadians, and
you, millions of Canadians who disagree with the idea of redefining
marriage, your opinions don't count." O'Brien had no doubts: the
Ontario Court of Appeal decision was the "worst example of judicial

activism in the history of this country":

> I want to make it very clear that I feel that whatever a person's
> sexual orientation, they are deserving of respect and dignity.
> But this does not mean we must redefine something as funda-
> mental and important to our society as marriage, which is held
> dear and cherished by millions of Canadians who are very
> fearful of what such a change would do. It does not mean that
> in treating people with respect and dignity we have to discard
> our own values, ignore our own conscience. That's just simply
> not on, Mr. Chairman, not for me and not for millions of
> other Canadians.

His colleague John Harvard lost no time in replying:

> It is time to exercise leadership. It is time to stop buck-passing
> and it is time for parliamentarians to face up to our responsi-
> bilities ... The Ontario court has been anything but arrogant; it
> has faced up to its responsibilities. Perhaps we parliamentari-
> ans have not done so. I have heard from social conservatives
> that it's time for parliamentarians to face up to their responsi-
> bilities. Yet it is the very same social conservatives who say,
> "Oh, let's pass it on to those activist judges who, by the way,
> we don't have any confidence in, but we want to pass on the
> issue to them for final adjudication."

For Richard Marceau, the most important thing was to send a message
not just of tolerance, but of acceptance. "Voting for this motion would
be a wonderful way to end this parliamentary session, and join in
expressing our best wishes for all the same-sex couples who will be getting married in the next days and weeks," he said.

The discussion became more intense as it stretched into the afternoon.
"Those who vote against marriage for homosexual people will have to
accept the fact that it is a discriminatory act," warned Bloc Québécois MP
Réal Ménard. "I will go even further and say that it is evidence of institu-

tionalized homophobia." He probably did not make many friends by pointing out that it was opposite-sex couples who, by divorcing in ever-increasing numbers, had "dealt the most mortal blow to the family."

More moderate, Liberal MP Hedy Fry pointed out that society had, for many years, opposed the right of women to vote, interracial marriages and the abolition of slavery: "So each time, it is fundamentally about protecting the status quo, about protecting the old ways, about saying things must be because they have always been, thus they must continue to do so ... That is another reason I want to support this. Always we deal with the same thing: something is going to happen, the sky is going to fall, and harm will occur to society. And it never does." Opening up the institution of marriage to gay and lesbian couples would simply make it stronger, she suggested. Then she spoke about her own three sons, all heterosexual:

> But they all have told me very clearly, all three of them, "We would be so disappointed in you, Mother, if you did not vote very strongly to change the definition of marriage, because we want to get married not because of its religious connotations but because we think it's a valuable institution. And to deny other couples who love each other and want to form lasting bonds, or the children of those couples, the ability to be in a family that is recognized and accepted by society ... we would be really disappointed in you."

MP Chuck Cadman, at the time a member of the Canadian Alliance, considered that a vote in favour of Robinson's motion amounted to a vote to "throw the whole works in the garbage can." His Liberal colleague John McKay deplored the Ontario Court of Appeal's "sledge-hammer approach," clearly intended to "shut down what Parliament would like to say on this issue."

Alliance MP Stockwell Day took the debate a step backward by questioning the courts' inclusion of sexual orientation as a prohibited ground for discrimination under the Charter. "The framers, including Pierre Trudeau, looked at the question of sexual orientation, so-called,

and said we are not putting that in. They very specifically left it out,"
he said. According to Day, Parliament was free to reexamine this question. The former Alliance leader even went so far as to quote the
famous words Trudeau pronounced when he decriminalized homosexuality — "the government should stay out of the bedrooms of the
nation" — to justify his point of view.

Following this spirited debate, the MPs in favour of recognition of
same-sex marriage felt that it was time to put the issue to a vote. At the
express request of the Liberal whip — responsible for discipline within party ranks — they craftily made sure that some of their more sympathetic colleagues were called in to replace Liberal opponents of
same-sex marriage. In other words, it was time for a little political
manoeuvring. According to Marlene Jennings,

> We knew that several Liberal members of the committee were
> in favour of Svend's motion, but they didn't know it was sched-
> uled to be debated that day. They were out of town, and so I
> had to make sure I could find substitutes who were also in
> favour. I phoned the whip's office and suggested some names.
> Those people [Sue Barnes and Anita Neville] were taken off the
> committees where they were sitting on at the time, and sent
> over to our committee. Until they arrived, though, the oppo-
> nents were in the majority. We tried to drag the debate out to
> avoid a vote. When everyone had spoken, I encouraged the
> members in favour of the motion to leave the room. We stayed
> outside to make sure there wasn't a quorum until our substi-
> tutes arrived. From time to time I stuck my head in the door
> and Richard [Marceau] made signs to let me know what was
> happening in the room, all this in full view of the TV cameras.
> And then our substitutes arrived. We had to bring the discus-
> sion to a close and call for a vote as quickly as possible, because
> another Liberal MP [Derek Lee], who was against, was tied up
> in another committee. We knew that when he finished there he
> would come over. In the end, we managed to call for a vote
> before he arrived. He turned up less than five minutes later.

The interesting point here is that only ten days previously, Jennings had suggested that the government refer the marriage question to the Supreme Court while the committee was preparing its report, to ensure that "all options remained open." It appears that the immediate application of the Ontario Court of Appeal decision caused her, as a longtime supporter of same-sex marriage, to change her mind on this question.

Well aware of what was happening, one of the MPs opposing the motion, Pat O'Brien, asked committee chair Andy Scott to check whether the newcomers were entitled to vote. This was rapidly confirmed. Shortly afterward, his Liberal colleague Joe Peschisolido tried to persuade the other members of the committee to wait until Lee's arrival before voting, "as a courtesy." In vain. Jennings took a not entirely disinterested position: "Maybe it's a problem I could attribute to my legal training, but the question has been put; now, in my opinion, once the question has been put, we must proceed with the vote." Scott agreed with her and called the vote.

The result was entirely representative of the division existing within the broader public on the issue: eight MPs voted in favour of the motion (Liberals Sue Barnes, Hedy Fry, John Harvard, Anita Neville and Marlene Jennings, Bloc MPs Richard Marceau and Réal Ménard, and, of course, Svend Robinson) and eight voted against (Alliance MPs Chuck Cadman, Stockwell Day, Grant McNally and Kevin Sorenson, as well as Liberals John Maloney, John McKay, Pat O'Brien and Joe Peschisolido). The supporters of a redefinition of marriage could live with this result: they knew that the chair would have a casting vote, and that he would come down "on the right side." Scott now spoke:

> The rules of the House allow me to make a statement now. I've paid a great deal of attention over the course of these hearings in every part of Canada. I had a forum in my own constituency, which had 675 people there, and I listened. In 1999, I voted to keep the definition of "marriage" as it had existed. I have listened. I've listened with great respect to my colleagues, with a variety of views. I also have been informed by a num-

ber of judgments of the courts. I don't feel compelled to vote in any particular way because of what those judgments have said, but I also feel that I feel informed by them. It's a part of this process, in my opinion. Therefore, I will be voting in support of the motion of Mr. Robinson.

Scott's position was bound to create waves, especially since his remarks were broadcast live on the TV news channels, providing wall-to-wall coverage of this dramatic finish. "Who gets to do this, the judges or Parliament?" asked the chair, before answering his own question to general applause, "I believe this is Parliament."

The battle was not over yet, however. MP Pat O'Brien, unhappy with the outcome, tabled a second motion requesting that the government appeal the decisions of the British Columbia and Ontario appeal courts. After an hour of futile discussions and obstruction by the MPs in favour of same-sex marriage (Ménard and Jennings even dragged the names of Lucien Bouchard and René Lévesque into the debate), O'Brien agreed to postpone the vote on the motion, and, in fact, it never took place. Parliamentary tradition generally prohibits the adoption of two directly contradictory motions within a short space of time.

Marlene Jennings, the daughter of an Italian mother and an African American father, had not always been a fervent supporter of the right of gays and lesbians to marry. Only after voting in favour of the Alliance motion in 1999 did she begin to think seriously about the question:

> I said to myself, "Hold on there, Marlene! Your reaction so far has been a pure reflex, but now you should do your homework!" I started to talk things over with people, to read everything I could lay my hands on. And the more I thought about it, the more I said to myself, "It's really about minority rights." As a woman and member of a visible minority myself, I couldn't do otherwise but support same-sex marriage. And not just support it: I had to promote it too.

Her biggest surprise was to hear her mother, who was then 72, say, "God created marriage, so it should be open to same-sex couples too!"

* * * * *

Of course, whatever the "opinion" of the committee, the government could do whatever it liked. Opponents of same-sex marriage, however, could feel the ground slipping from beneath their feet, perhaps permanently. Even today, they have not forgiven their colleagues for smothering their protests. "It was one of the most horrible days I've ever seen on Parliament Hill," recalled Pat O'Brien. "It was disgusting. It really was politics at its worst and on a very important issue. The work of the committee was reduced to a pathetic farce and that's what it became. The best way to show that is that the committee never did its report."

Vic Toews is unreconciled as well. "We would have won that vote had the committee remained as it was," he said. "I think it demonstrated a lack of good faith on the part of the chair of the committee and the government generally." Toews still resents the actions of Justice Minister Cauchon: "I trusted him and I thought that there would be a full open hearing on this matter and that he would do nothing to preempt the examination of this matter by the committee, and I can't tell you how disappointed I was. My trust was betrayed." What the opponents of same-sex marriage found particularly galling was that the court decisions had shifted the balance of power. Toews said,

> Those who were advancing the proposition that the definition of marriage would be changed bore the onus of demonstrating that such a change would not be detrimental to society. You don't change fundamental institutions in a country that has by and large functioned very well unless there is some kind of powerful, almost overwhelming, reason to do so and quite frankly, the evidence that I heard at the justice committee did not convince me that there was any such argument. After the courts' decisions, the onus was on us.

Few MPs changed sides in the course of the committee's work. However, when they realized that legislation on same-sex marriage was practically inevitable, some adopted a more flexible position. "I was pretty much opposed to civil unions for homosexuals at the beginning," O'Brien acknowledged. "I became convinced during the hearings that, even though I might not necessarily like that, it was going to be a necessary compromise, if you will, or recognition that we would have to accept in law. But then I would never support the destruction of the term *marriage*. I think that most of the Canadian public has come to that opinion as well."

Nevertheless, there was one dramatic conversion: committee chair Andy Scott. Initially a ferocious opponent of same-sex marriage, he was the person who eventually tipped the scales in favour of change. The many meetings he had with Martin Cauchon and close advisers of Jean Chrétien probably had some connection with his change of heart, but the strictly legal arguments repeatedly invoked by Bloc Québécois MP Richard Marceau had the most influence. "Generally, in politics, you receive more insults that anything else," Marceau said. "So to be told by a Liberal MP that I had had a strong influence on his position was quite flattering. In the end, I told myself, it was possible to make a difference as a politician. It was possible to have an effect on people's lives."

8

JEAN CHRÉTIEN'S CONVERSION

The days after the vote of the standing committee were the decisive period in the process that would eventually lead to the expansion of marriage to include same-sex couples. Martin Cauchon and the government were in a hurry: within a few days it had to decide whether or not to appeal the decision of the British Columbia court handed down six weeks earlier. And in Ontario, there was already a steady flow of same-sex couples getting married.

Before the Ontario Court of Appeal ruling, the Minister of Justice had not yet "come out of the closet" and made his position known to his boss, Jean Chrétien. Not that he was gay — Cauchon is the straightest man imaginable. However, he had not yet stated clearly to the prime minister that he personally supported same-sex marriage. When he eventually made his case, Chrétien reacted badly. "Cauchon, you want to change the definition in the dictionary!" the experienced politician told his young minister, who realized he was facing an uphill battle. The Prime Minister nevertheless agreed to allow Cauchon to present the various possible solutions during a cabinet "retreat" scheduled for the following Tuesday, June 17, 2003.

"As Minister of Justice, I was in a situation where I had to juggle the classic definition of marriage, which was also the position of my own party, a parliamentary committee that had yet to make up its mind and a court decision that I could theoretically appeal," recalled Cauchon.

However, the immediate effect of the Ontario judgment was to make his task easier: "It meant that I could move forward faster. It didn't take away the political initiative I had taken, but it allowed me to move ahead faster. I made it a major issue. As a result, it became one of the government's priorities, and I took advantage of this opening."

An appeal of the Ontario decision "would have been feasible," according to Cauchon, but the problem was that "I would have had to file a motion to suspend execution of the judgment, which would have prevented any new marriages. That was unthinkable! I couldn't do that to people! I would never have done that!" In any case, the more days went by, the less realistic this option appeared. In other words, time was on the minister's side.

After getting the green light from Jean Chrétien, Cauchon met with officials from his department to draw up a game plan. "That's when we decided we wouldn't appeal," he says. "Then we started to define the idea of a bill." Three options would be presented to cabinet: appealing the court decisions, introducing draft legislation to legalize same-sex marriage while referring the question to the Supreme Court and immediately introducing a bill. "My proposal, draft legislation, appeared more reasonable than the other two," Cauchon explained.

It would have been far too risky to broach the subject in cabinet without preparing the terrain beforehand. "Before the meeting, I called I don't know how many ministers — probably 20 [out of a possible 38] — to get their support," Cauchon recalled. "I called them one by one, myself. We had never really discussed the underlying arguments before. But I realized that the support was there. I was actually quite surprised." Everyone suspected that because the government had not acted swiftly to suspend the effects of the Ontario decision, it had already implicitly revealed its real intentions.

At a more mundane level, Cauchon was busy "collecting IOUs," asking his fellow ministers for tacit support in return for help he had provided in various areas in the past. "In politics, being a member of cabinet is a little strange," explained former heritage minister Sheila Copps. "If you want support for your own projects, you always agree to the projects put forward by other ministers. It's not in your interest to

JEAN CHRÉTIEN'S CONVERSION

oppose them, because when your turn comes people will remember what you did."

The support of a majority of ministers, whatever their motives, was an encouraging sign. But nothing is achieved in cabinet without the backing of the prime minister. Cauchon and Chrétien's inner circle began preparing him for the small revolution they were promoting. Paul Genest, Chrétien's chief adviser on the marriage question, recalled,

> The Prime Minister had approved the decision to have the standing committee deal with it, but he had not declared himself on the issue. He was very careful with decision-making and his decision was to watch the process unfold, gauge the dynamics of the debate. He could see what the courts were saying and could follow the arguments, but he was not coming down anywhere at that particular time. He was listening hard to it, but before June 2003, he hadn't made a decision yet. For him, there was a bit of a personal tension between where he conceived Charter logic was going and his own roots in rural Quebec, still a practising Catholic, all of that. Mr. Chrétien, you couldn't push him when it wasn't ready. So my approach in the year previous to that was just to keep him informed and not to ask a decision.

According to a source quoted by the *Toronto Star*, in the spring of 2003 Chrétien even toyed with the idea of leaving the whole question of same-sex marriage to his successor, due to be chosen in November. Irritated by slow progress in other areas, the Prime Minister, who did not need any new problems, is said to have shouted to his staff, "We're not going to do that [redefine marriage]!" Obviously, Martin Cauchon and his allies were worried.

The Ontario Court of Appeal decision forced Jean Chrétien to rethink his position — for several reasons, it was this decision that made him change his mind. It came into effect immediately and confirmed three other decisions from three provinces. Nevertheless, at the time the Prime Minister was not pleased that gay and lesbian couples could suddenly get married, especially since the manoeuvre had been partly orchestrated by Chief Justice Roy McMurtry, an old friend. Chrétien had gotten to know McMurtry when the latter was attorney general in Ontario's Conservative government. As federal justice minister, Chrétien was in charge of the negotiations to repatriate the constitution in 1980–81, and at the beginning Ontario and New Brunswick were the only provinces supporting his efforts. (After obtaining the agreement of all the provinces except Quebec during the legendary "night of the long knives," Ottawa was able to secure the return of the precious document from London, with the addition of the Charter of Rights and Freedoms.) And now Roy McMurtry, one of the key players in the constitution drama, was sending his former ally a clear message: the Charter of Rights is more than just words. According to Genest,

> They had worked several years together on creating that thing, the Charter, and ironically, there was Mr. McMurtry as chief of that court, saying: same-sex marriage is the logic of the Charter. For Mr. Chrétien, the ruling was highly credible. It had profound implications for him. It was a bit of a coincidence in some ways, but he had no doubt in the wisdom, the decency and the legal knowledge of Roy McMurtry. Moreover, Mr. Chrétien's personal connections have always mattered enormously.

Despite everything, Genest recalled, the prime minister had not yet made a definitive decision:

> He listened to a lot of people, but he didn't say a lot himself. I could see there was some discomfort. But he could see that the marriages were happening as he was considering the issue. So what do you do? So what do you do? Do you turn the page back? What's your position going to be? Are you going to argue that these marriages are null and void? So he could see a political reality taking shape before his eyes. And what he said is:

"I'm going to think about it." And he said, "Let's see what the ministers have to say at the cabinet discussion."

Jean Chrétien had an opportunity to reflect on the topic during Question Period in the House of Commons in mid-June, when Liberal MP Marlene Jennings addressed at length the idea of a referral to the Supreme Court. "He was very receptive," she noted.

* * * * *

After taking the weekend to reflect, the cabinet came together on Tuesday, June 17, 2003 at the Lester B. Pearson Building in Ottawa, the home of the Department of Foreign Affairs. This is where the cabinet met two or three times a year for its "retreats" — long planning sessions. The session had been previously scheduled, but came at a useful time given the importance of the subject on the table.

The discussions went on at length, but Martin Cauchon was confident throughout. One or two ministers were still unwilling to redefine marriage, but all the others were strongly in favour. "I had widespread support," recalled Cauchon. "The Clerk of the Privy Council, Alex Himelfarb, and Mr. Chrétien's other advisers could see that I had done my homework, that I had prepared the ground with my colleagues."

"Some lost courage in the weeks after, but at the cabinet meeting it was unanimous that we should not appeal," recalled an observer who prefers to remain anonymous. "Appeal was not really considered."

The justice minister and Jean Chrétien's inner circle were in for a surprise, however: a majority of ministers were not only in favour of same-sex marriages, but also wanted to skip the referral to the Supreme Court to save time! This was the third option: to introduce legislation to legalize same-sex marriage immediately. "I was astonished, because I expected many of them to be firmly against same-sex marriage," recalled Sheila Copps. "It was astounding."

It is important to note, however, that some ministers had a pragmatic reason for taking this approach. Those who were fervent supporters of Paul Martin in the Liberal leadership race wanted Jean

Prime Minister Jean Chrétien, in the amphitheatre of the Lester B. Pearson Building in Ottawa, June 17, 2003. "We will not be appealing the recent decision on the definition of marriage," he announced.

Chrétien to deal with same-sex marriage right away, to save the incoming team from having to address this contentious issue. This "ideal" scenario was a little overly optimistic: it was June 2003, and Martin was expected to take over the helm at the end of the year, after the formality of his election as Liberal leader. It would have been practically impossible to pass such controversial legislation in less than six months, especially since the long summer recess was about to begin. Whatever the reasons that made the plan seem attractive, it would have allowed gay and lesbian couples across the country to marry earlier. But it was not to be.

"I would say there was a slight majority, in the talk around the room, that would have favoured going right away. The view was, 'Get it out of the way before the election so this isn't an election issue,'" the anonymous observer confirmed. "But Mr. Chrétien said, 'You're rushing the issue too much.' He steered the discussion towards the reference as the more prudent political decision. He could see where it was going, but he said, 'Don't force it down people's throat.'"

Martin Cauchon was not convinced by the arguments of the people who wanted to move forward without delay. He wanted his approach to appear "reasonable." He explained, "I didn't think Parliament was ready at that time. The subject was too new, too untested. There had been no society-wide debate; people had not had time to discuss it. I thought that if we rushed ahead we would actually harm our cause, that we would shoot ourselves in the foot." Once again, the tension created by the leadership race was a factor: Cauchon did not necessarily want to allow the Martin clan, of which he was not a member, to score a victory.

Of course, the idea of a referral to the Supreme Court did not please everyone. "We chose this solution to calm the opposition, but it didn't help us much because all we got was an oracular decision from the Supreme Court that leaves various points open to interpretation," noted another cabinet member, Bill Graham.

When everyone had had a chance to speak, Jean Chrétien pushed his chair back and made an astonishing statement: "I hear what you are saying, but I haven't made my mind up yet." A press conference was scheduled to begin in a few minutes. He added, "I just want to say that if we decide to move in the direction you have indicated, don't think it's not going to be wavy and bumpy down the road. We'll have a fight on our hands." Thus ended the cabinet meeting that would change the definition of marriage for the benefit of gay and lesbian couples.

"Mr. Chrétien is not someone you can push into making a decision," commented Martin Cauchon. "But I think he's always been able to distinguish between himself, his values and his position as head of the government. I'm sure he asked himself, 'What is best for the Canadian people, based on our values?' He did what he had to do as Prime Minister, even if it went against what I believe were his personal values. However, if we had found a way to avoid it, he would have accepted with pleasure." Paul Genest added a little nuance: "He never complained about what came his way. It was not typical of him to bitch about being in a situation. For him, it was 'Deal with the situation.'"

* * * * *

There was more for Jean Chrétien to do that day. He still had to
announce the decision, which was even more difficult for him than the
decision itself. Chrétien and Cauchon retired to a small room adjacent
to the amphitheatre where a crowd of reporters waited to see how this
extraordinary day would unfold. Paul Genest, Alex Himelfarb and
Chrétien's chief political adviser, Eddie Goldenberg, were also present.
Their goal was to draft the text that the Prime Minister would then read
out to the press. The negotiations were difficult, to say the least.
According to one witness, Chrétien was like "a caged lion." In fact, he
refused to pronounce the words *same-sex marriage*, which was the
essence of the announcement he was to make. He stuck to his position
and wrote down *same-sex unions*. Cauchon was disappointed, but
already had a solution: he would speak to the reporters immediately
afterward and dissipate any remaining ambiguity.

"It was a torture for him," a close associate of Chrétien's said off the
record. "What was harder was getting ready to go out. He had his stride.
I had never seen him like that. He was upset, but he knew where he was
going. It really came out of the cabinet meeting. But he didn't declare
to us where we were headed! I knew he'd listened and I knew we were
making progress in the conversation."

Jean Chrétien did not take lightly the future of the party whose leadership he was about to relinquish, but he felt he had some room to follow his own instincts. One of his close confidants recalled,

> He had an attitude of "I don't need to be elected again, I'm
> going to call things as I see them." He was not cavalier
> towards the electoral hopes of the Liberal Party in the future
> and he did argue in the cabinet meeting, "Remember, you
> have colleagues who have to campaign in rural Canada — this
> is not a big winner or an easy sell there." That was on his
> mind. It wasn't just "Screw the rest of you, I'm going to do

things how I feel." But he was certainly freed up from future electoral calculations for his own personal benefit. Plus, given that he was under attack, he recognized that the best thing he could do to keep things at bay was to be doing important things, to be aggressive in a policy context. It was a very creative and aggressive policymaking period for him.

In fact, even though Chrétien had announced almost a year earlier that he would give up his leadership in February 2004, many Martin supporters in the Liberal caucus were calling for an earlier departure. Chrétien's reaction was to become hyperactive. He got involved in the decriminalization of marijuana possession, the ratification of the Kyoto agreement to reduce greenhouse gas emissions and the reform of political financing, followed by the refusal to go to war in Iraq and the same-sex marriage debate. "While you're discussing Kyoto, same-sex, you're not debating Jean Chrétien, even though it wasn't solely political calculation," recalled the same confidant. "These were deeply principled decisions. It was: 'Controversy is fine, bring it on!' He felt very freed up in that environment and the best way to deal with the risk and the threat was to go on the offensive."

"We will not be appealing the recent decision on the definition of marriage," announced Chrétien. "Rather, we will be proposing legislation that will protect the right of churches and religious organizations to sanctify marriage as they define it. At the same time, we will ensure that our legislation includes and legally recognizes the union of same-sex couples. As soon as the legislation is drafted, it will be referred to the Supreme Court. After that, it will be put to a free vote in the House."

Bombarded with questions, the Prime Minister cited public opinion and legal arguments: "For me, we have a Charter of Rights, there is evolution in society and according to the interpretation of the courts, they concluded these unions should be legal in Canada."

Although only a few hours earlier he had not yet made up his mind, Chrétien was suddenly eager to bring the debate to a close. "We don't want there to be a long period of uncertainty," he said. "We want to complete this file and deal with it as quickly as possible, and as soon as we have the reference, then the House of Commons will vote." He was perhaps a little optimistic.

As planned, Martin Cauchon specified that it was "quite clear" that the government recognized same-sex marriages and would not appeal the Ontario and British Columbia decisions. "It's a great day for Canadians," Cauchon said. "I'm very proud to be part of this country." Much of his pride was personal: he knew that, thanks to the same-sex issue, his name as a minister would go down in history.

John Fisher of Egale Canada was also jubilant. "It's a historic day," he said. "The Prime Minister of Canada has finally said our relationships are equal. Same-sex marriages are here to stay." NDP MP Svend Robinson agreed: "The Prime Minister has shown courageous leadership on this issue. He's doing the right thing." As vigilant as ever, his Bloc Québécois colleague Richard Marceau wondered whether the referral to the Supreme Court was still really necessary. "We feel it is important to bring a referral before the Supreme Court to ensure that the debate is brought to a close and that the new legislation cannot be challenged," Cauchon responded. But however noble the intention, the approach was still naive. Opposition to same-sex marriage remained as virulent as ever in the ensuing months and years, even though a large segment of the Canadian elite approved of the change. The subject was too controversial for debate to be ended by a government decision.

9

THE FORCES REGROUP

With the decision of the Chrétien government not to appeal the judgments permitting same-sex marriages, the groups opposing the change lost their main ally. For years, Ottawa had echoed their arguments during court cases. Now they had to rely on their own devices and, not surprisingly, they felt bitter. "The federal government has abdicated its leadership role," said Derek Rogusky of Focus on the Family, a conservative lobby group based in the United States. "This matter has far-reaching consequences nationwide, and the nation's highest court should be permitted to consider the fundamental issues."

This was in early July 2003, and for several days a rumour had circulated to the effect that Ottawa would ask the Supreme Court to answer three questions, but not the main question posed by right-wing groups: was the traditional definition of marriage constitutional? The opponents' objective was clear: the Supreme Court had to be asked to broaden the scope of the debate. "This is a very limited action," was how Gwen Landolt of Real Women of Canada described Ottawa's approach. "It is not settling the matter at all."

Focus on the Family, the Association for Marriage and the Family in Ontario, the Interfaith Coalition and Landolt's organization came together to petition the Supreme Court for leave to appeal the court decisions that had cleared the way for same-sex marriages. The Canadian Alliance could only support this initiative that, although unusual, was not unprecedented. In October 2003, however, five Supreme Court judges rejected the petition.

Janet Epp Buckingham, of the Evangelical Fellowship of Canada, acknowledged later that the termination of court proceedings did not help the adversaries of same-sex marriage: "It is clear that the government's decision not to appeal made our task more difficult. We suddenly had less latitude: there were no more cases in which we could intervene before the courts. This is why we adapted our message to the political forum and turned our attention to Parliament."

On July 8 came more bad news for the opponents of same-sex marriages: the British Columbia Court of Appeal lifted the suspension included in its May 1 decision, allowing same-sex couples to marry immediately. To wait any longer before authorizing same-sex marriages would have resulted in "an unequal application of the law as between Ontario and British Columbia," the judges ruled. Half of the population of Canada was now suddenly living in provinces where same-sex marriages were legal!

Since most of the couples who had launched the original case before the B.C. courts had already married in Toronto during the Lesbian and Gay Pride Week that followed the Ontario Appeal Court judgment, another couple was found to break the ice in western Canada. Less than an hour after the B.C. Court of Appeal decision was announced, Tom Graff and Anthony Porcino tied the knot in front of the Vancouver courthouse. Tim Stevenson, a United Church minister and gay member of Vancouver City Council, officiated.

The gay couple had no difficulty obtaining a marriage licence from the city offices, except that the draft document listed Anthony Porcino as the "intended bride." The document was quickly changed to name both men as the intended spouses. "Being first was not what was significant to us; it was just being able to do it," Porcino said. "That's two provinces down, and may they all fall quickly like dominoes now," said Jane Hamilton, who with her partner Joy Masuhara was part of the B.C. lawsuit.

While gays and lesbians were celebrating this new victory, Prime Minister Chrétien continued to feel the effects of his decision. His close adviser Paul Genest recalled,

It was still a difficult moment for him, because when he went back to his riding, people who had grown up with would literally say, "You're crazy, you know. What on earth are you doing?" So there was a bit of a disconnect between his cultural roots and what he'd created and the thinking of the people for whom he had a very high regard. But sitting on the front porch of his cottage in Lac des Piles, he would answer back, "You know, guys, things change and you've got to be willing to adjust."

Jean Chrétien had always been a combative politician who enjoyed challenging his opponents and even his allies. He always listened to arguments that contradicted his views, but did not mind proving that he was right. It is probably this trait of character that explains Chrétien's behaviour at the Progressive Governance Summit held in Bagshot, England, in mid-July 2003. "It was just a couple of weeks after the decision had been taken, and by that point, he was boasting behind closed doors to these guys, who all styled themselves left-leaning governments," said one observer. The world leaders present included British Prime Minister Tony Blair, Brazilian president Luiz Inácio Lula da Silva, South African President Thabo Mbeki and former U.S. President Bill Clinton. "He was very proud that he had done it, that Canada had done it, so we were out in front of the lead on these guys," recalled the observer. "They were looking at him and he told them frankly, 'If you had told me I was going to do this 40 years ago, when I started politics, I would have dropped dead on the spot! But you know times change.'"

However, on the plane trip back to Ottawa, Chrétien expressed some of his doubts. According to one reporter, "He said, 'It didn't come naturally to me. Some people thought I was crazy — including myself! I was surprised at what I had done, given my own education.'" As usual, though, Chrétien did not look back; instead, he stood by his decision.

* * * * *

On Thursday, July 17, 2003 Martin Cauchon introduced his much-anticipated draft legislation. The short text stipulated that "marriage, for civil purposes, is the lawful union of two persons to the exclusion of all others." In response to his detractors, the Justice Minister reiterated that the future legislation would not remove any rights from heterosexual couples, but would "enrich" the definition of marriage.

"This is a more generous and inclusive definition, based on the values of Canadians," he insisted. "By broadening the definition of marriage to recognize unions between people of the same sex, we recognize that all Canadians have the right to equal treatment." Like the final version of the bill, introduced 18 months later, the draft version clearly specified that religious authorities could continue to refuse to marry same-sex couples if it ran counter to their beliefs.

For opponents of a redefinition of marriage, the problem was not so much the draft bill as the three questions that the government referred to the Supreme Court to validate its approach:

1. Is the definition of marriage within the exclusive legislative authority of the Parliament of Canada?
2. Is same-sex marriage consistent with the Canadian Charter of Rights and Freedoms?
3. Does the freedom of religion guaranteed by the Charter pro tect religious officials from being compelled to perform a marriage between two persons of the same sex that is contrary to their religious beliefs?

The first question was practically an insult to the judges' intelligence: nobody, whether in provincial governments or among the bill's opponents, had suggested that the definition of marriage did not fall under federal jurisdiction. The goal of the question, though, was to obtain confirmation from the Supreme Court that, despite what Judge Ian Pitfield of the British Columbia Supreme Court had suggested, a constitutional amendment was not required to change the criteria for marriage.

The second question was ingenious: it asked the Supreme Court to approve same-sex marriage without looking explicitly at any other possibilities. The supporters of a traditional definition of marriage have never forgiven Ottawa for moving the judicial debate in this direction. Instead, they would have preferred the Supreme Court to rule on the constitutionality of excluding gay and lesbian couples as candidates for marriage, even though three lower courts had already given their opinion on this matter.

The third question was a sort of consolation prize for the opponents of same-sex marriage, whose main demand had been ignored. The government wanted to provide reassurance for religious groups by asking the Supreme Court to confirm that the section of the Canadian Charter of Rights that guaranteed freedom of religion would protect them from any obligation to perform same-sex marriages.

In short, for anyone already acquainted with the decisions of the lower courts, it was unlikely that the Supreme Court's answers would contain any surprises. It would still take several months, however, before they were announced, since the hearing was scheduled for mid-April 2004. To demonstrate his good faith, Cauchon decided to go one step further. First, he asked the Supreme Court to hear the referral promptly, which it refused to do. Next, he contacted his provincial counterparts. "I'm asking the provinces and territories to go ahead and act on the basis of the draft bill I have just introduced," he announced at a press conference, reiterating his position of one month earlier. "It is up to them to do something." However, the legal community and the provincial governments greeted his proposal with skepticism. "We can't act right away," said Quebec Justice Minister Marc Bellemare. "When Ottawa changes the legal definition of marriage, Quebec will respond." In the meantime, Quebec's gay and lesbian community had to bide its time.

* * * * *

In the days immediately following Ottawa's decision not to challenge same-sex marriages, the Canadian Conference of Catholic Bishops (CCCB) had voiced its concerns. "Altering the definition of marriage in order to include same-sex partners discriminates against heterosexual marriage and the family, which are thus deprived of their social and

legal recognition as the fundamental and irreplaceable basis of society," said the conference's chair, Bishop Jacques Berthelet of Saint-
Jean–Longueuil, in a letter to the Prime Minister. "I would very much
hope that the legacy you are leaving does not include legislation that
represents an assault on common sense, an assault on the values of
societies which are advanced but not amoral, and an assault on the lib-
erties of men and women of good will."

Although comments such as these may appear radical, they were, in
fact quite subdued compared to the official Vatican position, as
defined by the Congregation for the Doctrine of the Faith, led by
Cardinal Joseph Ratzinger, who would become Pope Benedict XVI in
April 2005. "Marriage is holy, while homosexual acts go against the
natural moral law," stipulated a document approved in late March
2003 by Pope John Paul II but only made public two months later, in
June. After all, according to this proclamation of doctrine, homosexuality was "deviant behaviour," and to allow homosexuals to be parents
was "doing violence" to children.

Aware that several other countries were considering legalizing same-
sex marriages, the Vatican felt the need to address parliamentarians:
"When legislation in favour of the recognition of homosexual unions
is proposed ... the Catholic law-maker has a moral duty to express his
opposition clearly and publicly and to vote against it. To vote in favour
of a law so harmful to the common good is gravely immoral." Asked
about the tone and content of the papal declaration, the president of
the Assemblée des Évêques du Québec (Quebec Assembly of Bishops),
Raymond Saint-Gelais, admitted that "the language used does not
match the current culture." In fact, many people criticized the church's
initiative, seeing it as interference in the affairs of government.

Claude Ryan, a former leader of the Quebec Liberal Party who, from
1945 to 1962, had headed the French section of Catholic Action in
Canada, did not agree. "I believe that Rome has exercised its incon-
testable right to intervene in the debate on the future of same-sex
unions and marriage," he wrote in an open letter published in early
August 2003. Ryan opposed same-sex marriage: "If I were a member of
Parliament, I would vote against the bill introduced by the Chrétien

government because it seeks to establish uniformity, whereas the realities it attempts to cover with a single definition are clearly different."

With hindsight, the Catholic hierarchy acknowledged that it had to adapt its message to combat the success of the opposing side. Archbishop André Gaumond of Sherbrooke, who was vice-chair of the CCCB, explained,

> We had to make our arguments more specific over time and support them better, especially in terms of anthropology. The marriage debate was like a dialogue with our adversaries: we countered the arguments they put forward, and tried to refute them. Our own arguments became more refined, as was natural. For example, we had to coordinate them with the precepts of civil law, which were not taken sufficiently into consideration in our original position. We had to gain clearer understanding of society's legal apparatus in order to discuss same-sex marriage on an equal footing with its supporters, who had the Charter on their side.

Clearly, the opinion of the church had a decisive influence on a number of federal MPs who were also practising Catholics. Jean Chrétien, on the other hand, remained unimpressed by the decrees of religion. On July 30, for example, Bishop Fred Henry of Calgary warned the Prime Minister that he risked burning in hell if he supported same-sex marriage. "He doesn't understand what it means to be a good Catholic," Bishop Henry told the *Globe and Mail*. "He's putting at risk his eternal salvation." Bishop Henry repeated the same message to Paul Martin less than a year later, in the middle of the election campaign.

"I'm a Christian and I pray, but I'm also Prime Minister of Canada and, as such, I behave as somebody with responsibility for the whole country," Chrétien retorted in mid-August. "I deal with my religion in other circumstances … In Canada, there is a major division between the state and religion."

At the same time, Chrétien recognized that he would probably not have agreed to legalize same-sex marriage if he had not been forced to do so by the Ontario court decision. "If there had been no court ruling making it legal that very day in Ontario, things would have been different," he said. "We were facing an emergency." If the government had filed an appeal with the Supreme Court, it would have halted any further same-sex marriages in Ontario and borne the stigma of withdrawing a right from a minority group. Chrétien probably calculated that this approach was not profitable in political terms.

In citing the separation of religion and the state in his response to Bishop Henry, Chrétien was following an old family tradition. The MP for Saint-Maurice was fond of telling his colleagues the story of his ancestors' resistance to Catholic authority in Quebec before the Quiet Revolution. At the beginning of his autobiography *Straight from the Heart*, he boasts that his family have always been Rouges and Liberals, in the anticlerical, antiestablishment and freethinking tradition of the nineteenth century. For a long time, he says, people were excommunicated for supporting liberalism that, among other radical measures, advocated the separation of church and state.

Fred Henry was not the first bishop to brandish the spectre of eternal damnation before a member of the Chrétien family. This distinction probably belongs to Mgr. Louis-François Laflèche who, in 1896, demanded that Chrétien's paternal grandfather, François, travel to the diocesan headquarters in Trois-Rivières to obtain absolution for his sins: he had distributed alcohol free of charge while working as a Liberal Party organizer. François Chrétien, however, refused to confess to a Conservative bishop. The bishop eventually relented and authorized the rebel to confess in his hometown, before a lower-ranking priest.

In 1960, it was the young Jean Chrétien's turn to lead the battle against the religious authorities in his region, who had called on their parishioners to support the Union Nationale in that year's Quebec election.

* * * * *

Summer is an ideal time for prime ministers to announce major decisions on controversial subjects: during the two-month vacation period, they can avoid facing their MPs. But all good things come to an end. A

Liberal caucus meeting was scheduled for August 19 to 21, 2003, in North Bay, Ontario. There was no doubt that same-sex marriages would be the main focus, especially since the MPs who opposed the change were planning a "revolt" to force the government to change course. "Our constituents are forcing us in that direction," explained Joe Volpe, later a minister in the Martin cabinet. Even Wayne Easter, then one of Chrétien's ministers, had gone so far as to criticize his own government's decision. "There is a difference between heterosexual couples when they get married; it's procreation," he said. "That can't happen with same-sex couples." Other ministers, including Claudette Bradshaw, Herb Dhaliwal and Robert Thibault, stated publicly that they had not yet made up their minds. Strangely enough, none of them had actually opposed same-sex marriage during the cabinet discussions two months earlier.

With this determined opposition coming from within the Liberal Party, Paul Martin kept all his options open, seeking to please as many people as possible. The former finance minister was campaigning openly to succeed Jean Chrétien as Liberal leader and did not want to lose the vote of even one of his supporters. However, many of them were fiercely opposed to any expansion of the concept of marriage to include same-sex couples. "I support the government's move in this area, but I do believe that in the course of discussion other options may well be put on the table," Martin declared on arriving in North Bay. "I think that those other options are going to have to be examined very carefully." He was clearly referring to the two other possibilities envisaged by the opponents of same-sex marriage: the elimination of civil marriage and the establishment of civil unions.

Like many opponents of same-sex marriage, MP Pat O'Brien, a long-standing Liberal, had always believed that Paul Martin was on his side: "I'm not convinced that he believes that in his heart at all [the redefinition of marriage]. I think he's come to the conclusion that we had to follow the courts on this. He was not prepared to overrule the courts on that. I think he was wrong."

Unlike the "little guy from Shawinigan," who was not afraid to impose his own decisions unilaterally, Martin preferred to leave his supporters free to discuss the marriage question. He never encouraged them to support the government's position, at least not before he moved into 24 Sussex Drive. Martin even aimed a barb at Chrétien concerning this different approach to leadership. "You'd better get used to this," he said. "I believe that members of Parliament do have a right to make their voices heard." Sheila Copps, the former heritage minister, saw things differently: "When there was a split in the party, Martin did what he could to make it worse, instead of trying to reconcile the differences."

Aware of Martin's strategy, Martin Cauchon was quick to set the record straight: in his opinion, he said, civil unions did not provide an adequate response and it would be unacceptable to end civil marriage. "We have a constitutional responsibility, that of defining marriage," he insisted. "For example, people who don't want to marry religiously — how could they marry?"

In his opening speech that evening, the Prime Minister admitted that the question had been "difficult" for him, as it still was for many MPs. "I'll tell you this: I would have preferred not to deal with it," he confided in a departure from his prepared text. "But you know me: I never walk away from a problem." Next, the Liberal leader attacked the statement by the Canadian Alliance that the redefinition of marriage was a result of the "activism" of the judiciary: "It is code for their profound opposition to the Charter of Rights — a Charter that was passed by Parliament and that Liberals and all Canadians respect and cherish." Chrétien's attachment to a part of the Constitution that he had helped create showed through. He continued,

> So let us not fall into their [the Alliance's] trap on this issue. This is not about weakening Parliament. It is not about weakening traditional religion. It is not about weakening the Canadian social fabric. In fact, it is about giving Parliament its rightful voice. It is about protecting religious traditions and rites. It is about giving force and effect to Canadian values. Values of mutual respect, justice and equality.

Visibly convinced he had made the right decision, Chrétien borrowed the U.S. school segregation analogy used by his justice minister and gay and lesbian groups to exclude the possibility of civil unions: "The courts have been telling us that the notion of separate but equal has no place in Canada." Once again straying from his text, Chrétien pronounced words that still echo in the hearts of gays, lesbians and other members of minority groups: "I'd rather see an interpretation guarantee rights than take away rights." The assembled MPs could not restrain their applause.

The Prime Minister delivered a stirring plea for change:

> So I urge you all to give this careful consideration at the appropriate time. To cool the rhetoric. Not to fall into traps set by the opposition. Believe me, for someone of my generation, born and brought up in the Catholic rural Quebec of my youth, this is a very difficult issue. But I have learned over 40 years in public life that society evolves and that the concept of human rights evolves often more quickly than some of us might have predicted — and sometimes even in ways that make some people uncomfortable. But at the end of the day, we have to live up to our responsibilities. And none of these are more essential than protecting the constitution and the fundamental rights it guarantees to all Canadians.

Laurie Arron of Egale was in the room and was profoundly moved by what he heard: "That speech was an emotional experience for me. It was a really powerful speech that brought tears to my eyes. I mean to watch the Prime Minister of Canada understand our position, understand that stigma that we face and understand that it was important not just for gays and lesbians but for society to embrace those who are different was a wonderful experience. I was so proud to be Canadian."

Whatever the impact of Chrétien's speech, it failed to convince everybody. The next day, Senator Céline Hervieux-Payette and a small group of MPs brought up the possibility of holding a referendum on the redefinition of marriage. "Let's leave it up to the population to decide what the word *marriage* means," she pleaded, pointing out that if the need to respect the rights of gays and lesbians had gained widespread acceptance, there was not yet a consensus within society on the need to change a centuries-old institution.

The Prime Minister wasted no time in condemning this strategy, even drawing a parallel between gays and lesbians and French culture in Canada. "To have a referendum to decide on the fate of a minority, it's a problem," declared Chrétien, specifying that it would not be healthy to give the general public a veto over the rights of a minority group. "The majority will prevail on everything," he pointed out. "Perhaps the French language would have been banned in Canada for a long time if it had been a question of the majority deciding." Paul Martin agreed. "There are some issues that are suitable for referendums," he said. "There are other issues for Parliament to deal with. This is something for Parliament to deal with."

Foreign Affairs Minister Bill Graham was pleasantly surprised by Chrétien's firm stance:

> During the 1993 election campaign, I was walking with Mr. Chrétien in my Rosedale riding, on Church Street, and I remember telling him, "You know, Mr. Chrétien, we're right in the middle of the gay and lesbian community of Toronto." And he replied, "Bill, you can talk about that if you like, but I won't talk about it." That was back in 1993. In 2003, you have the same person saying, "We won't hold a referendum on human rights!" He went through a dramatic transformation.

Other MPs reiterated the idea that the government should simply abolish civil marriage, leaving the institution of marriage to religious authorities. Paul Martin, who did not want to completely disappoint his fiercest supporters, did not reject this proposal out of hand. Jean Chrétien, in contrast, was firm. He pointed out that Ottawa would have to amend the constitution to relinquish its responsibility for marriage.

That the issue was still far from settled for most Liberal MPs and senators was reflected in their first working session in North Bay, which was entirely given over to the marriage question. They tried to find a "compromise" that would be acceptable to all parties and would still

give equal treatment to gays and lesbians. The MP for the Montreal riding of Mount Royal, Irwin Cotler, who would later replace Martin
Cauchon as justice minister, said that it was possible to reconcile all
opinions. He was an expert in constitutional law, but could still only
suggest civil unions as a possible option, a path fraught with political
and legal obstacles. He suggested doing more to "sell" same-sex marriage by stressing that it was primarily a civil institution, and not necessarily religious.

In the morning, at the Quebec caucus meeting, Martin Cauchon
delivered another vibrant speech to promote the redefinition of marriage. Hélène Chalifour-Scherrer, the MP for the Quebec City riding of
Louis-Hébert, recognized that the minister's comments would encourage further reflection among those who still resisted the change. "I'm
probably an old fossil, but I still have reservations," admitted Scherrer,
who later became Prime Minister Paul Martin's principal secretary.

On the last day of the meeting, August 21, the tension was palpable,
and the excess of emotion had to find an outlet. "That kind of discussion in our Liberal caucus should have taken place six months earlier,"
MP Pat O'Brien said later. In a plenary session, many MPs and senators
took the floor to denounce the very idea of a marriage between spouses of the same sex, as well as the government's approach. Some did not
hesitate to display their homophobia: they accused gays and lesbians
of "deviancy" and of seeking only to satisfy their "unbridled lust."
According to several observers, the most virulent speaker was Senator
Anne Cools, who did not mince words.

Deeply shocked by what she heard, the African Canadian MP
Marlene Jennings addressed her colleagues. "I find it hard to believe
that in the third millennium people could still make such hateful comments about a minority," she said later. "The people who, like me, were
part of a minority, were thinking, 'Okay, if this is what you think, what
do you really think about me?' It was not long ago that similar comments were made about my family and ancestors. It was hard to take."

Senator Laurier LaPierre, at the time the only openly gay member of
the Liberal caucus, took the floor. With trembling hands and a voice
shaking with emotion, he related what a 70-year-old gay man had had

to endure over the course of a lifetime. "I told them about my personal situation," he later explained. "I told the MPs and senators that they
couldn't just give themselves rights because they were straight and deny
them to us because we were gay. It was ridiculous, unthinkable.
Somebody had to put a stop to it. I pointed out that we had been mis-
treated, treated differently from other people, and that it was time to
allow everyone to be treated equally."

Most of the MPs and senators in the room were deeply moved by
LaPierre's words. Some even had trouble holding back their tears.
"People were affected," LaPierre recalled, "because nobody, within the
Liberal caucus, had ever admitted they were gay. I was one of the first
to come out [among federal parliamentarians] but after that, nobody
else followed." In this regard, the political world of Ottawa is staunch-
ly conservative, much more so than many other spheres of activity in
Canadian society. This probably explains why the debate on the redefinition of marriage lasted so long.

In North Bay, a small majority of the Liberal caucus supported the
change. The problem was that the most ardent critics of same-sex marriage would not give up easily, especially since, with the support of the
Canadian Alliance, they still had a good chance of sinking the project.
"The opponents who spoke the most vehemently against the change
were like crusaders hoping to win a place in heaven by condemning
anything they considered contrary to their faith," recalled Liberal
Senator Serge Joyal. Within the Liberal caucus, there was the so-called
"God squad," made up of around a dozen MPs who systematically
opposed abortion, new reproductive technologies and same-sex marriage, among other things. This group supported Paul Martin in his
leadership bid, in the hope of steering the party to the right on moral
issues. This would turn out to be a mitigated success.

One of the most agitated representatives of the God squad is Senator
Cools, who crossed the floor to the Conservatives during the 2004 election campaign. In North Bay, she was so aggressive in her remarks that
several people were afraid the confrontation would end in blows. "In
all my parliamentary experience, this was the time we came closest to
a physical fight within caucus," says Sheila Copps. Shaken, a sobbing

Laurier LaPierre fled from the room, refusing to speak to reporters. Jean Chrétien finally took the floor to calm the situation and, more importantly, to make his troops listen to reason. "Even if the bill is defeated, the law stands," Chrétien said, in the voice of one stating an incontrovertible truth. "That's the reality."

Since most Liberal MPs and senators supported the right of gay and lesbian couples to marry, some of them left the caucus meeting with the idea that the bill should be introduced without waiting for the opinion of the Supreme Court. "It's a human rights issue," said Ottawa-Vanier MP Mauril Bélanger, a future minister in Paul Martin's cabinet. "I think that as legislators we have a responsibility to act, to express our will, and that it should be done this fall. There comes a time when action is necessary." A few days later, NDP leader Jack Layton also asked the government to take this path.

The idea even garnered some support among the opponents of same-sex marriage, who saw it as an opportunity to debate the bill before the election scheduled for the spring of 2004. Paul Martin had no choice but to take into consideration this unexpected consensus. His one condition remained the same: to give everyone a chance to take part in the debate: "When I look at this caucus, I see that the debate is already engaged. That's important. And if we continue that way, this is an option the government could consider."

Jean Chrétien, however, could not accept this approach, which would have contradicted the decision he had encouraged the cabinet to make two months earlier. "We have chosen the means that will give a result as quickly as possible," he said at a press conference. "Politically, some people would prefer to vote right away. Maybe it would be better, but on the other hand, if it's just a way to avoid facing the real problem, it's not a solution." According to Chrétien, not waiting for the Supreme Court decision would open the way to legal challenges that would create uncertainty for years to come. "We want to have a bill that will not be challenged in court," he repeated.

One month after the North Bay meeting, Laurier LaPierre had no regrets about his caucus statement. In an interview with the Montreal daily *La Presse*, he pointed out that, even today, young gays and lesbians are more likely to be rejected by their family or to attempt suicide than their straight friends: "If we do it [recognize same-sex marriage] children will be able to say, 'There's still hope,' and their parents will realize that it's not as bad as they think. We will send a clear public message; we will be saying, 'It's okay to be gay.'" The former TV host also spoke about the homophobia and hypocrisy of some of the politicians opposing a redefinition of marriage: "When my colleagues speak about gays or gay marriage, they also add that they have nothing personal against gay people. They always look at me when they say it. I always reply, 'If you have nothing against me, why do you want to deprive me of a right that I am entitled to under the Charter of Rights and Freedoms?'" The question always makes some people feel uncomfortable. "It gets on their nerves," said LaPierre. "They are irritated by the same-sex marriage debate. They are irritated to have to talk about something dirty like homosexuality."

The senator, who retired in the fall of 2004, was married for 15 years. He and his wife had two children, and now have three grandchildren. "I got married because I wanted to have children and because I loved the woman I was with," he explains. "At the time, I thought about it [homosexuality] as basically as an illness. I had to find a cure. I enrolled in a seminary to try and cure myself, but it didn't work. I did nine-day devotions; they didn't work. That's when I thought if I got married, maybe that would work!"

He does not intend to repeat the experience with Harvey, the man he has lived with for the last seven years. "Once is enough," he laughs. "In any case, I've always thought that marriage was for straight people. It's all part of the plot to make us straight. No, I don't have any inclination to get married."

10

A HOUSE DIVIDED

The August 2003 Liberal caucus meeting in North Bay gave an idea of the kind of debate that was to follow. The opposition to same-sex marriage, until then poorly organized, began in earnest.

The first major demonstration took place in Ottawa on August 22, the day after the Liberal caucus meeting. Around 6,000 people, mainly from religious groups opposed to same-sex marriages, marched in silence over the short distance from the Supreme Court to Parliament Hill. Several carried placards addressed to their MPs that read "If you want my vote, say no to same-sex marriage." The organizers of the event were more outspoken. "The country is under threat," said one of them, Tim Dooling, a practising Catholic from Ottawa. "Marriage is more than just a word that can be redefined to suit fashion," added Father François Beyroui, from an Ottawa Melkite church. "We must keep our country glorious and free, whether from foreign domination or internal deterioration," proffered Rev. Rick Reed of the Metropolitan Bible Church. The speakers swore that God loved everyone, but some of them still managed to disparage homosexuality. "You can't call something good that is fundamentally evil," said Imam Gamal Solaiman, from Ottawa's Muslim community.

Some 20 supporters of the redefinition of marriage had assembled in front of the Parliament Buildings before the arrival of the marchers, but they were no match for the main demonstration.

To convince as many people as possible that his way was the right way, Martin Cauchon began a cross-Canada tour in early September, travelling to Ontario, British Columbia and Alberta to answer the arguments of opponents of same-sex marriage who were preparing to demonstrate in front of the riding offices of some 20 MPs who favoured the change.

The same week, Quebec representatives of the Canadian Conference of Catholic Bishops (CCCB) held a press conference to warn the government not to confuse equality with uniformity. "We remain convinced that a solution can be found without having to radically redefine marriage," the CCCB president, Bishop Jacques Berthelet of Saint-Jean–Longueuil, said reassuringly. However, this moderate message veered off course when the reporters asked the Archbishop of Montreal, Cardinal Jean-Claude Turcotte, what exactly straight people stood to lose if same-sex marriages were permitted. "You open the door to all kinds of things," he suggested, adding, "Should we allow marriages between brothers and sisters? Between a mother and her son? I don't want to be difficult, but —" Opening this door would destabilize society, he warned: "We don't know what consequences it could have in the future."

The following day, September 11, MP Roger Gallaway and Senator Anne Cools, both Liberals, filed an application with the Supreme Court for intervener status at the hearing into the federal government's referral on marriage. The MPs went so far as to request that the government reimburse their legal fees, which the Court refused. Nevertheless, the Liberal government allowed them to present their arguments to the judges.

* * * * *

At a purely political level, a new moment of truth occurred the following week. As soon as Parliament reconvened, on September 15, 2003, the Canadian Alliance moved "that, in the opinion of this House, it is necessary, in light of public debate around recent court decisions, to reaffirm that marriage is and should remain the union of one man and one woman to the exclusion of all others, and that Parliament take all necessary steps within the jurisdiction of the Parliament of Canada to preserve this definition of marriage in Canada." The text was identical to the Reform motion passed in June 1999 by a vote of 216 to 55. The goal was to embarrass the government by highlighting the profound division in the House of Commons — and especially within the Liberal Party — on this issue.

"It was complicated, because public opinion had not yet evolved sufficiently," said Martin Cauchon. "Not all MPs had had time to think about the issue, and in addition a majority of them had voted for the Reform motion [supporting the traditional view of marriage] in 1999. I had to fight hard for that vote."

"Civil" supporters of same-sex marriage were also expecting the coming fight to be a fierce one. They had therefore decided, on August 14, 2003, the day of the major power blackout in Ontario and the northeastern United States, to set up a broad coalition to promote their position. "We wondered what we should do and, more to the point, how to do it," recalled Alex Munter, at the time an Ottawa city councillor. "We realized that the best way to go about it was to form a coalition that would reach out beyond the gay and lesbian community. It was a comfort to know that we were part of a movement of people sharing important values with regard to the type of country they wanted to live in."

The objective of Canadians for Equal Marriage was both simple and ambitious: to mobilize the population to ensure that MPs backed the redefinition of marriage. The coalition quickly began to collect donations and to enlist the support of various organizations such as unions, ethnic and cultural associations, human rights groups and professional associations. Like the religious groups, the coalition relied extensively on the Internet and email to make its message heard: in the week leading up to the vote on the Alliance motion, it sent MPs no fewer than 1.5 million emails. "We knew that if we lost this first vote in the House, our adversaries would seize the opportunity to push back the gains made and call for a suspension of the right of same-sex couples to marry," Munter later explained.

Alliance leader Stephen Harper launched the parliamentary debate on September 16. He also set the tone for the discussion: "Let me begin by recognizing that this is an emotional debate, one where views are strongly held. We should be clear on what the debate is and is not about. It is not about human rights. The rights and privileges of marriage have been extended in law across this country to gay and lesbians and to nontraditional relationships of various kinds already. That is not in contention here." It is interesting to note that in 2000, the Canadian Alliance had been fiercely opposed to Bill C-23, which extended the advantages and obligations of marriage to same-sex couples. However, to avoid projecting an image of intolerance, the party took the opposite tack in 2003.

In a little over ten minutes, Harper carefully set out the position of the official opposition, which would be copiously repeated by his MPs in the course of the day. He spoke for a number of MPs, Liberal as well as Alliance, when he said that the burden of proof was on the supporters of redefining marriage and not the opponents:

> The question we should really be asking today in this debate is whether this institution should be redefined in law. We on this side of the House say, no, but if the answer to that question were to be yes, the responsible thing to do would be for those who believe traditional marriage should be abolished to argue democratically and openly that it is desirable and socially necessary to do so. However, opponents of traditional marriage have refused to do that. Instead they have gone to the courts to contort this into a human rights issue. They have chosen to make change without social consensus and, in doing so, they have articulated a position which I believe is wrong in law, is universally insulting, is very dangerous as far as real rights are concerned and, of course, has been done in a highly undemocratic manner.

Harper next focused on an argument that, until then, had received little attention. He said that, when the Canadian Charter of Rights and Freedoms was adopted in 1982, the government of Pierre Elliott

Trudeau had consciously decided not to include sexual orientation in the list of grounds on which discrimination was prohibited. (In fact, the Alliance leader refused to admit that sexual orientation existed as such, preferring to refer to "sexual behaviour.") However, in 1995, the Supreme Court, like the lower courts before it, had decided that sexual orientation was an "analogous ground" for discrimination under the Charter, a decision that opened the way for same-sex marriage. Harper said,

> Sexual orientation or, more accurately, what we are really talking about, sexual behaviour, the argument has been made by proponents of this position [same-sex marriage] that this is analogous to race and ethnicity. This position was not included in the Charter of Rights when it was passed by Parliament in 1982. It was not included, not because of some kind of accident or oversight, but deliberately and explicitly by all sides of the House of Commons. Sexual orientation was later read into the Charter. I would point out that an amendment to the constitution by the courts is not a power of the courts under our constitution. Something the House will have to address at some point in time is where its powers begin and where those of the courts end.
>
> However, even accepting the reading in of sexual orientation, the addition of sexual orientation unconstitutionally by the courts into the Charter does not in itself mean automatically that traditional marriage should be deemed illegal and unconstitutional.

NDP MP Svend Robinson was quick to respond to the Opposition Leader's attack. He pointed out that the judges had been guided in their decision by a group of MPs and not the reverse: "In 1985 a parliamentary committee made up of five Conservatives, one Liberal and one New Democrat, myself, travelled across the country to hear the views of Canadians about what section 15 should in fact encompass.

Should it include sexual orientation and other grounds? That parliamentary committee made up of elected representatives unanimously said yes, that section 15 should in fact prohibit discrimination based upon sexual orientation."

For many different reasons, not least the difficulty of amending the constitution, the government had never implemented the recommendation. However, it could not be said that MPs, or at least the MPs on the committee, had not intended to extend the scope of section 15. Vic Toews remained unconvinced. "If one wants to change the constitution there is a process and it does not simply involve passing a resolution of a committee," he pointed out.

Stephen Harper also felt the need to respond in strong terms to suggestions that access to the institution of marriage for same-sex couples could be compared to the civil rights movement. "For the Liberals or anyone in the Liberal Party to equate the traditional definition of marriage with segregation and apartheid is vile and disgusting, and a position that has no place [in this debate]," he said, before being interrupted by offended MPs. But he continued, "If the Liberals and some of their front bench people now say that the traditional definition of marriage is illegal, immoral, discriminatory and racist, what will stop them? Why would they ever tolerate those who, through their religious institutions, believe otherwise?"

As soon as Harper finished speaking, Robinson asked him why he had not mentioned the use of the Charter's notwithstanding clause to block same-sex marriage. After all, the Alliance motion referred to taking "all necessary steps" within the jurisdiction of the Parliament of Canada to "preserve" the traditional definition of marriage. The notwithstanding clause allows Parliament to override court decisions based on the Charter. Over the years politicians have become extremely nervous about using the clause, probably out of fear that they will be accused of infringing the fundamental rights of citizens. Aware of how controversial the clause is, Harper replied that in his opinion using it would not be necessary. A few minutes later, to silence its critics, the Alliance amended its motion to remove the reference to "all necessary steps" — saying, of course, that this manoeuvre was part of its original strategy…

Bloc Québécois MP Réal Ménard went to the heart of the matter when he said aloud what many people were thinking about Harper's motion: "Does he realize that, since 1993 and right up to now, the Canadian Alliance has demonstrated a homophobic feeling that is unworthy of a party leader?" Harper replied, "I can only say, as I did in my remarks, the idea of traditional marriage is not a homophobic idea, but a basic idea for all societies in every culture."

A few minutes later, Martin Cauchon rose to defend the government's position, which had taken a beating. "Let me remind members of Parliament that our attachment to long-cherished traditions and conventions is not the only, or even the best, measure of what is just or what is right," he said, citing the example of the long struggle for voting rights for women. Then the minister launched an attack of his own: "Let me be clear. A vote in favour of the Alliance motion means a vote to use the notwithstanding clause. The Government of Canada has never invoked this clause to override the Charter rights of a minority. I believe this would set a dangerous precedent."

Bloc MP Richard Marceau, one of the most effective supporters of same-sex marriage, dared to make a solemn appeal. "My wish in closing is for my five-year-olds to grow up in a society that is open and generous, not merely tolerant, a society which accepts and embraces difference. In voting against this motion, we will make it possible for them to grow up to vote in such a society."

Next, Svend Robinson remarked that, for gays and lesbians, the question went beyond mere politics: "It is an intensely personal debate as well because we are talking about our lives, about my life, about my partner and about my ability as a citizen of this country to enjoy equal status." His lesbian colleague Libby Davies went one step further: in her view, the fundamental importance of marriage for gays and lesbians practically required legislators to set aside their personal opinions. "What one's conscience says is one thing. It is a very important matter. But I believe that our duty as members of Parliament is to apply the law fairly and to apply the Charter fairly, without prejudice and without bias," she affirmed. She then cheekily added, "No one is forcing the leader of the Canadian Alliance to marry a man if he does not want to."

However, many MPs were unable to go against their conscience. Liberal MP Pat O'Brien responded to Davies's comments: "I wonder if the member honestly believes that one can draw a direct parallel between Martin Luther King standing up on his religious principles and fighting to defend the natural moral law that people are not unequal because of the pigmentation of their skin and a relationship called same-sex relationship which fundamentally goes against the natural moral law. Does she really believe that?"

Later in the debate, O'Brien quoted from a letter he had sent to Jean Chrétien two weeks earlier, on August 29. The letter contained an astonishing comparison: "Consider the evolution of Quebec's society resulting in the separatist movement. Does the change the separatists want make it inevitable and even a right to be defended? I think not, and so must you, based on your courageous fight against the separatists throughout your entire career." To avoid the polemics that could follow, he was careful to add, "Obviously I do not equate the demand for same sex marriage to the separatist movement."

As was to be expected, Alliance MPs did not miss this opportunity to rub in the Liberals' majority support for the 1999 Reform motion in defence of the traditional definition of marriage. MP Vic Toews quoted from the comments made at the time by Anne McLellan, then justice minister: "Important matters of social policy should not be left to the courts to decide. If Parliament does not address the issue, the courts will continue to hand down decisions in a piecemeal fashion, interpreting narrow points of law on the specific questions before them. This guarantees confusion and continuing costly litigation. Most worrisome, it risks removing us from the social policy process altogether."

Former Alliance leader Stockwell Day repeated his belief that human beings were "created by God." He ended his speech by stating that he was making his comments "encouraged by the majority view of my constituents and by the phrase in our Canadian constitution imploring me to recognize the supremacy of God and the conviction deep in my heart that Canada will not be able to handle financially or socially the effects and consequences of a parliamentary or judicial decree putting an end to marriage as we know it."

Liberal MP Clifford Lincoln, a former minister in Robert Bourassa's Quebec government in the 1980s, had to reconcile his rejection of same-sex marriage with the position he had taken at the time with regard to language legislation in Quebec. When Quebec decided in 1988 to invoke the notwithstanding clause under the Canadian Charter to avoid having to comply with a Supreme Court ruling that would have allowed languages other than French on commercial signs in Quebec, Lincoln resigned from cabinet in protest. "Rights are rights and will always be rights," Lincoln said in 1988. "There are no partial rights. Rights are fundamental rights. Rights are links in a chain of fundamental values that bind all individuals in a society that wants to be equitable, and just and fair. Rights are bridges that unite people in a society through a set of fundamental values, and the minute you deny those rights, you withdraw that bridge, and create a gap between members of that society."

However, freedom of speech for English speakers in Quebec and the right of gays and lesbians to equal treatment did clearly not have the same importance in the view of Lincoln, who called the decision of Ottawa to authorize same-sex marriage "hasty" and "autocratic":

> The contexts were totally different. In the 1988 case, the right of freedom of expression, a universal and fundamental human right enshrined in the Universal Declaration of Human Rights, was taken away by legislation ... What I said this time was very different ... I said that marriage in its traditional definition has been a universally accepted institution over the millennia. It is not just a matter of law. It is a complex web of social, legal, moral, religious, sociological and natural elements.

* * * * *

At the end of the day-long debate, the Speaker of the House called for a vote. It was 5:45 p.m. The first item was the amendment deleting the part of the motion that would have opened to door to the use of the notwithstanding clause to preserve the traditional definition of marriage. The opponents of same-sex marriage had agreed to support the amendment, while the remaining MPs were expected to vote against.

The result was a surprise for all concerned: 134 for and 134 against! It was only the sixth time in the history of the federal Parliament, and the first time since December 1963, that there had been a tie vote. The Speaker of the House of Commons, Peter Milliken, had to cast a vote — a rare occurrence. He said,

> The Clerk has announced that there is an equality of votes for and against the motion. In these circumstances the duty of the casting vote, as it is called, now falls on me as your Speaker. I should make it clear that I am casting my vote tonight on purely procedural grounds. The precedents and practice of the House of Commons are designed to ensure that if the House cannot make a definitive decision on a question, the possibility should be left open for the question to come again before the House if members so choose. Therefore, since the House has been unable to take a decision tonight, I will vote so that members may be given another opportunity to pronounce themselves on the issue at some future time and, accordingly, I cast my vote in the negative. I declare the amendment defeated.

Things were looking bad for the main vote, on the motion asking the government to prohibit same-sex marriages. Tension was electric in the august lower house. This time, however, two MPs, Liberals Roy Cullen and Alex Shepherd, suddenly switched sides, and a third, Liberal Nancy Keretak-Lindell, showed up at the last minute. As a result, the motion was narrowly defeated, 137 to 132. "I declare the motion lost," confirmed Milliken, to a storm of reaction from both sides. No fewer than 50 Liberal MPs had voted against their government. If ministers had not been required to follow the party line, the number of opponents would doubtless have been greater, perhaps enough to allow the motion to pass.

An independent MP, Jim Pankiw, rose immediately on a point of order and asked the Speaker to reconsider his vote on the amendment, but in vain.

This dramatic result provided a vivid demonstration of the way the political mindset concerning same-sex marriage had rapidly evolved, while highlighting the strong resistance that still remained — and that remains to this day. "Parliament spoke and spoke in the same way the nation is speaking — it's split," acknowledged Chrétien spokesperson Jim Munson, now a Liberal senator.

For Martin Cauchon, however, there was only one possible course of action: to declare a brilliant victory. He saw the result as a "vote of confidence for the process" established by the government. "Look where we were a few years ago, and the vote this evening," he said as he left the House of Commons. "It is clear that society is changing."

Paul Martin, who had not yet been elected leader of the Liberal Party, voted against the Alliance motion, but remained cautious when speaking to the press. "This is an issue I've had to wrestle with and I must say this has not been an easy decision," he said. "What has certainly tipped the balance is the decision that the courts have taken is that this is a rights issue and you cannot discriminate." Martin even suggested that the institution of marriage was strong enough not to be weakened by the admission of gays and lesbians, but after these comforting words he decided to muddy the waters. "The much more fundamental debate is yet to come," he said, specifying that civil union should not be excluded from the debate. He then added, "One thing is clear — that 'separate but equal' is not an option." The only explanation of his position that makes sense is that the MP for LaSalle–Émard was deliberately hedging his bets to avoid displeasing any of his supporters.

Interviewed later for this book, Martin swore that the court decisions had persuaded him that civil union was not a satisfactory response: "When the courts said, 'Separate but equal is not really equal,' I said, 'That's fine, it's time to move ahead.' It didn't take long." The only possible conclusion is that Martin's long public hesitation was solely designed not to upset those of his supporters who opposed same-sex marriages.

Even though two NDP MPs, Bev Desjarlais and Peter Stoffer, had missed the vote despite clear instructions to attend, party leader Jack Layton did not miss the opportunity to tell off the future prime minister: "It's time for Paul Martin to step up and show some leadership. This man has been sitting on the fence on a fundamental issue. That's clearly not going to be acceptable." Layton, however, never punished his two dissident MPs. Stoffer later came round to the idea of same-sex marriage, while Desjarlais obtained permission to abstain.

Stephen Harper, visibly disappointed to have lost a vote he believed he could win, blamed Chrétien's decision to force his ministers to follow the party line. Backbenchers were free to vote as they chose, and no one from the Prime Minister's Office had made any serious attempt to win over the opponents. But at the same time, some 30 MPs from all parties had abstained, which probably aided the cause of same-sex marriage, as many of the abstainers were opponents. In any case, even though his motion was defeated, Harper said that the Liberals did not have the legitimacy they needed to legalize same-sex marriage, and he promised to introduce a bill that would prohibit it.

Liberal MP Pat O'Brien blamed the prime minister for asking the Liberal caucus not to vote for the amendment deleting the part of the motion that would have opened the way to use of the notwithstanding clause to prohibit same-sex marriages. This order, in his view, had muddied the debate. He was probably right: after voting for the amendment, Roy Cullen and Alex Shepherd voted against the Alliance motion, as though to signal that they opposed use of the notwithstanding clause, but not same-sex marriage.

* * * * *

In the end, September 16, 2003, was a key date for Canada's gays and lesbians. Aware of the difficulty of the road ahead, Alex Munter, spokesperson for Canadians for Equal Marriage, avoided sounding too triumphant. "The closeness of this vote is a wakeup call to the millions of Canadians who believe in Canadian values of inclusion and dignity and respect," he said. "It is not enough that the cause is just, that the constitution is clear, that public opinion has changed. The message today is we can never take our basic rights for granted."

Votes on opposition motions could only have a minimal effect on court decisions. In the eyes of the judiciary, Parliament expresses its will through the legislation it adopts. But for Martin Cauchon, the September 16 vote was politically crucial. A defeat would have had untold consequences. "I was under such a lot of pressure," he recalled. "In my mind, I had already decided to resign if I couldn't see it through. For me, it would have been a disavowal by the House and I would have said, 'Okay, if you won't support my policies, that's too bad, but you won't see me again.' For me, it was such an important, fundamental question."

In Jean Chrétien's immediate circle, the Justice Minister's tenacity did not go unnoticed. "Martin Cauchon deserves a huge amount of credit," recalled Chrétien's close adviser Paul Genest. "He was the force. He was dogged, he was determined, the controversy didn't bother him, and he was willing to do cross-country tours. He did everything that was necessary to manage the political process in a very skilful way. He was deeply committed about that and he didn't rush the issue either. He took his time."

Cauchon noted a major difference between the redefinition of marriage and the decriminalization of marijuana, the other controversial file for which he was responsible at the time: "Cannabis is not something that creates a gut reaction. I began to realize that the question of same-sex marriage affected people in terms of their deepest values, their inner self. That is why the discussions with other MPs were so difficult: if they were against, they were fundamentally against for reasons that I could only respect. That is why we really had to give people time. Let's not forget that for many people, the whole idea was revolutionary."

* * * * *

Cauchon's patience was to be put to the test in the following weeks. The day after the vote on the Alliance motion, Health Minister Anne McLellan, a close ally of Paul Martin, said that the future prime minister was under no obligation to continue on the course set by the

Justice Minister Martin Cauchon after the Canadian Alliance motion on mar-
riage was defeated on September 16, 2003. "I was under such a lot of pressure,"
he recalled. "In my mind, I had already decided to resign if I couldn't see it
through. For me, it would have been a disavowal by the House and I would have
said, 'Okay, if you won't support my policies, that's too bad, but you won't see
me again.' For me, it was such an important, fundamental question."

Chrétien government. "Unless this bill is presented to the House and
voted on before the change in leadership, I don't think anyone should
assume this draft legislation is the legislation that will ultimately be
presented to Parliament," she said as she came out of a Liberal caucus
meeting. "I think that we need to keep working on possible options."
She then mentioned a scenario that the supporters of same-sex marriage feared like the plague: "There may be other ways of looking at
this, other questions to submit to the Supreme Court."

For several weeks, MPs opposed to the redefinition of marriage had
been putting pressure on the government to add a fourth question to
its Supreme Court referral: would the introduction of civil unions for
same-sex couples be enough to satisfy the Charter requirements?
Obviously, four courts had already ruled that the answer was no, but

the skeptics wanted to be told so by the highest court in the land.

Martin Cauchon rejected this idea out of hand and challenged the Martin camp to respect his plan: "What is true today for this government will be true as well in the future for another government ... and I believe as well the next government will keep going in the same direction." Only a few weeks remained before the election of the new Liberal leader, and Paul Martin did not want to risk alienating the more conservative MPs in the Liberal caucus. It came as no surprise, then, when Martin continued to float the idea of abolishing civil marriages for both same-sex and heterosexual couples, even though this option appeared impractical for the vast majority of Canadians.

* * * * *

Later that day, September 17, MPs had to vote on third reading of another controversial bill involving gays and lesbians, this one making hate propaganda against homosexuals an offence under the Criminal Code. As expected, the result was close: 141 votes for, 110 against. The bill's sponsor, Svend Robinson, was more than a little proud of this second consecutive victory, especially since private members' bills are seldom passed by the House. The NDP member had been working on this specific issue for 20 years. "I hope that this bill will send a message that the lives of gays and lesbians are just as valuable as the lives and safety of all Canadians," Robinson declared after the vote, barely holding back his tears.

In the flush of victory, he probably gave little thought to the 110 MPs who had voted against his bill, invoking the freedom of expression of religious groups that strongly opposed the bill on the grounds that, if it passed, they could no longer preach against homosexuality without running the risk of prosecution. Some even went so far as to say that some passages of the Bible could be considered hate literature. To appease these fears, the bill was amended to exclude any "opinion on a religious subject," which still failed to persuade the Alliance, around 40 Liberal MPs and a handful of Conservatives.

This episode provides a striking illustration of the current gay-rights paradox: although a small majority of Canadians support same-sex marriage, a large minority want to retain the "privilege" of disparaging homosexuality. Whatever some optimists may think, the question of gay rights remains as controversial as ever. Concrete proof of this was provided a couple of months later, in late November 2003. A man physically attacked Liberal MP Andy Scott who, as chair of the House of Commons justice committee, had cast the deciding vote in support of redefining marriage in June. Terrance Allen Curtis struck Scott with such force that he had to spend several days at home recovering. The assailant, who had mental problems, was given a nine-month suspended sentence.

Next, Alliance MP Larry Spencer suggested to the *Vancouver Sun* that homosexuality should once again become a criminal offence. Spencer said, among other things, that gays and lesbians had orchestrated a plot to attract young people in playgrounds and changing rooms to convert them to their "lifestyle." Although Spencer apologized, Stephen Harper swiftly suspended him from the Alliance caucus and refused to allow him to return after the merger with the Progressive Conservative Party in 2004. Then, on November 27, David Kilgour, Secretary of State (Asia-Pacific), said that the legalization of same-sex marriage was a "slippery slope" that could "lead to all kinds of things," such as "mothers marrying their sons." Paul Martin, who had just been elected Liberal leader, was quick to demand an apology but did not punish Kilgour publicly.

Luckily, not everything that happened in November 2003 was bad. On November 18, by a narrow 4-3 margin, the Supreme Judicial Court of Massachusetts ruled that it was against the state constitution to exclude same-sex couples from the institution of marriage. As was only fitting, the judges referred to the main judgment existing at that time on the question in common law: the decision by the Ontario Court of Appeal. Martin Cauchon saw this as proof of the avant-garde nature of Canada's courts. "The message this sends is that the leadership exercised by Canada at the national level, and now at the international level, is a positive role that is moving in the right direction" he boasted in an interview with Canadian Press. Massachusetts gays and lesbians were free to marry as of May 17, 2004.

11

PAUL MARTIN'S DELAYING TACTIC

After years of waiting in the wings and a furtive campaign that finally managed to unseat Jean Chrétien as leader of the Liberal Party, Paul Martin became prime minister on December 12, 2003. As though to justify what some people called an internal putsch, the MP for LaSalle–Émard attempted to distance himself from some of his predecessor's decisions. Martin and Chrétien had never been close — to say the least. It surprised nobody that same-sex marriage became one of the issues that Martin chose to redirect, or rather send on a long detour.

At first sight, supporters of same-sex marriage considered Martin's appointment of Montreal MP Irwin Cotler as justice minister a positive step. Cotler is a lawyer with an international reputation in the field of human rights. In 1974, he had represented a group of gay students who wanted to add sexual orientation as a prohibited ground of discrimination in Quebec's Charter of Human Rights and Freedoms.

The gay and lesbian community, however, was soon disappointed. On his way out from Rideau Hall, where he had just been sworn in by Governor General Adrienne Clarkson, the new minister showed that he was as hesitant as Paul Martin. "I believe that gays must have all the rights arising out of marriage" said Cotler, careful not to equate this with the right to marry. Next, he evoked a scenario that had become a frightening possibility in the preceding months: the Martin government would ask the Supreme Court to answer a fourth question as part of the referral: whether the establishment of civil unions would satisfy the rights of same-sex couples. The three questions submitted by Martin Cauchon had been intended only to ensure that the draft bill legalizing same-sex marriages complied with the Charter.

"I'm saying that the broad framework of options is something that I'm hopeful that the court will [consider]," Cotler said, adding that Parliament would then be in a better position to pass the best possible legislation. However, at least three lower courts had already examined the concept of civil union and rejected it on the grounds that it perpetuated the segregation imposed on gays and lesbians.

This was enough to incense Michael Leshner. "I want the politicians out of my life!" shouted the newlywed. "It's an obscene interference in my marriage to Michael [Stark]." The opinion of Leshner and other supporters of a redefinition of marriage did not have much influence on the Martin government's decision. Above all, the new Liberal leader wanted, before the summer of 2004, to obtain the legitimacy that only the electorate could provide. This meant an election, and it also meant getting as many contentious issues as possible out of the way. Same-sex marriage was clearly a target. As campaign cochair David Herle told the Liberal caucus in January 2004, this hot potato needed to be kicked out of the way.

The best way to get same-sex marriage off the election radar was to postpone the hearing of the referral by the Supreme Court, scheduled for mid-April. To achieve this, Ottawa simply had to add a fourth question to the list submitted the court. The federal government lawyers, and all the other parties, would then need more time to prepare their case and the hearing would be pushed back to the fall.

The Prime Minister's Office timed the announcement carefully: it was made on the same day as two other key announcements, no doubt to ensure that they would compete for media coverage. On January 28, 2004, Ottawa revealed the total value of the contracts obtained by Paul Martin's business interests between 1993 and 2002 ($160 million!) and stated its intention of establishing a commission to investigate the role played by Canadian authorities in the deportation of Maher Arar to Syria, where he was imprisoned and tortured even though there were no charges against him.

Less than an hour and a half later, Justice Minister Cotler confirmed at a press conference that he would submit a fourth question to the Supreme Court, as provided for in an order-in-council adopted two days previously. The only surprise was the actual wording of the question: the Court was not asked to examine the question of civil unions, but rather to rule whether the traditional definition of marriage infringed the Canadian Charter of Rights and Freedoms.

"This is not a retreat," said Cotler to a skeptical crowd of reporters. "While the government's position has not changed, adding this question will allow for a more comprehensive opinion by the court." In another press conference, Paul Martin repeated the same message. "This is not an attempt to delay," he stressed. "It's a very important element of information for the debate in Parliament and the debate in Canadian society. A lot of Canadians are very concerned about this and they want this basic question asked." Cotler, however, admitted that the extra question would push the hearing back to the fall. He even predicted that the first vote on the same-sex marriage bill would not take place before the fall of 2005. As a result, some Liberal MPs saw this fourth question as squandering the gains made by Martin Cauchon.

"In my opinion, this decision was a mistake because of the time we lost," Bill Graham said later. "We could have settled the issue a year earlier if we hadn't got sidetracked. But if you ask the office of the [Liberal] whip the same question, I'm sure they'll say that it was the fourth question that garnered some extra support. It's easy to criticize after the fact, but perhaps it was worth it in the long run."

Not surprisingly, supporters of same-sex marriage reacted badly to this new delay. "Why should gay and lesbian couples outside of Ontario and British Columbia have to wait to have the same rights as other Canadians?" asked Svend Robinson. "Today they are simply saying they are going to put gay marriage on a back burner for a year or more ... It's quite clear that the last thing that Paul Martin wanted in the middle of an election campaign was a bitter debate about same-sex marriage."

In the eyes of Robinson and his Bloc Québécois colleague Richard

Marceau, what the Liberals were really doing was appealing the lower court decisions by the back door." Paul Martin promised us that he wouldn't appeal the judgments by the Ontario and B.C. courts of appeal," Marceau said. "Adding a question to the referral is really a disguised appeal."

The activists at Egale and Canadians for Equal Marriage (CEM) were careful to rein in their feelings in public, but some heartfelt comments were made. "Would the Prime Minister be doing this if one of his children fell in love with someone of the same sex?" asked CEM spokesperson John Fisher. "This is a basic human rights issue, one that has been debated over and over again. It is simply unacceptable to add another delay to passing this legislation."

In fact, the supporters of same-sex marriage came to realize that their mission had just become more complicated and would now take longer to achieve. "In August 2003, after the bill was introduced, we thought everything would go quite quickly, and that the Supreme Court would deal with the referral right away," recalled CEM's Alex Munter. "We even thought that the whole issue might be over before Christmas! We were working in a short time frame. We couldn't know that there would be a fourth question! When it was announced, we realized that we were in for a far longer campaign."

MPs opposed to redefining marriage were, in general, pleased by the addition of a new question, even if some wished they could go back and persuade the government to appeal the lower court decisions. "I'm hopeful that the top court in this country will uphold probably the most important institution in this country, and that's marriage as we know it," said Liberal MP Pat O'Brien. Some comments were more critical. The chair of the Canada Family Action Coalition, Charles McVety, deplored the government's removal of the marriage question from the upcoming election campaign. "It is not only hypocritical, but cold and callous in its political intent," he said.

Even in hindsight, Irwin Cotler continued to stand by the government's official position: the addition of a fourth question was not a delaying tactic and was not pointless, even though the Supreme Court eventually refused to answer it. He also refrained from blaming Paul

Martin, even though several sources have indicated that the leader was at the origin of the manoeuvre. "I take responsibility," Cotler said later. "Why did we do it? Because I wanted to give the opponents of same-sex marriage an opportunity to address the Supreme Court. I didn't want them to be able to say, 'We were never given the chance to express our position.' It seemed more democratic to me." When asked about this period, Paul Martin gave the same answer.

Despite his ambivalent statements about marriage during the summer of 2003, Cotler swears that he supported the inclusion of gays and lesbians when be became justice minister in December of that year. His ambition to join Martin's cabinet had perhaps made him more cautious in public. Still, the conversion of the member for Mount Royal occurred well after that of Martin Cauchon, who rallied to the cause shortly before the first court decisions. Irwin Cotler was eventually persuaded by the accumulated weight of the court rulings: "That's when I said, okay, this is a question of minority rights, compliance with the Charter and the rule of law."

A number of observers report that Cotler was astonished by the immediate effects of the Ontario Court of Appeal judgment. Later, he did not hide the fact that his preference would have been for the Chrétien government to appeal the judgment. "I thought there was a need not to rely on the decisions from the lower courts, or even the Court of Appeal, but to have a decision from the Supreme Court," he explained. "In my view, a Supreme Court decision would have helped persuade the population of the importance of recognizing same-sex marriage. After all, the Supreme Court is the cornerstone of our democracy. But another part of me, the part that acts as an MP, thought that the people should be given a chance to express their opinion through Parliament. From this point of view, a simple referral to the Supreme Court was the most advantageous solution. It was perhaps the best way to go."

Cotler often discussed the matter with Paul Martin. "I shared my personal viewpoint with the Prime Minister concerning this issue," he recalled. "I understood perfectly that the question was a difficult one for him. I was aware of the divisions within society. Paul Martin is a man of conscience, of commitment. He is also a man of faith, a fact that I respect. He goes to church every week. However, he's also a man who respects the rule of law and who sticks closely to the charter. Like me, the Prime Minister was won over by the rule of law."

Bill Graham was able to observe that Cotler's path was not an easy one. "Irwin himself was not particularly in favour of the change to start with," he said. "I remember having a long conversation with him. I have a lot of respect for Irwin, but it was a difficult issue for him. His Jewish community was against it, his wife was against it. Irwin had a hard time. As soon as he saw that, legally speaking, there was no other solution, he became a key player in the debate. And I believe he had a major influence on Mr. Martin."

* * * * *

While the politicians were trying to find a way out of the maze, the judges continued to press ahead. In Quebec, the case of Michael Hendricks and René LeBœuf had still not been settled. In fact, it was in an unusual situation: following the decision by the Chrétien government not to appeal the judgments by the Ontario and B.C. courts of appeal, the federal attorney general had basically withdrawn from the case. But the Ontario-based Catholic Civil Rights League (CCRL) had taken it upon itself to appeal Louise Lemelin's Quebec Superior Court judgment in Ottawa's place. This type of appeal is possible in Quebec, although it is an exceptional occurrence in English Canada. For example, in October the Supreme Court had rejected an application from religious groups that wanted to appeal the decision of the Ontario Court of Appeal. Had it not been for the CCRL, Michael and René would have been free to marry as early as July 2003.

The Quebec Court of Appeal hearing was set for late January 2004. The Hendricks-LeBœuf couple tried to have the date postponed to give the judges of Quebec's highest court time to take into account the arguments made before the Supreme Court as part of the referral, initially scheduled for April. The problem was that the chief justice of the Court of Appeal, Michel Robert[1], wanted the exact opposite: for the Supreme

Court to take note of the Quebec decision before beginning to hear the referral. The legal community today is not afraid to say openly that the country's magistrates were in a race to see who could hand down the swiftest, most profound decision on same-sex marriages.

The lawyer for the Hendricks-LeBœuf couple, Anne-France Goldwater, was between a rock and a hard place. "I could hardly contradict Justice Robert, whose ambition was to render a swift decision," she later explained, without too much bitterness. In a dead-end situation, the couple dismissed Goldwater and hired the lawyer representing several Ontario couples, Martha McCarthy, who retained the services of two Montreal colleagues, Colin K. Irving and Catherine McKenzie. Despite all the upheaval, the hearing was still held on January 26.

The decision was handed down on March 19. It did not focus on the constitutionality of excluding same-sex couples from the institution of marriage. Instead, it ruled on the motion presented by the couple's lawyers to halt the proceedings instituted by the CCRL. Five judges, including Chief Justice Robert, first mentioned the "complex and unusual, even unprecedented, legal situation" resulting from the withdrawal of the attorney general. "Neither the Court nor counsel were able to find precedents drawn from Canadian constitutional disputes," they noted.

In the end, their unanimous decision was that the CCRL had no "genuine interest" in the case and that, in any event, it could always make its arguments as part of the referral to the Supreme Court. "The issue before the Court [of Appeal] has no consequence for the rights of the appellant [the CCRL]," the court ruled. "In this case, the respondents' [Hendricks and LeBœuf's] rights now recognized by the Quebec Superior Court and by the courts of appeal of two other provinces are said to be affected," they continued. On the next to last page of the decision, the Court pointed out that the federal government no longer opposed the immediate marriage of same-sex couples. In short, the political decision had already been made. The court therefore felt it was able to lift the moratorium imposed by the Superior Court, scheduled to end only in September 2004. On the last page came the long-awaited words, "There is no longer any obstacle to the solemnization of the respondents' marriage by a competent officer."

"This is a day of immense joy," said Michael at a press conference. "We feel a bit like heroes," added René. "The generations that follow us will now be able to lead their own lives, rather than the lives someone else has chosen for them." In the end, the pair had had to wait five years to achieve their goal, which was still less than the ten years they had originally envisaged.

In Quebec City, Justice Minister Marc Bellemare reacted almost as euphorically as the people directly concerned. "This is judgment of the greatest importance," he declared. "I believe it marks a historic day in Quebec's development." In an interview with the Montreal daily *La Presse*, he added, "It's one thing to say that, since June 2002, civil unions have existed in Quebec, but everyone understands the enormous symbolic value of marriage. There's a huge gulf between civil unions and marriage." Richard Bastien, Quebec coordinator of the CCRL, was outraged. "We firmly believe that the change to the definition of marriage will have grave consequences for the family," he said.

Ironically, Michael and René hoped that Ottawa would appeal the decision. "All the political and other problems we had were caused by the fact that there was no Supreme Court decision," Michael said later. "They chickened out. Why were we prevented from going to the Supreme Court, where we could have consolidated our status? Because of that, a future government led by Stephen Harper could easily drag us back into the past."

* * * * *

The Quebec government had made concrete preparations for the change. In the morning, all the courthouses in the province had been alerted that they could now allow gay and lesbian couples to begin the process leading to civil marriage. As soon as the judgment was made public, a modified version of the marriage registration form, adapted for both same-sex and heterosexual couples, appeared on the Justice Department's website! Only one problem remained: there was no easy way to dissolve the civil unions formed by gay and lesbian couples to allow them to marry, now that they could legally do so. The situation was rectified a few months later through an amendment to the Civil Code.

Needless to say, Michael and René lost no time in going to Montreal's Palais de Justice to file their application. They even asked the authorities to waive the 20-day period for other people to object to the marriage (corresponding to the publication of banns), and their request was granted. The wedding date was set for April 1 — no April Fool's Day joke.

Around 200 people — friends, bystanders and a large number of media representatives — crammed into one of the small rooms in the Palais de Justice set aside for civil weddings. When the couple arrived, a little before 11 a.m., everyone present jumped to their feet and broke into applause. More applause followed the time-honoured words "I do," and the ceremony ended, as was only fitting, with Mendelssohn's Wedding March. "Everything was perfect," Michael told reporters after the 15-minute ceremony, while friends jostled for position to have their photo taken with the newlyweds, both the picture of elegance in their tails and bow ties — pink for one, a flowered pattern for the other. "I found it so moving to say 'I do,'" said René.

"Everything is different now," explained Michael. "We will be recognized as a couple ... I'm not getting any younger, and for me, marriage is for life. I feel at last as though I will be able to die in peace, with no bureaucratic worries." On their wedding day, Michael was 62 and René was 48; they had been together for 31 years.

The happy day ended simply, with a wedding reception in Chinatown. It is important to remember that the entire venture cost some $350,000, of which the couple paid about $20,000 out of pocket. Michael and René were still able to afford a honeymoon to South Beach, near Miami. Eventually, a large part of Anne-France Goldwater and Marie-Hélène Dubé's legal fees was paid directly by Ottawa. "I made a scene," recalled Goldwater. "I wanted to be reimbursed the same amount as the other lawyers in the other provinces. Some had obtained at least $600,000, in other words at least two thirds of what they were owed."

Despite the happy ending, a certain bitterness remains. "Suddenly, when we got married, everyone was on our side," recalled René. "We had been pushing ahead for years, but once we had smoothed and paved the path, everyone wanted to follow: suddenly we were the golden couple, that had done so much for the gay community."

One thing is certain: anyone who thought the two men were on a strictly personal campaign was wrong. Within 20 days of the Court of Appeal ruling, eight same-sex couples — six gay and two lesbian — had applied to be married at the Palais de Justice. In 2004, according to Quebec's statistical institute, there were 226 same-sex marriages in Quebec, 131 gay and 95 lesbian, more than the number of civil unions registered the same year (47 gay, 32 lesbian and 95 straight). The wheel had come full circle. During the first year and a half during which civil unions were available, in 2002–3, the new option had attracted mainly gay and lesbian couples (224 gay, 200 lesbian and 79 straight). Less than three years after their introduction, civil unions appeared to have fallen from favour, perhaps illustrating what some gay activists have been saying all along: that nothing can replace marriage.

The merchants in the temple were quick to grasp the message. The first show for prospective gay and lesbian brides and grooms in Canada was held in Toronto in February 2004. The event's spokesperson, Marni Milks, was not afraid to promote a cliché. "Our surveys have shown that gay couples have more expensive tastes than straight couples," she told the Montreal weekly *Voir*. Montreal's first show was held five months later. Questions were quickly raised about the relevance of shows "reserved" for the gay community. "Many business people do not want to do business with gays or lesbians," Mario Thiffault, the promoter of the Montreal event, told the daily *Le Droit*. If this is true, then the expansion of marriage to include same-sex couples has not yet eliminated discrimination.

The Panthères Roses (Pink Panthers), a self-styled "radical queer movement," demonstrated during the Montreal show to question the need for same-sex marriages. They were quickly expelled, but not before they had distributed an inspired press release. "In the late 1960s, we all applauded when Trudeau kicked the state out of the bedrooms of the nation, and strangely enough, here we are all again, this time applauding the reappearance of the state, through marriage, in our emotional lives," read the press release, signed by "a proud believer in systematic doubt."

12

ON THE CAMPAIGN TRAIL

If Paul Martin hoped to avoid a debate on same-sex marriage during the election campaign by adding a fourth question to the Supreme Court reference, he was only partially successful. And he had only himself to blame.

The MP for LaSalle–Émard had been honing his plan for months: after being elected leader of the Liberal Party in November 2003, he would take over the reins of power, bring down an enticing budget and then call a snap election to obtain his own mandate from the voters. However, the sponsorship scandal, exacerbated by Auditor General Sheila Fraser's damning report in February 2004, quickly upset this rosy scenario. But after months of hesitation, Martin asked Governor General Adrienne Clarkson to dissolve Parliament on May 23, in preparation for an election on June 28.

Paul Martin wanted to use the campaign to depict Conservative leader Stephen Harper, the former head of the Canadian Alliance, as an extremist who would threaten Canada's social programs by introducing U.S.-style income tax cuts. Martin, of course, would play the role of saviour of the Canadian health-care system. A week into the campaign, however, the strategy was apparently not working. The Liberals continued to slide in the opinion polls, while the Conservatives and the Bloc Québécois, powered by the sponsorship scandal, forged ahead.

Luckily, by the end of the first week, controversial statements by

Conservative MPs came to the Liberal leader's rescue. Scott Reid, the official languages critic, was first off the mark, raising the possibility that the scope of government services in French could be reviewed. Next, Health Critic Rob Merrifield said that women would have to obtain third-party counselling before going ahead with an abortion. On a similar note, Cheryl Gallant compared abortion to the beheading of hostages then taking place in Iraq. These comments provided the Liberals with ammunition for several days. In the second half of the campaign, though, the topic that evoked the most controversial outbursts from Conservative MPs was gay and lesbian rights.

Before these comments, however, another overwrought partisan decided to show his muscles. The incident occurred during a June 3 meeting in Guelph, Ontario, where Stephen Harper was about to make a speech to 600 people. A spokesperson for Canadians for Equal Marriage (CEM), Laurie Arron, had just asked Harper if it was reasonable to use the notwithstanding clause to prohibit same-sex marriage, when a Conservative activist punched Bob Smyth, a 58-year-old CEM volunteer. The crowd chanted their leader's name to drown out Arron's question.

The previous day, Harper had announced that, if elected, he would withdraw the Supreme Court reference on marriage and introduce a bill to define the institution of marriage as the union of a man and a woman, which would then be subject to a free vote in the House of Commons. "If Parliament expresses its views clearly on this, which is something that Parliament refused to do under the Liberals, then I am quite certain that the Supreme Court will understand that and respect Parliament's competency to deal with such a matter," he said.

On June 6, Gallant again made waves when she maintained, in an interview with the CTV network, that the listing of hate propaganda directed at homosexuals as an offence under the Criminal Code (Svend Robinson's Bill C-250, passed by the Senate a few weeks earlier) should be repealed. "The danger in having sexual orientation just listed [is] that it encompasses, for example, pedophiles," Gallant said. "I believe that the [Conservative] caucus as a whole would like to see it repealed." It is important to note that she was only repeating, in cruder terms, the official position of her party. Practically all the Alliance MPs had voted against Bill C-250 in September 2003. When asked to comment on the new crisis, Stephen Harper spoke in politically cautious terms that were completely at odds with his vote eight months earlier. "I'm certainly not opposed to having hate protection against gays and lesbians," he said. "I think that is a reasonable thing to have in law, but I think those protections have to be crafted carefully to ensure no ambiguity, ensure that the rights of others are not negatively impacted."

On June 9, an Ontario Conservative candidate, Frank Luellau, went even further than Gallant. "I think that the biblical teaching is that [homosexuality] is not a natural kind of relationship," said Luellau, a former executive director of the Canadian Council of Christian Charities. "I think it is inappropriate for Christians, especially Christian leaders, to live that lifestyle." He also refused, in the name of freedom of religion and freedom of association, to criticize the practices of his former organization, which reserved the right to dismiss any homosexual employee or volunteer. However, he said, "I'm not running for public office in order that I can impose my will on the country, or on Parliament." The same day, the chair of a Toronto Conservative riding association, Tamara Kronis, resigned in protest against the intolerance that she perceived within the party. "Stephen Harper's willingness to entertain private members' bills on abortion and capital punishment, to weaken laws that protect gays and lesbians from hate crimes, and to override Charter rights on these and other issues has shaken beyond repair my confidence that a Conservative government led by Mr. Harper will respect the fundamental rights of Canadians," she wrote in her letter of resignation.

It is true that the Conservative leader did little to avoid this kind of criticism. With regard to the statements by Luellau, Harper merely said that they concerned "religious teachings" and that he had warned the candidate to "respect the decisions and the lifestyles of consenting adults." However, he promised that "any candidate who won't pledge that clearly will be removed as a candidate." Harper's habit of referring to homosexuality as a "lifestyle" eventually caught up with him. During a gathering on Parliament Hill to celebrate the first anniversary of the Ontario decision that made same-sex marriage possible, Alex Munter, spokesperson for CEM, made it a point of honour to respond to Harper's terminology. "Wintering in Florida is a lifestyle," he said ironically. "Drinking heavily is a behaviour. People's loving, committed relationships are neither lifestyles nor behaviours and people are entitled to your respect if you want to be the prime minister of Canada."

The Conservative leader's conception of gay rights was another source of worry for the gay and lesbian community. On June 10, for example, he stated that the whole issue was "not part of" his election campaign: "What consenting adults do is their own business, and it's not up to me to comment on it one way or another, and it's not what people want from government officials." When reporters asked what he really thought about the topic, they were booed by Conservative supporters.

Liberal strategists eventually realized that the Conservatives were getting bogged down in social issues and tried to take advantage of the situation. A few days before the leaders' debate, Paul Martin began to defend same-sex marriage with a little more vigour. During a stopover in St. John's, Newfoundland, the intelligent questions posed by a group of young people forced him to make his clearest statement yet. "It is absolutely a question of human rights and under those circumstances there is no way that anybody should be allowed to discriminate or prevent same-sex marriage," he said to loud applause. All of this was part of a broader strategy. Throughout the meeting, also attended by NDP leader Jack Layton, Martin tried to win over left-wing voters by expressing his agreement with the major themes of the NDP program. The Liberal leader stuck to this approach for the rest of the campaign. He had to persuade NDP supporters that a vote for the Liberals would allow them to block the election of a Harper government and the threat to social programs and minority rights. A TV advertising campaign reinforced this message.

The Liberals were not entirely innocent, however. Paul Martin was not as credible criticizing the Conservatives on gay and lesbian rights as he was attacking them on abortion. After all, 50 or so government

MPs had voted against same-sex marriage in September 2003, while a smaller number opposed abortion. Seven ministers in the Martin government had supported the Alliance motion on marriage: Albina Guarnieri, Joe McGuire, David Pratt, Judy Sgro, Bob Speller, Joe Volpe and Hélène Scherrer, cochair of the Liberal pre-election campaign. Four ministers had even opposed the inclusion of hate propaganda against homosexuals in the Criminal Code: McGuire, Speller, Volpe and Tony Valeri. Two of the most right-wing MPs in the Liberal Party, Roger Gallaway and Tom Wappel, even predicted that the government would lose a free vote on the recognition of same-sex marriage. Another, John O'Reilly, was seeking reelection (he eventually lost) by buying full-page advertisements supporting the traditional definition of marriage.

* * * * *

The subject again raised sparks during the TV debates in June. In the first debate, in French, Harper refused to reply when Martin asked him if he intended to use the notwithstanding clause to halt same-sex marriages. The following day, in the English debate, Harper swore that he would not invoke the clause, pointing out that Martin had already shown willingness to use the clause to protect the freedom of religious institutions not to marry same-sex couples. The prime minister replied firmly, "I would never use the notwithstanding clause to take away the rights that are enshrined in the Charter." He had just found the slogan he would use until the end of the campaign. The formula was clear, and had the advantage of not specifically mentioning the underlying question: the legalization of same-sex marriage.

In the English debate, Jack Layton called Martin to order. "That's not leadership," he said, referring to the prime minister's hesitant attitude. When Harper commented that Martin had supported the traditional definition of marriage in 1999, Layton interjected, "It's back-of-the-bus human rights for same-sex couples," referring to the racial segregation that persisted in the southern United States through much of the twentieth century.

During the second half of the campaign, the Conservative leader had less difficulty controlling his troops, for the simple reason that party authorities had ordered them to stick closely to the official platform. The rule was ineffective, though, against prerecorded slips. On June 25, three days before the election, it was learned that MP Randy White had granted an interview to a documentary filmmaker three days before the start of the campaign. "If the Charter of Rights and Freedoms is going to be used as the crutch to carry forward all of the issues that social libertarians want, then there's got to be for us Conservatives out there a way to put checks and balances in there," he said. "I think you'll see more uses for the notwithstanding clause in the future." He added that he had "very little, if any regard" for the country's courts: "I think our courts are much misguided and miss the conservative social reality of our times. To heck with the courts, eh?" Stephen Harper was quick to distance himself from his MP's opinions, which he described as "not important."

Nevertheless, on countless occasions during the campaign, Harper himself was critical of the Charter, the goal of which is to guide the work of legislators. He said that, for him, an ideal Supreme Court judge was someone with a broad understanding of Canadian law and "someone who's committed to understanding the role of the judiciary, which is to interpret and to apply law, not to rewrite it."

On June 28, 2004, the Liberals obtained a rare fourth term in office, but the anger generated by the sponsorship scandal reduced them to a minority. Many analysts attributed Paul Martin's survival to his efforts to highlight the "intolerance" of his Conservative adversaries on moral issues. By draping himself in the Charter of Rights, a Liberal Party achievement to which Canadians have a strong attachment, Martin was able to save his political skin without even having to pronounce the words *same-sex marriage*, although this was clearly what he was referring to. This was a skilful approach, especially since an opinion poll published in May showed that 47 percent of the population was opposed to a redefinition of marriage, with only 43 percent in favour.

Asked about his strategy, Martin insisted he had talked about gays and lesbians during the campaign. "But there was another argument: Charter protection," he reiterated. "I wanted to make sure that all my decisions reflected the importance of the Charter, and make it clear for Canadians. I'll tell you one thing: it's not the last time the Charter will be used to ensure equality."

In the United States, four months later, the debate on same-sex marriage turned in favour of the right-wing candidate, Republican George W. Bush. On the day of the presidential election, 11 states held referendums to amend their constitutions to prohibit same-sex marriage. According to several analysts, this helped mobilize the conservative vote, providing extra support for Bush. It seems fair to say that the same thing would probably have happened in Canada if similar referendums had been held at the same time as the 2004 federal election.

"We absolutely did not expect our rights and the Charter of Rights and Freedoms to become key elements in the Liberal victory," says Alex Munter. "The catch is that this assistance in the election did not encourage the government to speed up its resolution of the issue."

* * * * *

The 2004 federal election still helped shed light on a new social trend, one that can be expressed as an equation: opposition to same-sex marriage = intolerance, sectarianism. Or: support for same-sex marriage = open-mindedness, a progressive attitude. This sea change gradually emerged in casual conversations. People started to say things like: "Of course, we know she's against abortion, for the death penalty and against same-sex marriage." Some went so far as to describe the pope's conservative attitude in the following terms: "He's against the ordination of women, married priests, contraception and same-sex marriage." In a short space of time, the question became a label of social acceptability for many people.

Denise Bombardier learned this the hard way. In September 2003, she lost her new job as an interviewer and commentator on the Radio-Canada TV show *Le Point* after a single broadcast. During an interview with gay activist Louis Godbout, Bombardier launched a particularly virulent attack against same-sex marriage. A deluge of accusatory emails from viewers followed, along with union protests from the

Syndicat des Communications de Radio-Canada and complaints to the Quebec Press Council, which the council judged to be well founded. In February 2004, Radio-Canada decided not to renew her contract for two other shows and dismissed her temporarily after 32 years of loyal service. "The lobby won their point and made me out to be somebody who was against everything," she told the Montreal daily *La Presse*. "You can still be against same-sex marriage without being homophobic."

* * * * *

The bitter debates of the election campaign did not stop gay and lesbian couples from demanding the right to marry or courts from granting them that right. On July 14, Justice Peter McIntyre of the Yukon Supreme Court declared that the traditional definition of marriage was unconstitutional, a decision warmly applauded by the small crowd filling the courtroom. "The new common law definition of marriage in the Yukon is the voluntary union for life of two persons to the exclusion of all others," said McIntyre, ordering the federal and territorial governments to reimburse the legal fees of the applicant couple, Rob Edge and Stephen Dunbar. Obviously, the judge had based his decision on those of the Ontario and British Columbia courts of appeal. He noted in passing that the Ontario justices had used the adjective *voluntary*, while their B.C. colleagues had used *lawful* instead. He opted for the first solution, stressing that it was the term used in the well-known 1866 definition of marriage.

This new victory should have been routine, since for the last year Ottawa had acknowledged that the exclusion of same-sex couples from the institution of marriage was unconstitutional. Nevertheless, in a move that appeared to be a judicial echo of Paul Martin's political strategy of delay since his election as Liberal leader, Ottawa's lawyer had asked the Yukon Supreme Court to adjourn the proceedings until the federal reference had been heard by the Supreme Court of Canada. Ottawa claimed that the Yukon court would not be able to hear sufficient proof, that the applicants had "provided no evidence of real prejudice" if they were refused permission to marry, and that to hear the matter would be "a waste of scarce judicial resources"!

In the British Columbia and Quebec appeal courts, the government had agreed to the immediate legalization of same-sex marriage, without mentioning the reference. Ottawa had even applied to the Supreme Court to prevent religious groups from appealing the decision of the Ontario Court of Appeal. It should be noted, however, that with the exception of the Hendricks-LeBœuf case these decisions were made while Martin Cauchon was still justice minister. In his written decision, Justice McIntyre lost no time in rejecting the federal request, pointing out that by refusing to formally appeal the judgments to the Supreme Court, Ottawa had agreed that they would take effect immediately and be binding on the government. After all, the federal government had already given its political support to redefining marriage!

The judge even gave the government a mild scolding: "I do not consider it open to the Attorney General of Canada to ask this Court to defer to the Reference and to Parliament. The Attorney General is not divisible by province ... As a result of the action or inaction of the Attorney General, in my view were I to agree with the request for an adjournment, a legally unacceptable result would be perpetuated in the Yukon."

The couple were naturally delighted with the decision. "It's a combination of being thrilled, of relief, of a lot of pent-up emotion," said Dunbar, who married Edge the following Saturday in the presence of friends and members of their families.

* * * * *

A few days later, there was an unexpected twist in the long-running soap opera. It was announced that a lesbian couple had filed a motion for divorce before the Ontario Superior Court. M.M. and J.H. (identified only by their initials in compliance with a publication ban) had seized the opportunity to marry on June 18, 2003, a week after same-sex marriage became legal in Ontario. They had naively believed that by making their seven-year partnership official, they would be able to save it. This was not the case: they separated five days after the wedding. Divorce is never enjoyable or simple, but for a same-sex couple it is even more complicated. At least, this was the case in 2003–4, before the law was amended to take same-sex couples into account.

One of the spouses hired Martha McCarthy, the lawyer who had been in the forefront of the fight to recognize same-sex marriage in Canada. She had lost none of her verve. "It doesn't really make a lot of sense, it really doesn't," she explained. "I find it a bit concerning when this government was elected after trumpeting its commitment to the Charter." The lawyer for the other spouse, Julie Hannaford, added, "You can't say to people that we're going to punish you for being in a same-sex marriage by never allowing you out of that marriage." After attempting to obtain an adjournment, Ottawa finally gave McCarthy and her colleagues some assistance. In the documents filed with the court, the government conceded that the definition of *spouse* in the Divorce Act — "either of a man or woman who are married to each other" — was unconstitutional. However, it refused to ask Parliament to amend the legislation until it had adopted the new definition of marriage.

Detractors of gay and lesbian rights were quick to see this marriage breakdown as proof that same-sex couples were "impostors." "It's clearly a set-up case after five days where they are intentionally trying to push their agenda," said Brian Rushfeldt, executive director of the Canada Family Action Coalition, who could not understand why a court would agree to hear the case before the Supreme Court had ruled on the reference. In an interview with the *Globe and Mail*, M.M. denied the accusations: "It was important to me to be able to legally dissolve it. It was a personal need, and I reluctantly became part of a bigger cause. I wasn't going to shy away from it because of the possibility of it becoming a bigger issue. But I didn't start out to make a crusade."

Two months later, on September 13, Justice Ruth Mesbur ruled that the definition of *spouse* in the Divorce Act was "unconstitutional, inoperative and of no force and effect" in Ontario. Martha McCarthy saluted the judgment, however sad the circumstances. "We believe that this is not just the first gay or lesbian divorce in Canada, but actually the first gay or lesbian divorce in the world," she said as she left the courthouse.

* * * * *

The summer of 2004 was also marked by manoeuvrings surrounding appointments to fill two vacancies on the Supreme Court prior to the October hearing of the reference. In the spring, two judges, Louise Arbour and Frank Iacobucci, had unexpectedly announced their departure from Canada's highest court, Arbour to move to a prestigious position as the United Nations High Commissioner for Human Rights and Iacobucci to become interim president of the University of Toronto.

However, Prime Minister Martin had undertaken, during the Liberal leadership campaign, to reform the process for appointing judges to the Supreme Court. Taken by surprise by the two resignations, the Liberals fell back on a temporary procedure that nevertheless allowed MPs to question Justice Minister Cotler on the qualifications and probity of the replacements proposed by the government, Rosalie Abella and Louise Charron. The Conservatives were not afraid to establish a link between the government's intention to legalize same-sex marriage and the two candidates, who had both handed down judgments favourable to gays and lesbians in the past (Charron had drafted the majority opinion in *M. v. H.* at the Ontario Court of Appeal). "It is clear for everyone to see that this is part of the prime minister's agenda [to allow same-sex marriage]," said Conservative MP Vic Toews. After Martin had confirmed the appointment of Abella and Charron to the Supreme Court, the ineffable Conservative senator Anne Cools and her ally, Liberal MP Roger Gallaway, wrote to the court to ask them to recuse themselves from the reference because of their previous decisions! In the end, they were both sworn in only a few hours before the reference hearing.

* * * * *

Before getting to the hearing, it is important to note several other gains for same-sex marriage in Canada during these months. On September 16, 2004, Justice Douglas Yard of the Court of Queen's Bench in Manitoba made his province the fifth jurisdiction in the country to authorize same-sex marriage. Ironically, he found unconstitutional the definition that had been the unintended consequence of Richard North and Chris Vogel's unsuccessful legal bid in 1974. Before their high-profile case, the law in Manitoba made no mention of the sex of the spouses. Rich and Chris were one of three couples who, in August 2004, filed a new application to claim their right to marry. Less than a month later, Justice Yard handed down his decision: the "elegant, cogent and compelling" reasoning of the previous decisions could not but have an "overwhelming and cumulative effect" on the outcome of the case. The rapidity of his decision can be partially explained by the fact that, for the first time, Ottawa had not challenged the application.

"It's nice to wrap something up like this," Vogel said shortly after the decision was announced. The most surprising element is that, despite their — tardy but deserved — court victory, Chris and Rich have no intention of registering the marriage they celebrated in 1974 at the Unitarian church. After 30 years, they no longer feel the need for recognition for their union, which has stood the test of time.

As a result, it was Jordan Cantwell and Laura Fouhse, both United Church ministers, who were the first to take advantage of the new definition of marriage in Manitoba. In a ceremony that had been planned seven months previously, they married two days after the decision was announced, in the presence of their daughter Hope, aged six at the time. Fouhse was particularly pleased that her marriage not only took place in the presence of friends, relatives and "God," but was also recognized by the state. "It just makes the whole event seem so much more complete," she said. Hope was also overjoyed. "I want my mothers to get married because it looks like so much fun!" she said. Cantwell appreciated the more practical aspects: "Now our daughter will grow up knowing that her family is recognized and valued like those of her friends."

The Manitoba attorney general, Gord Mackintosh, felt the need to criticize the federal government for its slowness in ensuring a uniform definition of marriage. "We regret there remains this patchwork of rights across this country," he said.

The expansion of marriage to include gays and lesbians was not a

smooth process in the province: in the days following the Yard decision, at least two marriage commissioners resigned because they did
not want to preside at same-sex marriages and two others were considering a similar course of action. In all, almost a dozen commissioners
resigned in the ensuing weeks. "I will not perform a same-sex marriage,
so based on that, I am left with no choice but to resign, back out or
whatever," Gil Dube, the owner of a trucking firm and part-time commissioner, explained to the CBC. Another commissioner, Leo Tolledo,
said that he would retain his position but take steps, such as citing a
scheduling conflict, to ensure that he did not have to perform same-sex
weddings.

On the day of the decision, Manitoba's director of vital statistics,
Carolyn Kaus, sent a letter to each of the province's 600 marriage commissioners that addressed the issue directly. "In the event you are
opposed to performing marriages for same-sex couples, please return
your Certificate of Registration to Solemnize Marriages so we may can-
cel your registration and remove your name from our listings," she
wrote. "When we appoint you, we assure all Manitobans will be treated in an equitable manner," she continued, adding that people would
not notice a few resignations.

This was not the first time this kind of situation had occurred. In
British Columbia, at least ten marriage commissioners had resigned
once same-sex marriages became legal in the province. A few cases were
also reported in Ontario. Conservative MP Vic Toews was quick to
come to their defence. "These are principled people," he said. "They
have chosen to resign. They have failed to realize that there is a judicial
solution: a complaint to their province's human rights commission."
In his view, the freedom of conscience of employees of the state should
have prevailed over the right of citizens to equal treatment. Further
developments can be expected.

* * * * *

Whatever else was happening, the courts stayed on course. On
September 24, eight days after her Manitoba counterpart, Justice Heather
Robertson of the Supreme Court of Nova Scotia made same-sex marriage

possible for the first time ever in the Maritimes. Addressing the lawyers for the couples concerned, she added, "Forward my congratulations to your clients." Since 2001, the province had offered gay and lesbian couples domestic partnership registration, the model for Quebec's civil unions. The new option had left many people dissatisfied because of the restrictions it imposed compared to good old-fashioned marriage.

"It's time," said Ron Garnett-Doucette, who had applied to the courts along with his partner Bryan. "We waited 20 years for it. I knew it was eventually going to come ... I'm ecstatic it's today." As was to be expected, Brian Rushfeldt of the Canada Family Action Coalition deplored this new breach. "We've got more fools on the bench than we thought we had in this country, obviously," said Rushfeldt, whose self-imposed mission was to re-establish "the principles of Judeo-Christian morality" in Canada.

* * * * *

After months of waiting, the Supreme Court began to hear the reference on marriage on October 6, 2004, the day after the Martin government's second Throne Speech. No fewer than 28 lawyers were to plead before the assembled judges: 20 for and eight against the redefinition of marriage. The representative of the Ontario and Quebec couples, Martha McCarthy, decided to read out a unique affidavit, from Robbie Barnett-Kemper, age 12, the son of Alison Kemper and Joyce Barnett, who married in June 2003:

> The day of their wedding, I did not feel that anything was changing ... I didn't cry like my sister. But I do feel different now that my parents are married, and I feel that people treat me differently. I am beginning to feel like a regular kid ... I feel like my parents are just a little more like other parents ... Now other kids can't say that I don't have a real family.

This affidavit, and the experiences recounted by other couples, provided new evidence of the impact of marriage on gay and lesbian couples,

McCarthy argued. "The sky has not fallen," she said to the court, packed with lawyers and couples, with additional rooms provided to accommodate all the people who wanted to follow the case on closed-circuit TV. "Equal marriage has arrived and life marches on." The lawyer for the Metropolitan Community Church in Toronto, Douglas Elliott, was of similar mind, but added an ironic twist. "Despite the predictions of disaster there have been no negative impacts on heterosexual couples," he said. "Heterosexuality remains remarkably popular."

For the first time, the federal government had to defend same-sex marriage, instead of vehemently opposing it as it had done for many years or passively tolerating it as it had done since June 2003. "The exclusion of same-sex couples is discriminatory and cannot be justified," said Michael Morris, for the federal attorney general.

The strategy of the same-sex couples and the gay rights groups was simple: to persuade the court that the redefinition of marriage was irreversible and that it would be pointless to answer the fourth question submitted by the federal government on whether the exclusion of same-sex couples was in compliance with the Charter. After all, a reference is not an appeal. Even if the Supreme Court ruled against same-sex marriage, the rulings of the lower courts would still stand, unless Parliament passed a new definition of marriage excluding homosexuals using the notwithstanding clause.

"You ought to decline to answer the question," pleaded Cynthia Petersen, the lawyer for Egale. "Having explicitly accepted the correctness of the decision [extending marriage to same-sex couples], it is not now open to the attorney general to ask this court to revisit it." After her eloquent performance, during which she answered questions from the judges with aplomb, Petersen clarified her position even further by pointing out that many couples would not have got married if they had not believed in the solidity of the previous decisions made by 18 different judges: "The way that our system of justice works is that when you win a case, if it's not appealed it's final and you can rely on that and you don't have to relitigate it in perpetuity. Our clients won in British Columbia."

Petersen stressed her clients' incongruous situation: not only had they won their case before the courts, but the federal government had never appealed the decision. And yet, here they were again before the Supreme Court, not as parties to the case, but with intervener status and limited judicial rights. The lawyer even referred to an "abuse of process."

The judges — or at least five out of nine — were almost as critical as the assembled lawyers for gay and lesbian couples of the fourth question submitted by Ottawa. "Are you not describing a political role [for the Court]?" Justice Michel Bastarache asked Morris. "Basically, you are saying that Parliament can introduce and pass the legislation whatever else happens. You are saying that, politically speaking, it would be preferable for MPs to get a definitive answer to this question to help them in their deliberations. All of this sounds like the outline of a political role for the Court. [According to your way of looking at it,] there would be no legal role [for the Court]: you say that the bill would pass regardless!"

"My time is up," replied Morris, revealing that he was a little taken by surprise. The audience burst out laughing. "But I'm sure that the Court would enjoy hearing your answer," retorted Chief Justice Beverley McLachlin. The lawyer for the attorney general simply mentioned that the Supreme Court Act left the government free to choose the questions submitted to the Supreme Court in a reference. In addition, he added, the Court can always decide not to answer one or more of the questions. But with regard to marriage, an answer to the fourth question was "essential" and would have a "real impact" on the future.

The other lawyer for the attorney general, the well-known constitutional expert Peter Hogg, tried to come to his colleague's assistance by suggesting that a decision by the Supreme Court would be "a clear ruling that would encompass the entire country." In saying this, Hogg was forced to admit that the current situation constituted a legal "patchwork." "Surely if this proposed bill is passed the patchwork disappears," countered Justice Ian Binnie.

At least one supporter of same-sex marriage, Aaron Berg, representing the Manitoba Human Rights Commission, asked the Court to answer the fourth question. "We think it is important that the issue be laid to rest," he said.

The second and last day of the hearing centred on the comments presented by religious groups, but also on the astonishing arguments put forward by Alberta, the only province to oppose Ottawa's position on same-sex marriage. One of the lawyers for the Alberta government, Robert Leurer, claimed that a redefinition of marriage would necessarily require a constitutional amendment. In his view, the word *marriage* in the Constitution Act, 1867 had to be interpreted in its traditional sense, as the union of a man and a woman. Justice Rosalie Abella disagreed. "You don't look at 1867 as the end of the story," she said.

Leurer did not stop there. He said that extreme caution was needed before modifying a centuries-old institution like marriage. Twenty years of charter law did not, in his view, "obliterate in one fell swoop the wisdom accumulated since time immemorial." The lawyers for the religious groups agreed: marriage was not "a creature of the law." Justice Binnie was scathing in his reply: "Why is it that the divine right of kings had to give way to constitutional change, but an institution like marriage doesn't?"

The representatives of the Canadian Conference of Catholic Bishops (CCCB) and the powerful U.S.-based lobby group Focus on the Family, among others, presented the argument that the chief purpose of marriage was procreation. "Gays and lesbians are not excluded from marriage because of sexual orientation; they are excluded because of the biologic difference in sex," said William Sammon, representing the CCCB.

Justice John Major was quick to contradict this assertion, referring to the number of divorces and in vitro fertilizations. "The ideal you speak of becomes more and more idealistic, doesn't it?" he said. His colleague Ian Binnie stressed that same-sex couples could have the kind of loving, stable relationships that would allow children to flourish. Justice Abella pointed to the lack of serious studies of the risks encountered by children raised by gay or lesbian parents. "To reduce the whole thing to procreation seems to be an oversimplification," Binnie concluded, adding that "I have difficulty understanding why an extension of the institution to encompass this group will lead to the collapse of the whose edifice."

The most original intervention came from Quebec, anxious to defend its exclusive jurisdiction in the area of marriage ceremonies. The lawyer for the Quebec government, Alain Gingras, tried to show that in the second section of the draft bill, which gave religious institutions the right to refuse to marry same-sex couples, the federal government was using a power it did not have. "This section, if adopted, could effectively short-circuit any power of a province to restrict a fundamental freedom," he said, in this case referring to freedom of religion.

From Ottawa's point of view, section 2 was simply intended to reaffirm a form of protection already provided by the Charter. Peter Hogg had to admit that the federal government was not certain it would prove effective. He said that the courts would have to test it on a case-by-case basis. When Justice Louise Charron asked him how the Supreme Court could, without any facts before it, provide a "significant opinion" on the subject, Hogg surprised many people by replying, "Justice Charron, I have asked myself the same question." He conceded that it would be "difficult" for the Court to "drill too deeply" into the question without the facts.

This surprising admission provided unexpected ammunition for the opponents of same-sex marriage, who suggested that the change threatened the freedom of conscience and freedom of worship of the people who performed marriages. The judges responded angrily. "There are many religious institutions who are not in favour of divorce, but we have divorce available," Justice Abella told Peter Jervis, lawyer for the Islamic Society of North America.

Next, the Catholic bishops, Islamic congregations, Mormons and Seventh-day Adventists expressed their fear that they would be prosecuted for disseminating hate propaganda if they preached against same-sex marriage. "The federal government may not have the power to enact legislation that protects religion," said David Brown, lawyer for the Association for Marriage and the Family in Ontario, which included Focus on the Family. "If the definition of marriage is changed and constitutionalized as to include same-sex marriage it will be open season on religious institutions. It is going to be very serious stuff."

* * * * *

Usually the Supreme Court takes several months — from four to six months on average — to announce its decisions. In the case of same-sex marriage, however, barely two months elapsed between the hearing and the release of the opinion. Clearly, the judges already knew in which direction they were heading when they began to hear the reference. Of course, the hesitations of the Martin government had given them plenty of time to think. But even before the historic opinion was issued another judge had authorized same-sex marriage in another province: Saskatchewan.

On November 5, in a five-page document, Judge Donna Wilson of the Court of Queen's Bench endorsed the conclusions of the Ontario, B.C. and Quebec courts of appeal and ordered the provincial government to issue marriage licences to five applicant couples. "We love each other [and] now we'll be on equal legal footing with other couples," said Kelley Moore, who planned to marry Lenore Swystun in the fall. "It's time for people to understand this is an issue of human rights," said Swystun. Of course, Real Women rose to criticize this new "breach" in the institution of marriage. "This decision displays arrogance or ignorance about what marriage is," the organization declared in a news release. "The union of two same-sex persons is not equivalent to the union of one man and one woman."

Following in the footsteps of Justice Yard in the Yukon, Wilson ordered the federal and provincial governments to reimburse the legal expenses of the couples involved — $10,000 for the Saskatchewan case:

> The Attorney General for Saskatchewan was well aware of the decisions of the courts in other Canadian jurisdictions and, although those decisions were not binding statements of the law for Saskatchewan, the province did have the choice to act or wait for a decision of this Court ... The Attorney General could have taken the risk of advising marriage licence issuers in this Province to issue licences to same-sex couples.

This was a step that no province had dared to take, despite being encouraged to do so by Martin Cauchon and other legal experts.

13

THE SUPREME COURT HAS SPOKEN

Although six provinces and one territory already permitted same-sex marriages, the Supreme Court opinion of December 9, 2004, was eagerly awaited. Opponents of redefining marriage felt this was their last opportunity to regain control. Gay and lesbian activists, on the other hand, although generally confident of the outcome, were afraid that the Supreme Court opinion might contain some surprises. As is often the case, the judges provided ammunition for both sides.

Unlike the lower courts, the Supreme Court did not have much scope to express its opinion on the subject. Its role was primarily to answer the four questions submitted by the federal government in its referral. The goal of the exercise was not to reconsider each of the arguments put forward by the parties during the earlier court cases, but rather to assess the positions expressed on each of the four questions. This was no place for the lyrical outpourings on the injustices suffered by gays and lesbians that previous rulings had contained.

The Supreme Court opinion is barely 30 pages long and detached in tone, and it appears almost superficial in comparison with the lower courts' exhaustive examinations. It is true that the Supreme Court was facing what was practically a done deal: thousands of same-sex couples had already married, and the government had already said that it would legalize same-sex marriage whatever the court decided. Going with the flow, the judges had no other choice but to endorse the previous decisions and approve the Liberals' draft bill.

"The mere recognition of the equality rights of one group cannot, in itself, constitute a violation of the ... rights of another. The promotion of Charter rights and values enriches our society as a whole and the furtherance of those rights cannot undermine the very principles the Charter was meant to foster," states the opinion, signed by "the Court." This is a rare occurrence; in general, Supreme Court decisions are drafted by a single judge, supported by a majority of their colleagues. By openly stating their unanimity, the judges were sending a clear message.

The judges answered the first three questions swiftly. The first question was designed to confirm that the definition of marriage was within the legislative authority of the Parliament of Canada. This was a disguised way of asking whether a constitutional amendment was needed to change the definition of marriage, as some people had suggested. "The 'frozen concepts' reasoning runs contrary to one of the most fundamental principles of Canadian constitutional interpretation: that our Constitution is a living tree which, by way of progressive interpretation, accommodates and addresses the realities of modern life," said the Court. "Read expansively, the word 'marriage' in [the Constitution Act, 1867] does not exclude same-sex marriage."

The judges noted that the traditional definition used for marriages in Canada, taken from *Hyde* v. *Hyde* (1866), referred to "Christendom": "Hyde spoke to a society of shared social values where marriage and religion were thought to be inseparable. This is no longer the case." The "living tree" concept goes back to a Privy Council decision of 1930 in the "persons" case, concerning whether women could become senators. The judges also cited this historic case to reject another argument, that the definition of marriage could not be amended by law because it had existed from time immemorial. In the same way that it was formerly understood that "persons" referred only to men, so it was understood that marriage was available only to heterosexual couples. "The recognition of same-sex marriage in several Canadian jurisdictions as well as two European countries belies the assertion that the same is true today," the judges ruled, in a passive reference to the decisions of the lower courts.

The judges conceded that the extension of marriage to gay and lesbian couples would have repercussions for the provinces, which are responsible for the celebration and registration of marriage. But the effects were "incidental," they ruled, without addressing the question of officials who objected to performing same-sex marriages.

The Supreme Court confirmed the federal government's constitutional jurisdiction over the definition of marriage. It still had to assess whether section 2 of the bill, designed to protect the right of religious authorities to refuse to perform same-sex marriages, was also within the government's powers. This aspect of the opinion was probably the most surprising for Ottawa. "Only the provinces may legislate exemptions to existing solemnization requirements," the judges stated unambiguously, confirming the argument presented by Quebec.

The second question went to the heart of the debate, but was clearly biased towards gay and lesbian couples: was the bill, which made it possible for persons of the same sex to marry, consistent with the Canadian Charter of Rights and Freedoms? The Court's answer could not have been more direct: it could not be inconsistent with the Charter, since it flowed from it. No one had seriously predicted any other outcome, but the surprising element was the line of reasoning followed by the judges, which was practically circular:

> We note that [the recognition of same-sex marriage] embodies the government's policy stance in relation to the s. 15(1) equality concerns of same-sex couples. This, combined with the circumstances giving rise to the Proposed Act [the lower court rulings] and with the preamble thereto, points unequivocally to a purpose which, far from violating the Charter, flows from it.

In other words, since the lower courts had already authorized same-sex marriages and Ottawa had decided to legalize them, the Supreme Court had nothing further to add. The question was asked backwards, and the judges did not even bother to analyze the bill's consistency with section 15, which would have required a systematic examination in several stages.

In a subtle way, however, as part of a sentence concerning the juris-diction of the provinces, the Court took pains to rule that "civil unions are a relationship short of marriage," repudiating one of the proposals of the opponents of a redefinition of marriage — even though this question had not even been asked. To follow the logic of the Charter to its ultimate conclusion, the Supreme Court addressed the possibili-ty that the "Proposed Act may violate freedom of religion," specifical-ly by creating a "dominant social ethos" contrary to the precepts of the major religious denominations. The judges did not reject this fear out-right, but stressed that the Charter does not establish a hierarchy of rights. In other words, the right to equal treatment is not subordinate to the right to freedom of worship, and vice versa. "The right to same-sex marriage conferred by the Proposed Act may conflict with the right to freedom of religion if the Act becomes law, as suggested by the hypo-thetical scenarios presented by several interveners. However, the jurisprudence confirms that many if not all such conflicts will be resolved within the Charter."

Next, the judges dealt quickly with the third question, the goal of which was to test whether the extension of marriage to same-sex cou-ples would result in religious officials being forced to marry two peo-ple of the same sex despite its being contrary to their religious beliefs. The Supreme Court was clear: the powers of the state are limited to civil marriage and including same-sex couples could not "be interpreted as affecting religious marriage or its solemnization."

Of course, a decision by the government to force churches to marry same-sex couples would constitute an infringement of freedom of reli-gion. This was not the intention — and is still not the intention — of either the federal or the provincial governments. The conclusion was clear: "The Court is of the opinion that, absent unique circumstances with respect to which we will not speculate, the guarantee of religious freedom in ... the Charter is broad enough to protect religious officials from being compelled by the state to perform civil or religious same-sex marriages that are contrary to their religious beliefs."

The Court then came to the fourth question, added by Paul Martin and Irwin Cotler in January 2004, shortly after they assumed office. It was designed to appease opponents of the change by presenting the same question that had been examined by the lower courts: was the "traditional" definition of marriage in violation of the Charter? Even though several judges had already dealt with this question, it remained complex and controversial, and the Supreme Court judges could not treat it lightly. But this did not mean that they had to go back over the work of their predecessors, especially given that this was a referral rather than a full-scale appeal.

For this reason, they chose not to answer the question — an exceptional event, since the last time the Court had used its discretionary power not to answer a question referred by the federal government had been in 1929! Since then, the Supreme Court had specified in its jurisprudence the circumstances in which it could refuse to deal with a question: (a) when the question lacks legal content; (b) when the question is too ambiguous or imprecise to allow an accurate answer; or (c) where the parties have not provided sufficient information. The Court recognized that none of these situations applied to the fourth question on marriage, but ruled that "a unique set of circumstances is raised by Question 4, the combined effect of which persuades the Court that it would be unwise and inappropriate to answer the question."

The first reason given by the judges was that the government had already announced, and reiterated, its intention to legalize same-sex marriage, meaning that an opinion on the constitutionality of excluding gays and lesbians would serve no legal purpose. "On the other hand," they said, "answering this question may have serious deleterious effects."

The judges identified two major problems. First, they were afraid of creating legal confusion if they declared that the exclusion of homosexuals was constitutional: "The decisions of the lower courts in the matters giving rise to this reference are binding in their respective provinces. They would be cast into doubt by an advisory opinion which expressed a contrary view, even though it could not overturn them. The result would be confusion, not uniformity." This potential disorder would be especially threatening for same-sex couples who had already married, the Court noted: "The parties to previous litigation have relied upon the finality of their judgments and have acquired rights which in our view are entitled to protection." In any case, the parliamentarians would derive only a "hypothetical" advantage from an answer to the fourth question.

The judges also took the opportunity to indirectly criticize Ottawa's approach. "There is no precedent for answering a reference question which mirrors issues already disposed of in lower courts where an appeal was available but not pursued," they noted, corroborating the arguments of the supporters of same-sex marriage. "The Court was too clever for us politicians," Bill Graham later chuckled.

* * * * *

In the Supreme Court lobby, Martha McCarthy was unable to hide her happiness. She sent her clients an enthusiastic email via BlackBerry, typing, "It's a total victory."

In contrast, one of the lawyers for the attorney general, Peter Hogg, had to admit that the Supreme Court had not entirely settled the question of same-sex marriage. "It's true that the Supreme Court of Canada has not specifically said that opposite-sex marriage is unconstitutional," he told the *Toronto Star*. "They haven't said that. So to that extent there's a lack of clarity. But the lower courts have been absolutely consistent in saying that, so I think we can pretty much put in the bank that that is the position [of the Supreme Court]."

Justice Minister Cotler concurred, but as a politician he could not afford to be so candid and so his statement was less nuanced: "The opposite-sex requirement is unconstitutional because how else could we have said that the same-sex reference is constitutional? ... The only deduction we can make is that any attempt to exclude gays and lesbians from marriage would be unconstitutional." This was questionable reasoning, indeed almost sophistry. But it reflected the evident disappointment of the government, which would have preferred that the Supreme Court silence the opponents of same-sex marriage once and for all, at least on the legal level. "We knew there was a possibility that the Court would not give an answer," Paul Martin said later. "I thought we had more chance of getting the Supreme Court's opinion on the fourth question, but our lawyers told us there was always the possibility of a refusal."

An unassailably clear message from the country's highest court that the traditional definition of marriage was unconstitutional would have made the Liberals' task considerably easier. They would have been able to proclaim that they had had no choice but to expand marriage to include same-sex couples because of the Supreme Court opinion. Of course, politics being politics, the lack of a clear answer did not prevent some members of the government from proclaiming it anyway.

Opponents of same-sex marriage lost no time in exploiting the Supreme Court's silence on a question they considered fundamental. "This is an astute political judgment by the court," said lawyer David Brown, representing the Association for Marriage and the Family. Opposition Leader Stephen Harper said he was "encouraged" by the Court's decision. "This is a huge victory for the position of the Conservative Party on this issue and for Canadian democracy," he said at a press conference. "The court did not declare the traditional defini-tion of marriage unconstitutional. They have punted this issue back to Parliament to decide."

There was, of course, an element of calculation in his comments. They were intended to show that the Conservatives could still reverse the redefinition of marriage. But could they do it without invoking the notwithstanding clause? Aware of how dangerous recourse to the clause would be, Harper repeated that it was not inevitable.

Faced with the prevailing skepticism, the Conservative leader took pains to polish his plan to defend the "traditional institution" of mar-riage, carefully covering the plan with an artistic veneer. Harper pro-posed introducing a bill to end same-sex marriage, while preserving the "vested rights" of couples who had already married. One thing became clear: if his bill passed, the gay and lesbian community would begin the court fight again, a fact that the Conservatives grudgingly acknowl-edged. To round out his proposal, Harper suggested that provincial civil union and registered partnership schemes "be subject to the same rights, privileges and obligations as marriage." This would be a "compromise acceptable to a large majority of Canadians," he felt. However, only a few provinces have such schemes, even though they are under exclusive provincial jurisdiction. Harper's proposal therefore involved mainly provincial responsibilities, which seemed ironic given his claim to be a champion of provincial rights.

* * * * *

Two hours after the release of the Supreme Court opinion, Paul Martin seized the opportunity to attack Stephen Harper. "I would like to announce today that the Government of Canada will move forward with the bill to open civil marriage to same-sex couples," the Prime Minister declared solemnly as he left a cabinet meeting. As he was speaking, gay and lesbian couples could already marry in six provinces and one territory, home to 85 percent of the country's total population. In the remaining jurisdictions, however, this right was still not available. "The government agrees with the Supreme Court that uniformity is essential, and we will not permit the balkanization of marriage across the country," added Martin. "The other possibility would be to invoke the notwithstanding clause to deny Canadians a right guaranteed by the Charter, and I will never do that." The Liberal leader admitted that, for many citizens and parliamentarians, the question remained a difficult one, since it brought personal and religious beliefs into play and involved a profound transformation of an ancient social institution.

"This was not an easy decision for me," said Martin. "It is one that I've struggled with, but fundamentally it comes down to the equality rights under the Charter. I do not believe you can have two classes of citizen." Imploring MPs of all parties to support the bill, the prime minister continued in a more lyrical vein: "The Charter essentially says all Canadians must be treated equally, and I don't think that there's any other way to interpret the Charter, and I don't think there's any other way to look at our country." In other words, after helping win an election victory, same-sex marriage had become the symbol of national unity!

Liberal backbenchers had the option of voting according to their conscience, but not cabinet ministers, who were bound by the government's position. In the days following the release of the Supreme Court opinion, two ministers publicly expressed their reservations about supporting the redefinition of marriage. "The concerns of my constituents have got to be fundamental in my thinking when I make my decision on how I'm going to vote," said Joe Comuzzi, Minister of State (Federal Economic Development Initiative for Northern Ontario). His colleague from Newfoundland, Natural Resources Minister John Efford, even floated the possibility of resigning from cabinet over the issue.

Faced with a barrage of questions in the year-end interviews that the prime minister traditionally grants the TV networks, Paul Martin took the risk of explaining how he personally had been converted to the same-sex cause. He spoke of his conversations with a friend in British Columbia whose daughter was lesbian. She had suffered from depression and thoughts of suicide, but this sombre period ended after she came out at the age of 18. "It really does give you an insight that we've got to understand that we're all human beings and that all of us are brothers and sisters and cousins and daughters and sons and that, in fact, we can make life just a little bit better and a little bit fairer if we are prepared to recognize everybody for who they are," Martin told Global TV. These are some of the most philosophical comments Martin has ever made in public on the subject of marriage. He later acknowledged that it is the story of this young woman that had the greatest influence on him: "I must tell you that it had an enormous effect. Much more than people think."

In another TV interview, the Liberal leader confessed that he had attempted to persuade his aunt, Claire Guay, of the need to redefine marriage, emphasizing in particular that religious institutions would not be obliged to marry same-sex couples. He was unsuccessful. "Oh, she does not agree with me," he recounted. "She feels the traditional definition is the one that should remain. If you knew Aunt Claire, you'd know you don't change her mind easily." Claire Guay had already attracted attention by phoning Paul Martin in the middle of a September 2004 first ministers' conference on health care, to lecture her nephew on his language.

The Conservative government in Alberta would not be any easier to persuade than Paul Martin's aunt. In mid-December, Premier Ralph Klein announced that, to avoid having to issue marriage licences to same-sex couples, the province was considering relinquishing its responsibility to register civil marriages entirely. "That was the resolution [in cabinet]," he said. "How we do that, I just don't know." This approach, the brainchild of Advanced Education Minister Dave Hancock, would have resulted in Alberta registering only civil unions, open to both same-sex and heterosexual couples. Religious institutions would have had exclusive responsibility for marriage.

Klein, always willing to speak his mind, did more than just contradict Paul Martin's position. He also criticized his federal ally, Stephen Harper, for refusing to invoke the notwithstanding clause. "I'd like to see Stephen be more definitive in his actions," said Klein, who thought that same-sex marriage was "morally wrong." This was enough to make Paul Martin renew his attack of the Opposition Leader. "I think that, quite clearly, this is a lack of courage and a clear lack of leadership," Martin said after a cabinet meeting. "Mr. Harper has said he will change the law in the six provinces where the definition of marriage includes same-sex marriage and yet he refuses to say he would utilize the notwithstanding clause, which is the only vehicle open to him." In contrast, Ralph Klein had been "intellectually honest" when he recognized that use of the notwithstanding clause was a necessity.

Martin was enjoying this unique moment: after spending months fighting divisions within the Liberal caucus on the subject of same-sex marriage, he could at last take advantage of the beginnings of a split among the Conservatives. Harper, however, did not give up so easily. Only a few minutes after Martin's statement, Harper issued a vindictive press release in which he accused Martin of lacking courage: "In the past year, Mr. Martin has tried to hide behind the courts on the issue of marriage. The Supreme Court has refused to provide him cover. I support the traditional definition of marriage, Mr. Martin doesn't. It's that simple. I will work to ensure that most of my party can support my position, and I will allow all Conservatives a free vote. Does Mr. Martin have the courage to do the same?"

Faced with this uninspiring spectacle, NDP MP Bill Siksay, who had taken over Svend Robinson's riding of Burnaby-Douglas after Robinson admitted stealing an expensive ring during a trade show, tried to add a little perspective: "It's outrageous that Paul Martin should be accusing anybody of cowardice on the issue of same-sex marriage. After all he is the one who set up the pattern of never coming out with his own position on it for over ten years, of delaying the issue of going to the Supreme Court to get it off the agenda so he didn't have to face it during the election campaign."

Siksay's criticisms were justified since, despite their elevated sentiments concerning equality for gays and lesbians, the Liberals did not seem willing to take their line of reasoning to its logical conclusion. For example, a few days after the publication of the Supreme Court opinion, Irwin Cotler revealed that he would give government employees the option of not performing same-sex marriages if it went against their religious beliefs. "In the six provinces and one territory [where same-sex marriages are permitted,]" the minister admitted, "there have been no problems so far. But there are perhaps one or two people in the country who are civil, not religious, representatives and who have their own problems of conscience or religion. I believe that we can arrive at what the Supreme Court calls a reasonable accommodation." In his view, the Supreme Court had only stated that religious authorities could not be forced to marry same-sex couples, without mentioning government employees.

Cotler wanted to place the freedom of religion of these — provincial — government employees above the rights of all citizens to equal treatment. Since the problems involved only a handful of people across the country, Egale was not too indignant. "They [the provincial authorities] are going to have to issue licences to same-sex couples and make available solemnization services," said Laurie Arron.

* * * * *

On December 21, 2004, same-sex marriage became legal in

Newfoundland and Labrador. In a decision largely based on the previous rulings, Chief Justice Derek Green of the Supreme Court of Newfoundland and Labrador, Trial Division, authorized the marriages of Jacqueline Pottle and Noelle French and of Lisa Zigler and Theresa Walsh. As soon as the judgment was released, Pottle and French applied for a licence, which was issued. Their wedding took place two days later, with the mayor of St. John's, Andy Wells, officiating. "It's about the respect we will now get from society," said Pottle. "I'm sure there will be some legal and social benefits. But for us, it's about that next level of commitment; that lifetime commitment we can now make in front of our families and our friends." Despite Irwin Cotler's assurances, several marriage commissioners resigned following the court decision. In some cases, the commissioner who resigned was the only commissioner in their community.

Unlike the Conservative government of Alberta, Newfoundland's Conservative government did not challenge the expansion of marriage to include same-sex couples. In fact, Premier Danny Williams went so far as to make a personal statement two months later. "From a personal perspective, I actually support gay marriages," Williams said in an interview with Canadian Press. "I practised law for over 30 years and championed social justice and believed in minority rights and believed in the rights and freedoms of individuals under our Charter of Rights." After the comments voiced by Ralph Klein, Stephen Harper was now being criticized, for the opposite reasons, by another influential Conservative. The Tories were perhaps not as divided as the Liberals on the question of same-sex marriage, but a small split was apparent.

* * * * *

Although the right of gays and lesbians to marry was spreading across the country, there were — and are — still many places where their weddings could not be held. In January 2005, a lesbian couple filed a complaint against the Port Coquitlam council of the Knights of Columbus with the British Columbia Human Rights Tribunal. The two women had reserved the Catholic organization's hall for their wedding reception, but when the council realized it was a same-sex wedding they cancelled the rental contract. The women "want to make sure that no one else has to deal with that kind of an issue around their wedding," explained their lawyer, barbara findlay.

Their intention was worthy, but the final outcome of the legal process remains to be seen. In its December 2004 opinion, the Supreme Court appeared to say that religious organizations were free to refuse the use of their premises for same-sex weddings: "Concerns were raised about the compulsory use of sacred places for the celebration of such marriages and about being compelled to otherwise assist in the celebration of same-sex marriages. The reasoning that leads us to conclude that the guarantee of freedom of religion protects against the compulsory celebration of same-sex marriages, suggests that the same would hold for these concerns."

* * * * *

In early 2005, a new controversy on the redefinition of marriage was sparked by a statement in which Stephen Harper raised an old spectre. During a visit to Montreal, the Conservative leader expressed his concern that once same-sex marriage was legalized, "The next thing on the Liberal agenda will be polygamy and who knows what else."

Paul Martin, on a trip to China, felt duty-bound to respond. During a press conference in Beijing, reading from prepared notes, he called Harper's statement "absolutely ridiculous": "Polygamy is against the law, and as far as I'm concerned it will always be against the law." However, when a reporter asked him if he was ready to call an election on the marriage question, Martin became more aggressive. "I have no intention of calling an election," he said. "We're here to govern, and I intend to continue. We want to govern. But if you're asking me whether I'm ready to call an election to support the Charter of Rights against its attackers, then the answer is yes."

The Prime Minister's statement was astonishing, because the vote on the proposed marriage bill did not involve a vote of confidence — it would, in fact, be a free vote for all backbenchers. A government, even a minority government, cannot be defeated except on a vote of confidence. Quickly, Martin added the following clarification: the future of the government would not hang on the bill to legalize same-sex marriage, but on any future bill to use the notwithstanding clause to block its application. "If there is a vote on the use of the notwithstanding clause on this question, I will make it a vote of confidence," he said. "If the government loses the vote, an election will be called."

In putting forward this highly improbable scenario, Martin was clearly trying to trap the Conservatives. Harper, however, refused to be drawn into the argument: "While he [Martin] promised that the upcoming vote will be free for his backbenchers, he now appears to be threatening them with an election should they vote against his legislation ... I thought Mr. Martin had an agenda that he was planning to legislate, but if he wants to call an election on this issue, so be it. I am confident that our position on this issue is supported by a majority of Canadians." It is important to note that opinion polls commissioned by the Conservatives had shown a drop in support for same-sex marriage. In fact, according to several surveys, a clear majority of respondents preferred to keep the traditional definition, but to offer gay and lesbian couples the possibility of contracting a civil union with the same advantages as marriage. This was particularly evident in rural, mainly Conservative, regions.

Liberals who supported the expansion of marriage to include same-sex couples were nevertheless anxious about the impact of the new measure on their reelection prospects. Even an MP from an urban riding (Laval–Les Îles), Quebec caucus chair Raymonde Folco, expressed concern: "I think that there will be a price to pay on the part of the members of Parliament. There are always people who tell us if you do that, we won't vote for you." According to one survey, same-sex marriage was an especially sensitive issue for a fifth of Canadian voters.

Even if Harper had the public on his side, many of the country's elite continued to criticize his actions. A letter signed by 134 law professors from across the country, addressed directly to Harper, contained a stinging attack on the Conservative leader: "You must be completely honest with Canadians about the unconstitutionality of your proposal. If you intend to override Canadians' constitutional rights, you at least owe it to them to say this openly and directly. Canadians deserve better." Invited to respond, Harper thumbed his nose at the legal experts. "We've sought and received legal advice and the legal advice supports my position," he said at a caucus meeting in Victoria. "We're going to promote traditional marriage without [using] the notwithstanding clause, and lawyers can debate and speculate on the meaning of all this. But the only legal opinion that matters is the Supreme Court's opinion, and it has not ruled."

In the wings, the Conservatives were even more combative, pointing out that one of the main authors of the letter, University of Toronto professor Sujit Choudhry, had advised Paul Martin during his 2003 Liberal leadership campaign. "His record of Liberal partisanship makes him a biased observer," said Harper's director of communications, Geoff Norquay. "His mind is made up."

* * * * *

On February 1, 2005, almost two months after the publication of the Supreme Court opinion, Justice Minister Irwin Cotler introduced the long-awaited civil marriage bill, Bill C-38, in the House of Commons. Some people had hoped that the government would act sooner, but, in fact, Parliament had only sat for five days since the opinion was released, leaving little time to prepare and introduce legislation. A secret cabinet document obtained by the *Toronto Star* warned of the "polarization" created by same-sex marriage and hinted at the possibility of delaying introduction of the bill. "It is likely that the media will continue to highlight every example of diverging opinions within the Liberal caucus and in cabinet over what approach to adopt," noted the document.

Aware of this difficulty, Justice Minister Cotler was cautious during his press conference. "We have seen a trialogue between Parliament, the courts and the Canadian people, which has made it possible to apply the rights of gays and lesbians as part of the minority rights conferred by the Charter," he said in the emphatic tone he sometimes adopts.

The wording of the bill was clear: "Marriage, for civil purposes, is the lawful union of two persons to the exclusion of all others." The bill amended a total of eight acts, including the Divorce Act, which would now allow same-sex couples to dissolve their marriages. Despite objections from Quebec, which jealously guarded its jurisdiction over the celebration of civil marriages, the bill stated that "officials of religious groups are free to refuse to perform marriages that are not in accordance with their religious beliefs."

Cotler tried to place the bill in the broader context of human rights, which had been his specialty as a lawyer. "I hope that the bill [will] stimulate our awareness of the need to protect the rights of all minorities, including the rights of gays and lesbians," he said. "This [recognition for same-sex marriages] must have an impact."

To justify the approach used in the bill, Cotler completed the circular logic introduced by the Supreme Court, citing the passage from its opinion stating that the bill "points unequivocally to a purpose which, far from violating the Charter, flows from it." As we saw, this conclusion was based on the legalization of same-sex marriage, as instigated by the courts and endorsed by the government! Having disposed of this point to his satisfaction, the minister urged Canadians to follow him on the path towards a redefinition of marriage. "We know that some Canadians still have questions about this topic," Cotler conceded. "But Canada is founded on a tradition of tolerance and respect; it is rooted in a Charter that protects the equality rights of all Canadians."

To bolster his prediction that Bill C-38 would be passed into law before the summer, Cotler said, "I don't really foresee how one can put amendments to this." Astonishingly, Stephen Harper agreed with him on this question. "The bill is written in a way that will make it difficult to amend," he declared in a press release. The two politicians agreed on something else: that there should not be a referendum on marriage rights, even though two-thirds of Canadians, according to a poll published by CanWest in early February, wanted one. The same survey showed that 66 percent of respondents supported "keeping" the traditional definition of marriage. This result was probably attributable to the way the question was asked, but it still demonstrated the volatility

of public opinion. "You can't have a referendum to override the constitution of this country," said Cotler. The official opposition was not
completely against the idea of a referendum on marriage, but Harper
specified that it could not take place before a future Conservative government passed suitable legislation.

* * * * *

The introduction of Bill C-38 to recognize same-sex marriage rekindled
the debate, especially among Liberal MPs, and during the caucus meeting that followed, things got a little out of hand. An opponent of same-
sex marriage, Tom Wappel, accused the prime minister of deceiving the
Liberals by leading them to believe that the vote would be free for all
MPs, including ministers, since the question was a moral one. He was
so persistent that he was asked to sit down, and Paul Martin gave him
a lecture. "We're going to have differing opinions but you've got to
respect each other's opinions," he told his troops. "I might not agree
with [the opponents of same-sex marriage] but the reality is this is a
government initiative. And I still respect their opinion." Another fierce
opponent of the redefinition of marriage, Pat O'Brien, complained that
party officials had told him to "take a walk" when the time came to
vote on Bill C-38 to camouflage the dissension within the party. Liberal
whip Karen Redman denied the allegation.

There appeared to be more unity among the Conservatives, even if,
a few days after the bill was introduced, three MPs — Gerald Keddy,
James Moore and Jim Prentice — declared their support for the legislation, as Belinda Stronach had already done. Nonetheless, Stephen
Harper's party clearly remained the driving force behind the opposition to same-sex marriage.

On February 14, for example, it was reported that MP Jason Kenney
had made the following declaration to the Punjabi Press Club in
Brampton, Ontario: "Marriage is open to everybody as long as they're
a man and a woman. It doesn't say you can't marry if you're a homosexual. The fact is that homosexuals have been married [in heterosexual marriages] and do marry." He was referring to the 1993 decision by

Ontario judge James Southey. "Equality does not mean that everybody has to be treated in exactly the same way," he continued. "We are against unfair discrimination, but there are fair forms of discrimination. There are benefits for veterans, that you can't get if you're not a veteran. There are benefits for the elderly, that are just for them. There are benefits for students, reserved for students."

Kenney went so far as to cite the example of his NDP colleagues Svend Robinson and Libby Davies. Both lived for many years in heterosexual unions, although Davies never married. Davies, who had been living with another woman for the past six years, addressed this point at a press conference to mark Valentine's Day: "Marriage is about marrying someone you love. Why would you marry someone of the opposite sex if you love someone of the same sex? I object to the fact that he's drawing in my personal life. I look forward to the day when ... who my partner is, is not a political issue. Nobody questions Paul Martin and his wife."

Accompanied by two other openly gay members of the House of Commons, Réal Ménard and Bill Siksay, Davies released a letter that all three had sent to the leaders of the four parties represented in the Commons, emphasizing that gays and lesbians were not trying to transform the institution of marriage, but simply to have access to it.

14

A HUMAN RIGHT — OR IS IT?

In a rare departure from parliamentary practice, the Prime Minister himself launched the debate on Bill C-38 on February 16, 2005. Usually, the cabinet minister or MP sponsoring the bill delivers the inaugural speech in a debate. That Paul Martin took charge of it personally reveals how important the expansion of marriage to include gays and lesbians was. His speech could hardly have been more apt. Martin incisively laid out the main reasons for his own conversion as well as solid arguments aimed at convincing recalcitrant MPs — embellished with some partisan thrusts, of course.

"This is an important day," he began. "The attention of our nation is focused on this chamber in which John Diefenbaker introduced the Bill of Rights, and in which Pierre Trudeau fought to establish the Charter of Rights and Freedoms. Our deliberations will not be merely about a piece of legislation or sections of legal text. More deeply they will be about the kind of nation we are today and the nation we want to be."

Early on, Martin acknowledged the significance of the religious fears among some MPs. However, he repeated that no institution — "no church, no synagogue, no mosque, no temple" — would be compelled to marry same-sex couples. At the same time, he urged his colleagues to go beyond their beliefs: "Certainly, many of us in this House, myself included, have a strong faith, and we value that faith and its influence on the decisions we make. But all of us have been elected to serve here as parliamentarians. And, as public legislators, we are responsible for serving all Canadians and protecting the rights of all Canadians." It was not enough to "embrace freedom and equality in theory," he said. "We must also embrace them in fact."

The Prime Minister then explained why the establishment of a system of civil unions for same-sex couples, instead of marriage, would be insufficient. In such a scenario, he said, gays and lesbians "would be equal, but not quite as equal as the rest of Canadians," adding, "Put simply, we must always remember that 'separate but equal' is not equal." This phrase, echoing a slogan used by gay and lesbian groups, was greeted with applause. In any case, he reminded the House, the federal government does not have constitutional jurisdiction in matters of civil union: "Only the provinces could define such a regime, and they could define it in ten different ways, and some jurisdictions might not bother to define it at all. There would be uncertainty. There would be confusion."

In an effort to give the impression that same-sex marriage was inevitable, Martin pointed out that the definition of marriage had already been changed by the courts: "The issue is not whether rights are to be granted. The issue is whether rights that have been granted are to be taken away." Taking aim directly at Stephen Harper, while never mentioning the Conservative leader's name, Martin reiterated his position that the only way to prevent the redefinition of marriage would be to invoke the notwithstanding clause in the Charter of Rights:

> Some are frank and straightforward and say yes [to the notwithstanding clause]. Others have not been so candid. Despite being confronted with clear facts, despite being confronted with the unanimous opinion of 134 legal scholars, experts in their field, intimately familiar with the constitution, some have chosen to not be forthright with Canadians. They have eschewed the honest approach in favour of the political approach. They have attempted to cajole the public into believing that we can return to the past with a simple snap of the fingers, that we can revert to the traditional defi-

nition of marriage without consequence and without over-
riding the charter. They are insincere. They are disingenuous.
And they are wrong.

Use of the notwithstanding clause would send a message to all of
Canada's minorities that they could no longer turn to the government
"for protection, for security, for the guarantee of their freedoms," said
Martin emphatically:

> We would risk becoming a country in which the defence of
> rights is weighed, calculated and debated based on electoral or
> other considerations. That would set us back decades as a
> nation ... Our rights must be eternal, not subject to political
> whim.

Martin responded to Harper's controversial statement a few days earlier that same-sex marriage was an attack on ethnic-minority communities, evoking a very different relationship between same-sex marriage
and multiculturalism: "When we as a nation protect minority rights,
we are protecting our multicultural nature." He also linked same-sex
marriage to the establishment of official bilingualism in the 1960s,
noting the vigorous opposition that Lester Pearson's government faced
at the time:

> Today, we rightly see discrimination based on sexual orienta-
> tion as arbitrary, inappropriate and unfair. Looking back, we
> can hardly believe that such rights were ever a matter for debate.
> It is my hope that we will ultimately see the current debate in a
> similar light, realizing that nothing has been lost or sacrificed
> by the majority in extending full rights to the minority.

No gay or lesbian listener could have failed to be moved by hearing the
prime minister summarize the difficult struggle of hundreds of men
and women over the years to gain a measure of respect:

For gays and lesbians, evolving social attitudes have, over the years, prompted a number of important changes in the law. Recall that, until the late 1960s, the state believed it had the right to peek into our bedrooms. Until 1977, homosexuality was still sufficient grounds for deportation. Until 1992, gay people were prohibited from serving in the military. In many parts of the country, gays and lesbians could not designate their partners as beneficiaries under employee medical and dental benefits, insurance policies or private pensions. Until very recently, people were being fired merely for being gay.

Martin had to justify his own rejection of same-sex marriage five and a half years earlier, when he voted in favour of the Reform Party's motion:

My misgivings about extending the right of civil marriage to same-sex couples were a function of my faith and my perspective on the world around us, but much has changed since that day. We have heard from courts across the country, including the Supreme Court. We have come to the realization that instituting civil unions, adopting a separate but equal approach, would violate the equality provisions of the Charter. We have confirmed that extending the right of civil marriage to gays and lesbians will not in any way infringe on religious freedoms.

As recently as a year and a half earlier, Martin had still been skeptical about the need to legalize same-sex marriage, but he had come to see this change as an important step in Canada's collective life:

There are times when we as parliamentarians can feel the gaze of history upon us. They felt it in the days of Pearson [when they entrenched official bilingualism] and they felt it in the days of Trudeau [when they enshrined the Charter of Rights]. We, the 308 men and women elected to represent one of the most inclusive, just and respectful countries on the face of this earth, feel it today.

In sum, for Paul Martin same-sex marriage had come to represent progress that could not be held back: "If we do not step forward, then we will step back. If we do not protect a right, then we deny it. Together as a nation, together as Canadians, let us step forward."

The Liberals in the chamber gave Martin a thunderous standing ovation — none more so than Mario Silva, a young gay MP from Toronto who had taken his place at Martin's side. Even NDP and Bloc Québécois MPs joined in the applause, while the Conservatives remained seated, waiting for the next speech: Stephen Harper's.

To his credit, Harper gave the most detailed and, in a sense, the most rigorous speech of the day. You could feel the passion of someone who believed sincerely in the arguments he was putting forward. "My position ... is not derived from personal prejudice or political tactics, as some Liberal MPs would have us believe," he said, assuring listeners that his only motivation was the defence of "time-tested values."

He moved quickly to criticize Paul Martin for using nationalist arguments to sell the redefinition of marriage and appeared deeply insulted by this tactic: "The greater tragedy is the greater message in his speech, that if we do not accept his particular views on this legislation, then we are not truly Canadian. That is something that this party will never accept."

Harper then sought to gain political advantage from the Supreme Court's refusal to say whether the traditional definition of marriage was constitutional. He cited the court's judgment in the *Egan* case, in 1995, when Justice Gérard La Forest wrote that "marriage is by nature heterosexual." This statement "remains the only commentary on the fundamental definition of marriage in any Supreme Court decision," Harper said: "On this side, we do not believe that merely on the basis of lower court decisions, upheld only because the government refused to appeal them, a fundamental social institution must be abolished or irretrievably altered." He went so far as to accuse the prime minister of wanting to legalize same-sex marriage out of a "blind, ideological interpretation of the Charter."

Harper gave a detailed exposition of the danger that he believed recognition of same-sex marriage represented for religious authorities.

For the Opposition Leader, this was a point of honour: "What churches, temples, synagogues and mosques fear today is not immediately the future threat of forced solemnization, but dozens of other threats to religious freedom, some of which have already begun to arrive and some of which will arrive more quickly in the wake of this bill." He quoted an article by a Catholic priest, Raymond de Souza, that appeared in the religious journal *First Things*:

> That is the worst-case scenario of state expansion. But state expansion will likely pass other milestones on its way there, eroding religious liberty on questions related to marriage. First it will be churches forced to rent out their halls and basements for a same-sex couple's wedding reception. Then it will be religious charities forced to recognize employees in same-sex relationships as legally married. Then it will be religious schools not being allowed to fire a teacher in a same-sex marriage. Then it will be a hierarchical or synodal church not being allowed to discipline an errant priest or minister who performs a civilly legal but canonically illicit same-sex marriage.

Then, referring to Liberal cabinet minister Pierre Pettigrew's ill-considered remark that religious institutions should stay out of the marriage debate, Harper said, "This may only be the beginning of a chilling effect on religious freedom for those groups and individuals who continue not to believe in same-sex marriage."

Harper used his speech to lay out supporting arguments for his theory that it was not necessary to use the notwithstanding clause to stop same-sex marriage: "There are several precedents of Parliament passing statutes without using the notwithstanding clause to reverse decisions made by the courts including the Supreme Court under common law and the courts have accepted these exercises of parliamentary sovereignty." He noted that judges typically showed greater deference to laws passed by Parliament than to common-law jurisprudence. The court judgments on same-sex marriage represented a modification of the common-law definition of 1866. The Conservatives were gambling that if Parliament itself passed a law restricting marriage to heterosexuals, the courts would be less inclined to overturn it.

As an example, Harper mentioned Bill C-72, which Parliament passed in 1995 to reverse the Supreme Court's *Daviault* decision allowing extreme intoxication as a criminal defence. He also noted that in 1996 Parliament passed Bill C-46, reversing the Supreme Court's decision in *O'Connor*, which allowed the accused to have access to medical records of the victims in sexual assault cases. In a subsequent decision on this matter, the Supreme Court justices wrote:

> It does not follow from the fact that a law passed by Parliament differs from a regime envisaged by the Court in the absence of a statutory scheme, that Parliament's law is unconstitutional. Parliament may build on the Court's decision, and develop a different scheme as long as it remains constitutional. Just as Parliament must respect the Court's rulings, so the Court must respect Parliament's [decision] ... To insist on slavish conformity would belie the mutual respect that underpins the relationship between the courts and legislature that is so essential to our constitutional democracy.

"We have every reason to believe," Harper said, "that the Supreme Court, if it were eventually asked to rule on a new statutory definition of marriage combined with full and equal recognition of legal rights and benefits for same-sex couples, might well choose to act in a much more deferential manner toward the Canadian Parliament than lower courts showed toward ancient, British-made, common-law definitions." However, he neglected to mention the Quebec Court of Appeal's marriage decision, which had indeed invalidated a measure passed by Parliament, the Federal Law-Civil Law Harmonization Act, No. 1.

Then the Conservative leader turned to a demonstration of why opening marriage to gays and lesbians did not constitute a fundamental right. The government's attempt to present it as such a right was an "erroneous opinion and a totally specious argument," Harper said:

The Prime Minister cannot through grand rhetoric turn his political decision to change the definition of marriage into a basic human right, because it is not. It is simply a political judgment. It is a valid political option if one wants to argue for it; it is a mistaken one in my view, but it is only a political judgment. Same-sex marriage is not a human right. This is not my personal opinion. It is not the opinion of some legal adviser. This reality has already been recognized by such international bodies as the United Nations Commission on Human Rights.

Harper had done his homework. In 2002 the UN Human Rights Committee rejected a complaint in which it was asked to rule that New Zealand was in violation of the International Covenant on Civil and Political Rights because it refused to recognize same-sex marriage. "If same-sex marriage were a fundamental right," Harper said, "then countries as diverse as the United Kingdom, France, Denmark and Sweden are human rights violators. These countries, largely under left-wing governments, have upheld the traditional definition of marriage while bringing in equal rights and benefits regimes for same-sex couples, precisely the policy that I and the majority of the Conservative caucus propose."

Harper noted that the only other countries that had legalized same-sex marriage, the Netherlands and Belgium, had done so following political decisions and not judicial ones: "In other words, no national or international court, or human rights tribunal at the national or international level, has ever ruled that same-sex marriage is a human right."

He even reprimanded the Liberal Party for legalizing same-sex marriage while it "puts its business interests ahead of the cause of democracy and human rights in places like China." He charged that it was, after all, "the Liberal Party that said none is too many when it came to Jews fleeing from Hitler," that "interned Japanese Canadians in camps on Canada's west coast" and that "imposed the War Measures Act" during the October Crisis.

The Conservative leader concluded his nearly hour-long speech by linking multiculturalism with opposition to same-sex marriage. This argument had been criticized — even by some of his own MPs — when he had first made it some ten days earlier. "New Canadians know that their cultural values are likely to come under attack if this law is passed," Harper said in the House. " ... The Liberals may blather about protecting cultural minorities, but the fact is that undermining the traditional definition of marriage is an assault on multiculturalism."

This was an attempt to gain support from cultural-minority communities, which had long been Liberal bastions. However, a chorus of denunciations from ethnic communities began the next day. A typical statement came from Kristyn Wong-Tam, spokesperson for the Chinese Canadian National Council: "We want to say very clearly to Stephen Harper that he's wrong. In addition, we want him to know that it is condescending and insulting to us to imply, in the House of Commons, that ethnic minorities are monolithic in their opposition to the extension of civil marriage to gays and lesbians."

Tarek Fatah of the Muslim Canadian Congress accused Harper of "sectarianism":

> This bill does not involve religion but fundamental and universal human rights. These rights are a guarantee that all Canadians, whatever their ethnicity or religion, can feel that they are part of the same family. As a minority group it is incumbent on us to show solidarity with gays and lesbians in Canada even though many in our community believe that our religion does not tolerate homosexuality.

However, a larger Islamic group, the Canadian Islamic Congress led by Mohamed Elmasry, after initially supporting the government's initiative, changed its position and campaigned to have the government withdraw Bill C-38.

In a statement by its executive director, Anne Lowthian, the World Sikh Organization appealed to respect for the Charter of Rights:

> Extending the same civil rights and freedoms to those with

whom you disagree is not only the cornerstone of Sikhism; it is the foundation of democracy in Canada. Sending homosexuals to the back of the bus in Canada is wrong; it sends the wrong message to our fellow Canadians, it sends the wrong message to our international partners with whom we hope to trade. Whether we like it or not, refusing homosexuals equality in all aspects of Canadian society can only be viewed as wilful ignorance of the lessons of our own rich and diverse history.

Finally, the National Association of Japanese Canadians expressed indignation at Harper's attempt to link same-sex marriage with the treatment of Japanese Canadians during the Second World War. "Mr. Harper is resorting to cheap political shots at deceased politicians rather than facing the inconsistency of his position on human rights," said spokesperson Audrey Kobayashi.

* * * * *

Bloc Québécois leader Gilles Duceppe's speech, which followed Harper's, provoked less furor. "When a man or a woman realizes that he or she is a homosexual and faces discrimination, rejection and denial of rights, they suffer," he said:

> This can end in tragedy, driving some to suicide. One thing is certain: as long as the love shared by same-sex partners is not recognized as something totally normal and acceptable, this suffering will continue. Parliamentarians alone cannot eliminate this suffering, but we can certainly send a very strong signal, here in Canada and around the world, by passing this bill. In doing so, we will help alleviate human suffering. We will add a block to the democratic building which is slowly but surely being built year after year. We will help make our societies more just.

Duceppe repeated the seductive slogan initially used by Bloc MP

Richard Marceau: "The religion of some should not become the law for others." At the end of his speech, the Bloc leader tried to put things in perspective:

> To vote in favour of this bill is to embrace the progress that has been made in basic, universal rights. That is what we must do in all good conscience ... Of course some people will not be happy. But while this may go against their beliefs, they will not lose any rights. They will lose nothing but their illusions.

NDP MP Bill Siksay gave the final speech in this initial round of the Commons debate on Bill C-38. He replied to those who argued that expanding the definition of marriage to include gays and lesbians constituted a change that was incompatible with the role of marriage as an institution. The bill, he said, "does not fiddle with the ideals of marriage, the responsibilities of marriage, the obligations of marriage." Siksay also pointed out that without the support of the Bloc and the NDP, the Liberals hadn't a hope of passing the bill.

Towards the end of the debate, Bloc MP Gérard Asselin rose to say, "In 100 years, will we have to vote in this House to allow a mother to marry her son, a father to marry his daughter, a daughter to marry her brother?" Bloc strategists were visibly embarrassed by this comment, reminiscent of the remarks made a year and a half earlier by the Archbishop of Montreal, Cardinal Jean-Claude Turcotte — especially since the Bloc had repeatedly boasted about its avant-garde position on gay rights.

In the weeks that followed, many other MPs — almost 200 in all — spoke on the subject. Most of them opposed same-sex marriage. While lively at times, the debate contained few arguments that had not already been heard — perhaps because Stephen Harper had ordered all members of his caucus to submit their speeches to his office beforehand to ensure he maintained control. In a sense, this tactic worked: the speech that caused the most controversy was his own!

* * * * *

The close of proceedings before the Supreme Court in December 2004 gave new impetus to opponents of same-sex marriage, who quickly mounted energetic campaigns to gain support among the general public, and especially among federal MPs.

"Media tend to favour the perceived underdog," noted Janet Epp Buckingham of the Evangelical Fellowship of Canada. "And the media shape the public's perception. After the Supreme Court's opinion, we were glad to see the media talking more about preserving freedom of religion and the impact of gay marriage on the clergy. We felt that we could still make a difference."

MPs' offices were soon inundated with mail. In two months, Prime Minister Martin's office received no fewer than 22,000 letters and 26,000 emails, most of them generated by six separate offensives mounted by organizations opposed to redefining marriage. Hence a large majority of the messages were form letters, but some were handwritten messages with highly personal content. The Prime Minister's Office also received a large number of phone calls: about a thousand in December and January. About 90 percent of the writers and callers opposed the legalization of same-sex marriage. Epp Buckingham commented,

> We expected there to be a bit of fatigue but, rather, I'm finding there's new energy. People have been waiting for this moment. This has been in the courts for so long, and there was no forum. People feel their letter to their MP matters more because we're in a minority Parliament.

In terms of volume of letters and phone calls, this period was comparable to the weeks before the launch of the war in Iraq in 2003 or the time when Bill C-23, granting recognition to same-sex common-law partnerships, was passed in 2000. Following standard practice, staff members in Martin's office replied to messages with return addresses, explaining the government's position.

Both sides were preparing for the final battle. They collected money, planned demonstrations, refined their lobbying techniques. Each side, of course, suspected that the other was better organized and better financed. Each side boosted morale by maintaining that the people were behind them.

"We're the underdogs in terms of resources; they're the underdogs in terms of arguments," quipped Alex Munter of Canadians for Equal Marriage. "We think we have the support of the majority of Canadians," replied Derek Rogusky of the U.S.-based organization Focus on the Family.

One thing is certain: there were more organizations fighting against same-sex marriage. In addition to Focus on the Family, which was very active in the debate, there was the Defend Marriage Coalition, made up of the Canada Family Action Coalition, Real Women, the Campaign Life Coalition and the Catholic Civil Rights League. One secular pressure group, Enshrine Marriage Canada, even undertook to promote a constitutional amendment defining marriage as the union of a man and a woman.

In February 2005, the Montreal *Gazette* revealed that some of the organizations fighting same-sex marriage were being financed partly from the United States. The American headquarters of the Knights of Columbus, for example, had spent more than C$80,000 to print two million postcards distributed in Canadian churches. "Whatever it takes," commented Patrick Korten, Vice President for Communications of the Catholic men's group based in New Haven, Connecticut. "The family is too important."

Focus on the Family Canada benefits from at least $300,000 worth of services provided by its American parent every year. The organization's total annual budget is substantial — about $9 million — so that the American contribution does not appear to be decisive. In 2004 the organization spent at least $800,000 on advertising, primarily on the subject of marriage, and it mounted a similar effort in 2005. The marriage campaign included messages recorded by the founder of Focus on the Family, Dr. James Dobson, which were broadcast on some 130 Canadian radio stations. Expenditures of this sort are legal, since charitable organizations have the right to devote up to 10 percent of their resources to political activities. "We're funded by Canadians," Rogusky assured the Toronto *Star*. "It is not as though there is money flowing in from the U.S."

Nevertheless, Justice Minister Irwin Cotler was concerned by this development. "Clearly, we have free speech, but at the same time we want to protect the political equities in terms of the marketplace of ideas," he said in his characteristic style. "In other words, we don't want the public opinion to get mortgaged to the highest bidder in a certain sense."

By contrast, Canadians for Equal Marriage was able to raise only $90,000 between mid-December 2004 and mid-March 2005. It used the timeworn strategy of sending soliciting letters to members of Egale and others who were likely to support the cause. "Why did I drop everything to become National Coordinator of Canadians for Equal Marriage?" wrote Alex Munter in the letter. "Isn't equal marriage a done deal? Unfortunately, the answer is no." The letter emphasized the urgency of the campaign:

> Equal marriage must not fail. Please give today to ensure that equal marriage will become a reality everywhere in the country. It has taken us decades to get this far. But we're not finished yet — this isn't the time to be complacent.

However, some philanthropists did come to the aid of the pro–same-sex marriage coalition. The Public Service Alliance, the union representing civil servants, lent the group office space in Ottawa. Three commercials that drew a link between opposition to same-sex marriage and racial segregation in the United States were shown on PrideVision TV for several months. The commercials were created by a patron of gay and lesbian causes, David Moore, executive vice president and general manager of Leo Burnett Canada. They showed an escalator reserved for heterosexuals beside a staircase for gays and lesbians, a taxi with "straights only" written on the window, telephone booths segregated by sexual orientation and a bus shelter with a sign reading "No gays." At the end a call to reflection appeared on the screen: "If this is wrong, why is it right when it comes to marriage? Help us win the civil rights battle of our time."

Then, in early February 2005, Famous Players movie theatres began showing a promotional message suggesting that the meaning of "I do" doesn't change with sexual orientation. Moviegoers were invited to tell their MPs that they "support the Canadian Charter of Rights and Freedoms." The initiative was a gift from the president of Famous Players Media, Salah Bachir, one of the leaders of Toronto's gay community. The Canada Family Action Coalition did not appreciate it.

"For unsuspecting families who are accosted by same-sex marriage promotion, when all they're doing is going to see a movie, is unconscionable," said Charles McVety, president of the coalition as well as of Canada Christian College. Assuming it was a free promotion, presented by Famous Players, he demanded the same treatment for opponents of same-sex marriage. It turned out Bachir had paid for the message himself, and the company refused McVety's request. In response, McVety called for a boycott of the company's 79 theatres in Canada. Laurie Arron of Canadians for Equal Marriage was not surprised at the coalition's actions: "They're against equality; they're against freedom of religion [of churches who support same-sex marriage], and now they're going after another Canadian Charter right — freedom of expression."

Inoffensive as the promotional messages were, they caused too much controversy and Famous Players put an end to them. On February 20, less than a month after they were first shown, the company pulled the plug on the messages — and on any future "issue-driven" advertising. "We were starting to get emails that were threatening to our staff," explained Nuria Bronfman, vice-president of corporate affairs at Famous Players. "The phone calls were starting to get abusive." Bachir himself had received death threats. "So we thought it's not fair for our staff to have to go through that sort of thing," Bronfman noted. Not satisfied with this victory, however, the Canadian Family Action Coalition promised to continue the boycott until Famous Players agreed to present anti–same-sex marriage promotional messages.

* * * * *

Branded as intolerant during the 2004 election campaign, the Conservatives tried to soften their image. A key venue for this change was to be the party's policy convention in Montreal in March 2005, its first since it was formed out of the merger of the Canadian Alliance and the old Progressive Conservatives. Stephen Harper made it clear that he wanted party members to adopt resolutions in favour of official bilingualism and against any change in the way abortion is practised in Canada. These wishes were granted without too much difficulty.

It remained to be seen whether the rebranding of the party would go so far as to include same-sex marriage. A handful of Conservatives who favoured change, including Chris Reynolds, son of MP John Reynolds, tried to put pressure on their colleagues. During the debate Belinda Stronach, the high-profile MP who was one of the few Conservatives in favour of same-sex marriage, pleaded for the change on strategic grounds. "We want to form the government, so I think that to get there … we need to be inclusive," said Stronach, who became a Liberal minister less than two months later.

These efforts had little effect on the final result. Nearly 75 percent of the delegates voted for the resolution declaring Conservative support for "legislation defining marriage as the union of one man and one woman." A majority of delegates from every province voted in favour of the motion. Supporters of same-sex marriage were philosophical. "We will not abandon the party," noted Gary Mitchell, a British Columbia delegate. "We will keep up the battle from within."

Ten days earlier, Liberal activists had rallied behind the same-sex marriage bill, adopting a resolution supporting the bill by a wide margin. One Quebec delegate tried to link homosexuality to pedophilia, but it was the Young Liberals who stole the show with their provocative badges bearing the slogan "It's the Charter, stupid!"

* * * * *

Meanwhile, opponents of same-sex marriage saw the moment of truth rapidly approaching and stepped up the volume of petitions against changing the law. Over a period of months, MPs presented hundreds of such petitions — an average of five each day the House was sitting. The government replied to all the petitions with fairly direct statements, such as this one: "The Parliament of Canada is not called on to determine whether it should extend this right to this minority group, but rather whether it can withdraw this right, which is guaranteed by the Charter."

Opponents organized demonstrations, fundraising drives and rallies in front of MPs' offices. The largest event was a demonstration on Parliament Hill in Ottawa on April 9, 2005. Estimates of the crowd ranged from 4,000 (according to some reporters) to 15,000 (according to the organizers). Stephen Harper was there, and in the wake of the Gomery Inquiry's revelations about the sponsorship program, he linked the scandal to the redefinition of marriage: "Corruption is not a Canadian value. [Heterosexual] marriage is a real Canadian value." Archbishop Marcel Gervais of Ottawa was even more brutal: "Homosexuality is a private reality and cannot be the foundation of a social tie. Our government wants to make sodomy part of the norm, and we reject it."

Thousands of people opposing same-sex marriage demonstrate against Bill C-38 on Parliament Hill in Ottawa on Saturday, April 9, 2005. "Homosexuality is a private reality and cannot be the foundation of a social tie," said the Archbishop of Ottawa, Marcel Gervais. "Our government wants to make sodomy part of the norm, and we reject it."

15

IT'S THE LAW — FINALLY

No one expected that the bill extending same-sex marriage to all of Canada would enjoy smooth sailing. It took three votes before the bill was passed in the House of Commons, instead of the usual two. Proponents of redefining marriage were at least consoled that as a result of this new detour all doubt about the majority opinion of MPs had been eliminated.

The additional vote was on a Conservative amendment introduced to delay the process. The amendment sought to prevent second reading of Bill C-38 on the grounds that it "fails to define marriage as the union of one man and one woman to the exclusion of all others and fails to recognize and extend to other civil unions established under the laws of a province, the same rights, benefits and obligations as married persons."

The atmosphere in the House on April 12, 2005, the day of the vote on the Conservative amendment, was highly charged. It would be the first vote on same-sex marriage since the House defeated the Canadian Alliance motion of September 2003 and, more pertinently, the first one that would have some impact on how things played out. It would show where the MPs stood, including the new ones elected in June 2004.

The suspense was considerably reduced by the efforts of Clayton Chrusch, an Ontario computer science student who maintained an exhaustive website containing statements on marriage by federal MPs.

Thanks to his website (marriagevote.ca), it was known well in advance of the vote that 163 members were in favour of the bill, while 136 were opposed. This tally was extremely close to the actual result, which was that the amendment was defeated by 164 votes to 132. No fewer than 34 Liberals voted against the government's position. Three Bloc Québécois members (Gérard Asselin, Serge Cardin and Roger Gaudet) bucked their party's stand, while New Democrat Bev Desjarlais had to limit herself to an abstention, since party leader Jack Layton had forbidden his MPs to vote against same-sex marriage. There were no surprises in the Conservative caucus: 95 of the 99 MPs voted for the amendment.

"This has been a difficult subject for many, but I believe that Canada passed a very important test today," Prime Minister Martin said outside the Commons after the vote. Jack Layton spoke in similar terms: "Today is a day to celebrate, because it's the first time that Parliament has expressed itself this clearly in favour of gays and lesbians and human rights." Opponents of same-sex marriage acknowledged their defeat. MP Pat O'Brien said later,

> There is no question the gay lobby is very well organized. It's very well financed. It's very aggressive. They seized the agenda early on. Let me put it this way: on this issue, the Canadians who disagree with this change were too slow to wake up. They finally spoke out with great force, but they should have done that a year, two years ago, when this all started. It was only with the court rulings that people got a slap in the face. They realized, "Hey, this is actually probably going to happen in this country: they're going to change the definition of marriage." The barn was already burning with at least half the horses still in the barn. So it would have been better if people had woken up to this sooner, but it's difficult to get people to see something until it's pretty much too late. But it's what made the fight much more difficult for us. It was like a hockey game: it's far better to play three good periods than to wake up in the third period to find out you're behind three goals.

The pro–same-sex marriage side had won a real victory, but by no means a definitive one. The fragility of its success became all too clear in early April when Canadians learned that advertising executive Jean Brault had delivered a political bombshell with his testimony before the Gomery Inquiry into the sponsorship scandal. They heard about cash-filled envelopes from companies that had received federal sponsorship contracts finding their way illicitly to Liberal Party of Canada coffers. In the coming weeks, other witnesses would corroborate Brault's testimony. Liberal popularity plummeted, and the Conservatives and the Bloc Québécois quickly began to develop a strategy to defeat the government.

Spring election scenarios proliferated, sending fear into the hearts of those who hoped that the legalization of same-sex marriage would be wrapped up before the summer. With the Conservatives dangerously close to first place in voting intentions, political commentators confidently predicted that the bill would simply die. "It's a fear that plagues me," acknowledged Bloc MP Richard Marceau. "I would like to pass the bill as quickly as possible so that gays and lesbians everywhere in Canada have the right to marry on an equal basis with everyone else." Marceau's apprehension was well founded: Conservative MP Vic Toews welcomed the prospect of an election campaign, and not only because of the Gomery effect. "The vote [on marriage] is important," he said, "because it allows people to determine MPs' position, so that the voters can take care of them."

Canadians for Equal Marriage were aware of this danger. On the day of the vote on the Conservative amendment, they published the results of a poll showing that 76 percent of Canadians wanted to see a quick resolution to the debate on Bill C-38. Even Conservative supporters agreed: 75 percent desired a prompt end to the debate.

On the other hand, for the fiercely anti–same-sex marriage Ontario Liberal MP Pat O'Brien, things were going too fast. The MP for London–Fanshawe took advantage of the minority government's vulnerability to try to obtain concessions from Paul Martin. He threatened to quit the Liberal caucus, knowing full well that his threat would force the prime minister to meet with him to hear his complaints. After his audience, O'Brien said he had obtained Martin's "personal" assurance that the committee studying the civil marriage bill would hold "public hearings." It was a rather odd commitment: the MPs had already decided to put same-sex marriage under the microscope yet again by hearing from dozens of witnesses — many of whom had testified two years earlier.

As an illustration of the government's confusion at this stage, even Justice Minister Irwin Cotler admitted that he had "no idea" about the promise Martin had made to his recalcitrant caucus member. Faced with a confidence vote in which they could well be defeated, however, the Liberals did not want to take any chances. They had just lost Alberta MP David Kilgour, who had left the caucus because of the sponsorship scandal and because of same-sex marriage. Some personal attention from the most powerful person in the country was enough to convince Pat O'Brien not to drop Paul Martin — at least not right away.

* * * * *

As the government tottered through its crisis of legitimacy, the instigator of the sponsorship program, Jean Chrétien, went to Philadelphia to receive the International Role Model Award from Equality Forum, an American organization promoting gay and lesbian rights. The year before this same award had gone to Chrétien's minister of justice, Martin Cauchon. Even though he was never comfortable discussing same-sex marriage in public, in a speech before a queer audience Chrétien had no qualms about taking credit for his decision not to appeal the June 2003 Ontario Court of Appeal decision:

> This award acknowledges the progress we have made in Canada in the name of equality and in the name of respect for the relationships of gay and lesbian couples. Same-sex marriages are now a reality in Canada and I don't think there will be any turning back. [The debate] is not completely over but the direction is clear. It was not a matter to be settled by

polling or trying to be popular. This issue was about rights and respect. I prefer to live in a world where rights are expanding, rather than one where rights are contracting.

* * * * *

Back in Ottawa, the grip of political uncertainty was stronger than ever, and Bill C-38 had still not passed second reading. This vote, which amounted to official approval in principle of same-sex marriage, finally took place on May 4, 2005. Although it was an important moment, the vote on the Conservative amendment three weeks earlier had eliminated any suspense surrounding it. The result was very similar: 163 MPs in favour and 138 against. Thirty-five Liberals voted No, one more than on April 12. This was the first time the Commons had taken a stand on a positive motion favouring the redefinition of marriage: the three previous votes (in June 1999, September 2003 and April 2005) had all been on motions aimed at maintaining the traditional definition.

The only surprise came from the ranks of the Bloc Québécois. Instead of three or four Bloc MPs voting against Bill C-38, there were seven: the three who had supported the Conservative amendment plus Robert Bouchard, Odina Desrochers, Gilles-A. Perron and Louise Thibault. Gilles Duceppe's strategy of not putting undue pressure on his caucus in the hope that they would all come around to his position had failed miserably. Nevertheless, 87 percent of Bloc MPs had voted in favour of same-sex marriage, allowing Duceppe to have some fun at the Liberals' expense by pointing out the irony that it was thanks to support from the "wicked separatists" that the bill had survived.

The Martin government had won its bet on same-sex marriage, but it now faced a challenge that, at least in the short term, was even more critical: a confidence vote whose outcome was uncertain. After weeks of shocking Gomery Commission revelations, Conservative delay and Liberal manoeuvres, May 19 was established as the deciding date. In the meantime, the government had concluded a $4.6-billion budget deal with the New Democrats to gain their support for a few months. And Conservative MP Belinda Stronach had stunned the country by leaving the Conservative caucus — and her lover Peter MacKay — to become a Liberal cabinet minister. Her defection markedly improved Martin's chances of holding on to power.

Faced with this all-out Liberal effort to stay in power, the Conservatives tried to neutralize Stronach's departure by using same-sex marriage to bring MPs over to their side. In the hours preceding the crucial confidence vote, Conservatives contacted many of the 35 Liberal MPs opposed to Bill C-38. Their message was not a subtle one: help defeat your own government by abstaining or voting No on the budget measures and the redefinition of marriage will die on the order paper.

One of the Conservative targets was, of course, Pat O'Brien. "It started at eight o'clock in the morning in my condo," O'Brien told the *Toronto Star*. "And I had three phone calls, two little sit-down visits and two notes. So they tried me pretty hard." In all, seven Conservative MPs contacted O'Brien the day of the fateful vote. The Conservative director of communications, Geoff Norquay, did not deny that these kinds of attempted seductions were going on. "I suspect it may have happened on an MP-to-MP basis," he explained. "That's how this town works. People ride the buses on Parliament Hill together; they go to dinner with people ... The difference is we don't have the types of things to offer that the Prime Minister's chief of staff has." The Conservatives' efforts were in vain: no Liberal MP abandoned the party because of same-sex marriage, with the exception of David Kilgour, who had left the Liberal caucus a month earlier.

Just after 6 p.m. on May 19, tension was high in the House of Commons when independent MP Chuck Cadman stood up to vote with the Liberals, thereby confirming their survival. The Conservatives and the Bloc had failed in their attempt to defeat the government and precipitate an election. Pro–same-sex marriage activists were visibly relieved: they had taken for granted that this Parliament was effectively finished, but now there was once again a real chance of passing Bill C-38 before the summer.

* * * * *

After it passed second reading on May 4, the civil marriage bill was sent to a legislative committee for study. This was an unusual way of proceeding: typically a bill is sent to a standing committee of the House. But with many MPs growing tired of the issue, the government chose a legislative committee to speed things along, as in principle it could examine only the technical aspects of a bill. The Liberals carefully excluded all of their MPs who were opposed to same-sex marriage from membership on the committee. But the Conservatives had no intention of conceding defeat so quickly.

On May 16, only a few days before the confidence vote, Conservative MP Vic Toews manoeuvred to obstruct the committee's work. Officially, his aim was to add 22 people to the list of 41 witnesses, but his real purpose was to delay the process so that Bill C-38 would not be passed any time soon. This became clear when Toews requested that Bishop Fred Henry of Calgary appear before the committee to cast light on an improbable story. Several months earlier the media had reported allegations that a Canada Revenue Agency (CRA) official threatened Bishop Henry with cancellation of his diocese's charitable status because of his attacks on Paul Martin over abortion and same-sex marriage. In addition to Bishop Henry and the official involved, Toews also wanted to invite the prime minister's communications director, Scott Reid, to explain why he had dismissed the Bishop's allegation out of hand.

Toews's filibuster lasted two days. At one point Liberal member Françoise Boivin even accused him of "hijacking the committee." The filibuster would have continued longer had the other parties not been disposed to negotiate with the Conservatives. A compromise was reached on May 30, when MPs returned from a week's recess. Liberal, Bloc and NDP MPs agreed to hear 20 or so additional witnesses, not including Scott Reid and the CRA official. Ironically, Bishop Henry had not even asked to testify. For his part, Toews agreed to end his obstruction and follow a tight schedule aiming to send the bill back to the Commons on June 16 for a vote on third reading. Caustic observers concluded that the Conservatives, in a bad mood because of their defeat on the confidence motion, no longer had the stomach for a fight; Toews denied this interpretation. It is important to note that Liberal MP Don Boudria, with the support of the Bloc and NDP, had introduced a motion to send the bill back to the House on June 9, leaving the official Opposition with little room. "In the impasse, it was the least bad solution," was Bloc MP Richard Marceau's assessment of the situation.

Action was heating up outside the legislative committee as well. Focus on the Family launched an intense email and fax campaign aimed at MPs through a special website, Marriagematters.ca. Already drowning in mail, MPs now had to take extreme measures. Boudria informed Speaker Peter Milliken of the situation on the floor of the House on May 31:

> In the case of my office, whereby we normally receive 40 to 50 faxes from constituents in a day, we have been able to receive a grand total of five over the last two days. The rest of the time the equipment is completely blocked. A group calling itself Focus on the Family … is making it such that our telephone systems have been rendered inoperative this way.

Richard Marceau was swamped as well: "I have received more than 1,000 faxes in 36 hours. When this is done, people from the riding of Charlesbourg–Haute-Saint-Charles, who often communicate with my office in Ottawa by fax, are prevented from doing so by a group that is monopolizing an essential tool for all members of this House."

Conservative MPs played their part in the drama by rising to reply that citizens had the right to communicate with their elected members however they wished and that therefore the avalanche of messages did not constitute a violation of parliamentary privilege. If a sin had been committed, opponents of the redefinition of marriage were not the only sinners. In the days following Stephen Harper's speech in the Commons, Canadians for Equal Marriage boasted of having transmitted no fewer than a million and a half emails through its website.

Two days later, Boudria raised the matter again, complaining to the speaker of being a victim of cybersquatting. The Defend Marriage Coalition had taken advantage of his failure to renew the domain name registration for his website, www.donboudria.ca, and appropriated it. A

Web user who opened what was supposed to be the home page of the member for Glengarry–Prescott–Russell would find this message: "Can you trust Don Boudria?" A note indicated that this was not Boudria's official website, as anyone browsing the site would quickly realize from the repeated calls to action against the legalization of same-sex marriage. The Defend Marriage Coalition had been cybersquatting Liberal MPs' sites for months. (It had also taken aim directly at three ministers, John Efford, Anne McLellan and Joe Volpe, buying ads in newspapers and on television to recall their earlier objections to same-sex marriage.) Once again Conservative MPs replied that this was nothing to get excited about, since it was normal commercial practice on the Internet.

Boudria wondered about how actions of this sort fit with the values that opponents of same-sex marriage claimed to be upholding. "There is no doubt that what they're doing is extremely improper," he complained to the *Ottawa Citizen*. "What's exasperating is seeing people claim to do this in the name of religion. It's the modern equivalent of killing in the name of heaven."

Charles McVety, spokesperson for Defend Marriage and president of Canada Christian College, had no difficulty justifying such forceful tactics: "They are public figures who are representing people, many of them people of faith. We're putting forward these members' position on marriage." McVety even had the audacity to send a legal demand letter to an Ontario Liberal MP, Mark Holland, who had sent emails to his colleagues warning them against Defend Marriage's practices.

After deliberating on the flood of messages and cybersquatting practices for two days, Milliken assured the House that he considered the situation "of great concern," but concluded that it was not a breach of MPs' rights — they only had to put more paper in their fax machines.

* * * * *

While politicians and activists argued and debated, couples continued to seek to express their love publicly. According to some estimates, nearly 5,000 same-sex marriages were celebrated between June 2003 and June 2005, including nearly 1,000 involving Americans and other foreign nationals. Tourist offices were no longer shy about portraying Canada as not only a gay-friendly destination but also the ideal place to formalize a same-sex union with a minimum of delay. Vic Toews was not pleased with this development: "My concern is we're being used as the Las Vegas of the north for the gay community. This simply should not be."

But there have always been close ties between Canada and the United States. Because of the prevailing aversion to same-sex marriage south of the border (except in Massachusetts), gay and lesbian Americans who want to get married have no other option but to visit their northern neighbours, at least for the foreseeable future. Among those opting for this solution were 22-year-old Alex Ali and 30-year-old Lynn Warren, a California couple who were married in Ottawa on June 1, 2005. The wedding attracted unusual attention because Lynn and Alex were one of the most popular teams on the reality TV show *The Amazing Race 7*. The two men might have preferred to get married in their home state, but they weren't allowed to. On February 12, 2004, San Francisco mayor Gavin Newsom had decided to issue marriage licences to same-sex couples, but less than a month later the California Supreme Court annulled the 3,955 marriages that had been celebrated as a result of his decision.

The hundreds of gay and lesbian Americans who travel to Canada to get married are in themselves a demonstration of how strong a symbol marriage is. They return home with documents testifying to their pledge of mutual support, but few of them derive any benefit from these documents. The vast majority of American states do not recognize same-sex marriages. For these couples, marriage simply takes on its fundamental symbolic role as an expression of true love.

The negative attitude towards homosexuality in the United States is not always reflected on American television, which has put gays and lesbians in starring roles on some of its programs. But the first exclusively gay network, PrideVision TV, was launched in Canada, and a further step was taken when *My Fabulous Gay Wedding* began airing on the general-interest Global network on June 1, 2005. This show featured gay and lesbian weddings orchestrated by wedding professionals of all kinds.

The existence of such a show might suggest a high level of accept-ance of same-sex marriage. But the very day the show was launched, Fondation Émergence, a Montreal-based anti-homophobia organiza-tion affiliated with Gai Écoute, released the results of a poll showing that half of all Canadians considered homosexuality an "abnormal" state. Curiously, two-thirds of the respondents nevertheless said that they were "comfortable" with homosexuality. The survey also showed that two-thirds of Canadians would agree to attend a same-sex wed-ding, although only 57 percent supported the concept of same-sex marriage.

* * * * *

The parliamentary process leading to the passage of Bill C-38 was now in the homestretch. The Liberals were prepared to ask senators to cut into their vacation so that the bill could receive royal assent in July. The only two other bills given this special treatment were budget bills that the government needed to pass to maintain its deal with the NDP. "We're prepared to sit as long as we have to," said Jack Austin, the gov-ernment leader in the Senate.

This sudden haste did not win the approval of Liberals opposed to the redefinition of marriage, a dozen of whom met on the morning of Thursday, June 2, to organize their last stand. They briefly toyed with the idea of helping to defeat the government by voting against budget measures, as the Conservatives had tried to get them to do. But they quickly rejected this "bizarre concept," which would have undoubted-ly led to their expulsion from the Liberal caucus. Sooner or later, they realized, Bill C-38 would be passed. "I think we sort of concluded that delay for the sake of delay is not the best way for a win-win," said Ontario MP Tom Wappel. "Voting against the government is so ludi-crous it does not advance the issue." Indeed, some Liberal opponents of same-sex marriage had come to acknowledge that it would be better to put this divisive issue to rest. Later the same day, Wappel and Pat O'Brien met with Paul Martin to express their concerns and asked that the religious safeguards in the bill be strengthened.

However, this bargaining was not enough to keep O'Brien, probably the caucus member most resistant to the party's position on marriage, on board. On June 6, he called a press conference to announce that he was leaving the Liberal caucus and would sit as an independent. "For me, this question [same-sex marriage] is much more important than partisan politics," he said, accusing Martin of failing to keep the promises he had earlier made regarding the way the legislative committee would operate. O'Brien was so disillusioned that he was prepared to vote against the government on matters of confidence. "I will use all the possibilities at my disposal — with no exceptions — to defeat this bill," he promised.

With additional budget votes approaching, Martin feared losing more of his troops. The evening of O'Brien's departure, he took it upon himself to meet with the dissidents once again. Justice Minister Cotler also attended the meeting. He made no promises except to examine carefully the amendments proposed by the legislative committee "to the extent that they respect the principles of the bill."

When the committee conducted its clause-by-clause examination of the bill a week later, most of the amendments moved by the Conservatives clearly did not respect those principles. One amendment would have ended same-sex marriages in any province or territory "that has not enacted legislation to protect the freedom of individuals and religious and other groups in respect of their beliefs, practices and advocacy relating to the definition of marriage." No legislation with that degree of precision existed anywhere in Canada. In other words, the proposal was clearly just a delaying tactic.

Along the same lines, another amendment proposed by the Conservatives would have forced the government to allocate $10 million annually to a fund assisting religious groups "in the payment of legal and other expenses arising out of their involvement in public debate in respect of the definition of marriage." Rightly or wrongly, opponents of same-sex marriage feared — and continue to fear — that religious institutions would be the targets of innumerable lawsuits because of their position on the issue. They were especially frustrated because Egale and the Hendricks-LeBœuf couple had received tens of thousands of dollars from the Court Challenges Program of Canada (and considerably more in reimbursed fees) to finance a portion of their initiatives. The opponents did not have the same privilege.

None of the Conservative amendments was passed. The only amendment that received unanimous approval was initially conceived by Richard Marceau of the Bloc and then moved by Ontario Liberal MP Paul Harold Macklin. It stipulated that "no person or organization shall be deprived of any benefit, or be subject to any obligation or sanction, under any law of the Parliament of Canada" solely for having spoken out against same-sex marriage. In answer to criticisms that he was caving in, Marceau said, "Some people were afraid of losing their charitable status. If this amendment could calm their fears and stop them from playing the martyr, then it was worth the trouble."

Once the bill had passed the legislative committee stage, all that was left was a final debate in the House and then the decisive vote on third reading. The end of the session was approaching, but the government had promised that the same-sex marriage and budget bills would be approved before the summer recess. The Conservatives were well aware that the Liberals were committed first and foremost to the two budget bills, C-43 (implementing the 2005 budget) and C-48 (implementing the $4.6-billion deal with the NDP). They tried to persuade the government to drop same-sex marriage, at least for a few months, in exchange for their tacit support for Bill C-48 — despite their fierce opposition to that bill.

In the preceding weeks, the Conservatives had launched an all-out attack on Bill C-48, even arguing that it would plunge the federal government back into the deficit era. This was clearly a less frightening prospect for the Conservatives than extending same-sex marriage to the three provinces and two territories where it was not already legal. But the most disturbing part of this story is that the Liberals agreed to negotiate with their sworn enemies. Paul Martin even tried to use the Conservative manoeuvres to wriggle out of his commitment to wrap up Bill C-38 before the summer recess. "There is no guarantee in a minority Parliament," he said after a cabinet meeting. "Really, that is in the hands of the opposition ... If the opposition continues to filibuster, then that is in their hands."

This hesitation was the public expression of an argument that had been bubbling under the surface in the Martin cabinet. Speaking anonymously, one minister told the story:

> A few weeks before the bill was passed in the Commons, [Natural Resources Minister] John Efford came back to this topic during a meeting, repeating that same-sex marriage would cause problems for the Liberals in rural ridings. Scott Brison [the minister of public works, who is openly gay] answered him: "I represent a rural riding in Nova Scotia that has been Conservative since Confederation. It's not a question of being rural."

The wisdom of proceeding quickly was being questioned in the Prime Minister's Office as well. According to an informed source,

> There were people like Tim Murphy [Paul Martin's chief of staff] who said, "Let's let it go; it's not worth risking our life for." Others argued that we did need to risk our life for it, because otherwise we would pay the price later, for having dragged our feet. At the end, the problem wasn't the principle of gay marriage. It was determining the opportune moment to bring it to a conclusion.

Ironically, there was no serious risk to the government, since it was not a confidence vote.

The Martin government eventually got its nerve back and agreed to extend the session of the House to ensure the passage of bills C-48 and C-38. However, to make this happen, the Liberals needed the support of the Bloc Québécois, since the Conservatives — and 14 Liberals — had no inclination to work overtime for the sake of same-sex marriage, and there were not enough New Democrats to provide useful support. It was a curious reversal: the Liberals went to the Bloc, which had tried to defeat them a month earlier, to gain the passage of a bill that had far from unanimous support in their own ranks.

Bloc House Leader Michel Gauthier was suspicious and demanded a written promise from his Liberal counterpart, Tony Valeri. "When it comes to the Liberals, I'll tell you one thing: I believe only what's written and signed," Gauthier joked. Valeri wavered for a day before making up his mind to scribble "Michel, Yes absolutely" and put his signature on Gauthier's letter requesting "that Bill C-38 be voted on at all stages" before the House adjourned for the summer. It was the first time since the intense debates on free trade with the United States in 1988 that MPs had cut short their vacation. To demonstrate its good faith, the government even suggested the possibility of asking House Speaker Milliken to extend the parliamentary session through an extraordinary procedure reserved for national emergencies.

On June 23, the day the motion to extend the session was passed, gays and lesbians in yet another province won the right to marry. In New Brunswick, four couples had asked the Court of Queen's Bench to bring them "into the twenty-first century." For several months, the couples had said they were prepared to wait for the House of Commons to pass Bill C-38. However, with the delays in Parliament, they had resigned themselves to going through the courts.

Same-sex marriage continued to deepen its roots in the country. A few days earlier, it had been learned that the first same-sex wedding in the history of the Canadian Forces had taken place on May 3 in the chapel of CFB Greenwood, in Nova Scotia. A sergeant in the medical service married a warrant officer in a ceremony conducted by a United Church minister, with about 40 friends in attendance. While it was certainly not the first wedding between gay soldiers in Canada, it was the first to take place on a military base.

CFB Greenwood's head chaplain, coincidentally named David Greenwood, said he hoped that the couple's "courageous" decision would encourage others to get married within the military, which had excluded homosexuals until 1992. "Many people thought they would never have seen something like this in their lifetimes — and not in a negative way, but in a positive way," Greenwood commented in an interview with Canadian Press. "It was something that I was very proud to be able to be involved in." The chaplain recalled that when he had entered the Forces 29 years earlier, "It was actually a reason for firing people, if they had homosexual tendencies."

The top brass at the Department of National Defence were not caught off guard. In September 2003 they had promulgated guidelines according to which military chaplains "will receive all couples who come to them — regardless of sexual orientation — with respect and dignity." A chaplain who refused to officiate at a same-sex wedding would be obliged to call in a colleague "who will be able to respond in some way." This was in sharp contrast to the "Don't ask, don't tell" policy established by U.S. president Bill Clinton in 1993, which did not end discrimination against American gay and lesbian soldiers.

* * * * *

The day that thousands of gays and lesbians had been awaiting for years had almost come. In a little more than 24 hours, the Commons would pass Bill C-38 on third reading.

Conservative leader Stephen Harper was aware that defeat was now inevitable. A jarring statement indicated the depth of his bitterness. "Because this bill is only being passed with the support of the BQ, I think it will lack legitimacy with most Canadians," he said on June 27. "The truth is most federalist MPs will oppose this legislation."

Harper's statement may have sounded inadvertent, but he was deliberately reminding Canadians outside Quebec that the Conservatives would not abandon the struggle against same-sex marriage even after Bill C-38 was passed. Needless to say, this tactic undermined the party's efforts over the past year to win support among Quebec voters, and Harper's French-speaking advisers were opposed to it. But the Opposition Leader's anger at the "pact" the Liberals had concluded with the Bloc Québécois to extend the session was so intense that he had to turn up the volume. Harper couldn't wait to get back at the Liberals for having accused him of wanting to "get in bed with the separatists" to defeat the government in May.

Predictably, Liberal, Bloc and NDP members were quick to take advantage of Harper's gaffe. Jean Lapierre, the colourful transport minister, called the statement "totally idiotic." Jack Layton was only a little more polite: "Mr. Harper is essentially saying that Quebecers' votes don't matter — they aren't on an equal par with the rest of Canadians. So he wants to deny equality to same-sex partners, and he wants to deny equality to Quebec voters. Maybe Mr. Harper should think about why people aren't listening to him by just simply looking at what he says."

In the House, MPs gave their final speeches on same-sex marriage. Partisans of both sides repeated the same arguments that had been heard a thousand times, but with a bit more feeling than in the preceding weeks. Conservative MP Joy Smith even missed her daughter's graduation rather than pass up her chance to speak in the House.

It appeared that the final vote would be a mere formality; nevertheless, it contained one last surprise. On the morning of the fateful day, June 28, 2005, Joe Comuzzi, minister of state responsible for the Federal Economic Development Initiative for Northern Ontario, went to Paul Martin's office to tender his resignation. He preferred to return to the back benches rather than support the bill, even though he was not afraid of expanding the definition of marriage to include gays and lesbians: "I have no concerns about that [Bill C-38]. I'm just concerned about the commitment I made ... I committed myself to the people of Thunder Bay–Superior North that I would defend the standard traditional definition of marriage and today on the final vote of third reading I intend to fulfil that obligation to the people that elected me." Curiously, in the vote on second reading, the member for Thunder Bay–Superior North had had no hesitation in supporting same-sex marriage. Nonetheless, Comuzzi now took a more honourable course than those ministers who had doubts about same-sex marriage but stayed quiet to preserve their cabinet positions.

The government was all too aware of the early-summer sun shining outside. The request to its hard-working MPs to forego their summer relaxation was now wearing thin. Going back on numerous promises not to do so, the government cut off debate on Bill C-38. The final vote would take place around 9 p.m.

The Conservatives had moved yet another amendment — this one proposing that the bill be referred back to a legislative committee — and it needed to be disposed of first. It was defeated by a vote of 158 to 127, which augured well for the "real" vote, the one that would authorize the bill to be read for the third time and sent to the Senate. On this vote, proponents of same-sex marriage carried the day again, but by a slightly smaller majority: 158 to 133, or a margin of 25 votes.

As expected, about 30 Liberals — and five Bloc Québécois members — voted against the government, eliciting applause from the Conservative benches. Bev Desjarlais was the only NDP MP to defy her party's line. Jack Layton quickly punished her by moving her seat back several rows and removing her from her position as a party critic. However, circumstances were favourable to Desjarlais: Layton was in no position to lose even one of the 19 members of his caucus. Desjarlais explained her position after the vote: "You don't necessarily agree with everything within every party. I agree with probably 99.9 per cent of the policies in the New Democratic Party. I don't agree with this one and hopefully that can be accepted."

In the public galleries there was a mixed reaction. On one side a crowd made up primarily of young gays and lesbians applauded spontaneously before being asked to stop by parliamentary guards. On the other side there was silence, out of indifference or out of opposition to the bill. There was nothing like the electric atmosphere that had prevailed in the Ontario Legislative Assembly on June 9, 1994, when spectators booed MPPs after they rejected Bill 167, which would have recognized common-law same-sex unions.

Outside the House, Bloc MP Réal Ménard could not hold back his tears. "It's one of the most moving moments since I've been on the Hill," he said with a sob. "This represents the right to love. The meaning of this evening's vote is, 'Wherever you are, you have the right to love, even if you are homosexual.'"

Bloc leader Gilles Duceppe expressed considerable pride in this historic achievement. "It doesn't make me unhappy to see others happy — on the contrary!" he exclaimed. For the NDP, the legalization of same-sex marriage topped off a highly productive session. Just after the vote, they celebrated in a small room in the Parliament Buildings. "I think it will sound a clarion call around the world and perhaps reduce the hatred and the animosity and move us to a society where all are considered equal," said Jack Layton. "I think Canada is now sending out a signal that it is possible to provide full equality to people with different sexual orientations."

Of course, Paul Martin took credit for the bill's passage, but he was careful not to speak directly about gays and lesbians. Instead, he once again said that this was "about the Charter of Rights. We are a nation of minorities. And in a nation of minorities, it is important that you don't cherry-pick rights. A right is a right and that is what this vote tonight is all about."

The opponents of same-sex marriage were stunned. "It's a sad day," said Charles McVety, president of Canada Christian College:

> The great institution of marriage that has built this civilization and the foundation of our society has been defiled by our Parliament. And that is sad. It's sad for our children. It's sad for our grandchildren. It's sad for the young people. I have a seven-year-old daughter. When she comes of age to be married, will we still have marriage as we know it?

But McVety and his companions in arms were not going to let matters rest there. After all, wasn't same-sex marriage a symbol of the "moral degradation" of society, as McVety himself had indicated? He expressed the hope "that a pro-marriage Parliament will be formed after the next election so that [heterosexual] marriage will be restored."

The media quickly pronounced Canada the third country in the world to legalize same-sex marriage, but nothing becomes law in Ottawa without the approval of the Senate, which had not yet considered Bill C-38. Because of the delays in Ottawa, the third country to legalize same-sex marriage was not Canada but Spain. In April, the Spanish Congress of Deputies had approved in principle a bill opening marriage and adoption to gays and lesbians. The Senate had rejected the bill on June 22, but since the role of the Spanish Senate is purely consultative, the lower house was in a good position to revive the measure, which it did on June 30, two days after the vote in the House of Commons in Ottawa. In Madrid same-sex marriage carried by a vote of 187 to 147. The first people to take advantage of the change were Carlos Baturin German and Emilio Menendez, who got married on July 11, 2005, in a Madrid suburb.

As in the Netherlands and Belgium, recognition of same-sex marriage in Spain was the result of a political, not a judicial process. However, while in the Netherlands and Belgium the issue was relatively uncontroversial, in the country that produced Pedro Almodóvar, where 80 percent of the population is Catholic, there was an intense debate. Same-sex marriage was part of the Socialist Party platform, and when the Socialists were elected in March 2004 Prime Minister José Luis Rodriguez Zapatero worked to implement it. He saw full equality as a basic element in the "secular social revolution" the Socialists advocated. The extent of the change this represented can be seen from the fact that until 1978, three years after the death of General Franco, Spanish gays and lesbians were liable to be imprisoned or interned. Riding a wave of favourable public opinion, Rodriguez Zapatero was able to resist an intense campaign of denunciation by the Catholic Church. "Spain today is a more decent society, because a decent society does not humiliate the members that constitute it," he said after the bill was passed. He expressed confidence that his country would not be the last to redefine marriage: "It's true that [gays and lesbians] are only a minority, but their triumph is everyone's triumph, their victory makes us all better: it makes us all better." How different a tone from the one adopted by Paul Martin!

In Ottawa, senators returned to Parliament Hill after Canada Day to take their turn at examining Bill C-38. As in the Commons, the Liberals limited the length of debate on second reading, so that the senators had only one day — July 6, 2005 — to express their opinions. Either out of apathy or out of respect for decorum, their speeches generally stayed within the bounds of propriety, although one of them did raise the eternal spectre of same-sex marriage leading to the legalization of polygamy and incest. Liberal Senator Marilyn Trenholme Counsell offered a more original angle. "As a Christian, I often ask myself, what would Jesus do?" she said. "In this case, in this time, I believe he would say yes [to same-sex marriage]." Conservative senator Consiglio Di Nino responded, "Obviously, I do not have the same relationship with Jesus as does Senator Trenholme Counsell."

Liberal senator Tommy Banks was concerned about the negative impact he believed would result from gays and lesbians marrying. He was prepared to grant them all the rights associated with marriage, but without the name:

> Achieving that end by this proposed shortcut method does a disservice to our society, including, as I believe we will see some years down the road, the homosexual parts of our society. Homosexuals are proud. They are proud of the difference between them and others. This bill, if it were to become law in its present form, would require that homosexuals deny their identity, their right to distinct institutions and that there is a difference or a distinction.

His colleague Sharon Carstairs saw marriage more as a joy to be shared:

> It is based on making the very most of our talents and the encouragement of the other partner in that endeavour. It is a relationship of two soulmates who understand the heart of the other person. Honourable senators, how can I, someone who has had the glorious pleasure of 39 years of marriage, deny it to any other person? How can I do that? How can I say that two persons of the same gender have less opportunity than I have had? Honourable senators, I often wondered what I would do if one of my daughters had come to me and said, "Mom, I have chosen a partner, and that partner is of the same gender." I hope that what I would have said to her under those circumstances is, "I want you to have the same joy in your life that I have had with your father, so if that is your choice, that person will be accepted in my heart and will be loved."

The vote on second reading, which took place the same day, revealed a substantial gap between senators' point of view and that of MPs. The Senate approved the bill in principle by a vote of 43 to 12, a much wider margin than had been the case in the Commons. The bill then went to the Senate Legal and Constitutional Affairs Committee, which once again heard witnesses. There were about 30 in all, the vast majority of whom had already been heard before Commons committees and in public forums over the past three years. The star witness was Cardinal Marc Ouellet, Archbishop of Quebec and Roman Catholic Primate of Canada, who made a solemn appeal to the senators:

> As we reach the end of a political process that carries a grave risk of changing the essential nature of marriage and resulting in largely unforeseeable but assuredly negative consequences for Canadian society, we are turning to you, honourable senators, as the guardians of our country's highest interest in the hope that you will stop the adoption of this unjust law.

"It would be unfair and discriminatory to heterosexual couples, and offensive to the social order, to treat [same-sex couples] identically," he continued, adding that unions between gays and lesbians do not "fulfil the essential condition of sexual complementarity and openness to natural procreation which is characteristic of the institution of marriage."

Cardinal Ouellet noted that the church's arguments are rooted in the concept of natural law, which sees human-made rules as derived from a universal order. "The definition of marriage is based on that superior law," he said, "since God, and not the state, is the creator of human nature." Senator Serge Joyal replied that the Catholic hierarchy had resorted to natural law to attack the granting of the right to vote to women in Quebec in 1940.

This admonition did not particularly faze Cardinal Ouellet. Indeed, he found support for his theory based on natural law in the Charter of Rights, which, after all, invokes "the supremacy of God and the rule of law" in its preamble. In the course of the long debate on same-sex marriage, very few people had dared raise this point. Conservative Senator Pierre-Claude Nolin noted that even the Canadian Conference of Catholic Bishops had not invoked this argument before the Supreme Court.

Evoking a fear that numerous opponents of same-sex marriage had been noting for months, Cardinal Ouellet then expressed concern that people opposed to homosexuality were not able to speak freely, especially in schools. The Catholic Church, he reminded the senators, has "respect" for homosexuals as people while categorically condemning their "acts." He lamented that "when the state imposes a new standard affirming that homosexual behaviour is a social good, those who oppose it for religious motives or motives of conscience will be considered bigots, anti-gay and homophobes and will risk prosecution."

The coordinator of the Islamic Council of Imams–Canada, Abdul Hai Patel, made a similar point. He saw gays and lesbians as "small minorities" who were "excluding the majority by taking religion out of the schools." Janet Epp Buckingham of the Evangelical Fellowship of Canada quoted someone who "has gone so far as to say that Christians will have to inhabit the closets so recently vacated by gays."

However, the members of the Legal and Constitutional Affairs Committee did not heed the many requests by religious representatives to amend Bill C-38 by strengthening the "protection" it contained for religious groups, and they sent the bill back to the full Senate unchanged. July 19 was chosen as the date for debate on third reading. Government Leader Jack Austin was quick to threaten closure, but in the end it would be unnecessary.

This final round began with a speech by Senator Joyal. He began by noting that dictionaries were beginning to take account of the existence of same-sex marriage. Then he tried to persuade his colleagues to support Bill C-38 by going through the sad history of gays and lesbians: "This bill is about restoring the dignity of some human beings that we, as a country, as a government, have chased, humiliated, destroyed their lives and, in some cases, have pushed to suicide." One senator who was convinced by Joyal's speech was the entertainer Jean Lapointe. "In my case it is a question of humanity and minority rights," Lapointe said, although he acknowledged that he still had "some slight internal reservations."

After a full eight hours of debate, almost everyone had said what was on their mind. An amendment by Conservative senator Gerry St. Germain that would have postponed the vote on the bill by six months had been defeated. Noël Kinsella, the Conservative leader in the Senate, moved another curious amendment, which would have added a clause that Parliament "continues to recognize the traditional marriage of a man and woman" while retaining the new definition opening marriage to same-sex couples. This amendment, which Kinsella saw as a way to "heal the divisions which the bill presently causes among Canadians," was also defeated.

A little after 11 p.m., the senators agreed that the final vote would be held in 15 minutes. Since some opponents of same-sex marriage finally decided to show their hand, the vote was a little closer than it had been on second reading: 47 in favour, 21 against, 3 abstentions. Most of the senators marked this historic moment with thunderous applause. But because it was late, the celebration was a brief one.

In the end, four Liberals voted against the government, as did the independent Madeleine Plamondon. One Conservative and two senators who continued to call themselves "Progressive Conservatives" voted for the bill. Independent senator Marcel Prud'homme kept a surprise in store for the end. First he acknowledged that he did not like the bill because it could cause "a lot more problems." However, the colourful senator finally came around to supporting it, saying he was convinced that the institution of marriage would survive, although he could not resist the opportunity for a little moralizing:

> I waited, I thought, I consulted and I concluded that my conscience could sleep in peace tonight. Yes, I voted for the bill, but I left a message for young people. I said, "Respect your body. Be more respectful in your relationships. If you choose traditional marriage, be faithful to each other. If you choose another path, be faithful to one another."

And so one of the most tumultuous parliamentary sessions in the history of the Canadian federation came to an end. A session that combines a major political and financial scandal with one of the most significant moral debates of the last few decades clearly counts as exceptional.

Only one step remained for Bill C-38: royal assent. Normally it is the duty of the governor general to observe this formality, but Adrienne Clarkson was convalescing after having a pacemaker installed. Instead Chief Justice Beverley McLachlin, in her capacity as deputy governor general, signed Bill C-38 in the Supreme Court building at 4:56 p.m. on July 20, the day after it was approved by the Senate. In line with tradition, there was no ceremony. But now there was no doubt: the most controversial bill in recent memory had the force of law throughout the country.

A few short hours later, an Edmonton couple, Robert Bradford and Keenan Carley, obtained a marriage licence and so became the first people to benefit from the new law. A few days before the Senate had passed the bill, Alberta premier Ralph Klein had resigned himself to announcing that his government would comply with it. The most he promised to do was to introduce a bill that would allow anyone to refuse to perform a same-sex marriage if it went against their culture or religious beliefs. However, Klein did give vent to his frustration: "We have to obey the law of the land, and it's unfortunate that such a law would be passed."

Other opponents of same-sex marriage also expressed deep bitterness. The Campaign Life Coalition of Toronto set the tone in a press release:

> Usually, when a coup against a society is carried out, it is done under the cover of darkness, with silent forces working surreptitiously. However, the legal "redefinition" of marriage in Canada constitutes a public coup carried out in the full light of day and without any sense of shame. A cabal of parliamentarians, encouraged by activist courts and abetted by a compliant media, has foisted a new tyranny on Canadians — one that tramples on the true nature of marriage, harms families and ignores the rights of children.

The Canada Family Action Coalition was not much more restrained. "Canada is politically sick and democratically dysfunctional," the organization said, accusing the Liberal government of being "very dictatorial bordering on fascism." It made a point of distinguishing between "real marriage" and same-sex marriage, just as Cardinal Ouellet had a few days earlier when he spoke of same-sex marriage as "pseudo-marriage, a fiction, a derivative."

The Canadian Conference of Catholic Bishops (CCCB) called the fact that some Catholic politicians had supported same-sex marriage "serious and problematic." NDP MP Charlie Angus experienced the church's wrath more directly when the priest of his northern Ontario parish, John Lemire, refused him communion because of his support for same-sex marriage.

Paul Martin doesn't hide his view that the church's doctrine is too restrictive. He said in an interview,

> I'm a practising Catholic, but I've never had any difficulty making a distinction between being a legislator and being a believer. When you're a legislator in a country like Canada, where many religions and many cultures live side by side, you can't say, "I will be influenced only by my faith." That will never work. I understand very well those who find it difficult to accept the change in the definition of marriage — I had very long discussions about it with Catholics and people of other religions. I understand how difficult it is for a person to change their opinion. But fundamentally, for me, the Catholic religion is a religion of love. It's a religion that brings together, that doesn't exclude. And for me, my religion doesn't say that there are first- and second-class Catholics. Fundamentally it's a religion that loves and that says to everyone, "You must love your neighbour."

The CCCB's vice-president, Archbishop André Gaumond of Sherbrooke, admitted that the church's position has its limits: "We didn't find the knockout argument, the miracle formula for nailing our opponents to the floor. For many people the logic of the Charter is immune from attack."

Bruce J. Clemenger, president of the Evangelical Fellowship of Canada, acknowledged that religious power had been marginalized:

> The debate about the structure and nature of marriage and its religious significance prompted public discussion over the place of faith in politics and the role of the church in a plural society. Bill C-38 is symbolic of an ongoing shift in Canadians' understanding of the place and role of the church and, more generally, of religion in Canadian society.

Opponents pledged to make the redefinition of marriage a major issue in the next election campaign. The Conservative Party did not need much persuading to make the same promise. But the day Bill C-38 received royal assent, MP Vic Toews opened the possibility that the official opposition might abandon the struggle more quickly than expected. Instead of introducing a bill banning same-sex marriage, a Conservative government would only bring to a vote a motion stipulating its intention to introduce such a bill at a later time. This middle way could allow Stephen Harper's party to avoid losing face.

According to a poll conducted in early July for the Toronto *Globe and Mail* and CTV, no fewer than 55 percent of Canadians believed that the next government should leave the Civil Marriage Act as is, while 39 percent favoured a return to the previous situation. "The Liberals have been successful in defining same-sex as an issue of rights, not as a moral issue," commented Tim Woolstencroft of The Strategic Counsel, the firm that conducted the poll. A more apt summary of the debate could not be found.

CONCLUSION

The struggle for same-sex marriage has been described as the most important human rights battle of our time — an appealing suggestion, but undoubtedly an overly optimistic one. When you consider the innumerable injustices that millions of human beings on this planet suffer every day, the right of gays and lesbians to marry pales into insignificance.

And yet, every step forward that minority groups achieve has value in and of itself. Whatever one thinks of gays and lesbians' demand to participate in the age-old institution of marriage, it has resonated throughout the world. We hear frequently about the Netherlands and Belgium, the pioneers of same-sex marriage, but the movement is much broader than that. In the vast majority of Western countries, same-sex couples have begun initiatives aimed at having their unions recognized. Similar efforts have been undertaken in Russia, Latin America and Asia. However, almost all governments have flatly refused to legalize same-sex marriage. For most of the world's politicians, the idea remains both heretical and politically risky.

* * * * *

As we have seen, the movement in favour of same-sex marriage began in the United States in the early 1970s. But after decades of activism,

American gays and lesbians have obtained the right to marry only in Massachusetts — and politicians are threatening to overturn that decision later in 2006.

American states have strong constitutions that can be amended fairly easily, and this circumstance has been a significant obstacle to the recognition of same-sex marriage. No fewer than 18 states have held referendums leading to constitutional amendments that provide additional protection against any redefinition of marriage. In July 2004, an attempt was even made to amend the United States Constitution along similar lines, but the House of Representatives rejected the proposed amendment by a wide margin. Many legislators were uneasy with the idea of amending the constitution to take away rights. However, President Bill Clinton had cleared the way for such a development in 1996 by signing the Defense of Marriage Act (DOMA), aimed at restricting marriage to heterosexual couples. Since then, 41 states have passed DOMAs. Gay and lesbian activists have undertaken to challenge these measures in the courts, indicating that a long struggle lies ahead.

Canadian opponents of same-sex marriage also seek to end the practice through a constitutional amendment. Unfortunately for them, amending the Canadian constitution is such a perilous enterprise that no politician with even the slightest ambition wants to hear a word about it.

* * * * *

With a kind of immunity against the vagaries of constitutional amendments, the Charter of Rights and Freedoms has proven a highly effective tool in the struggle to legalize same-sex marriage in Canada. According to Michael Leshner of Toronto, it was "a wonderful revolution. The Charter worked brilliantly for us. It worked better for us than for the disabled, because equality for the disabled cost money, unfortunately."

There are few countries in which a minority group has been able to bring about permanent change in an institution such as marriage through the judicial system. In Canada, where the legal system was indeed used to institute such reform, the outcome is especially remark-able, considering that there was no significant mass movement in favour of same-sex marriage in the country, all of which does not detract from the significance of what the pioneers achieved in demand-ing their rights. They were able to use the legal-political system and the media to maximum advantage. "We were well connected, very power-ful, very articulate and we came at the right time," said Leshner. "We were like the Jews — I can say it because I'm Jewish."

The couples who sacrificed their private lives to carry on the struggle in the courts clearly played a fundamental role. But when you think about it, gays and lesbians would never have been able to enter the last bastion of heterosexual privilege, the institution of marriage, had it not been for the thousands of people who decided to come out to their fam-ilies and friends in recent decades. As Chris Vogel of Manitoba put it,

> The real forum of gay liberation was not Parliament or the courts or the streets: it was the living room, and the way we were successful quickly in part was because there was gays and lesbians in every family, church and community. It was the coming outs which caused gay liberation to be so successful so quickly.

The result of this increased visibility over the years was that most Canadians were no longer horrified by homosexuality. Hence, in the end, public opinion — and the judiciary — came to look favourably on the idea of legally recognizing same-sex unions, including marriage if necessary. This was no small accomplishment. One could conclude that a significant part of the population — decision-makers at least — came to define marriage in terms of a celebration of love and conjugal ties, and not in terms of procreation, even though many same-sex cou-ples do raise children. This says a great deal about how people cur-rently conceive of marriage.

Nevertheless, many Canadians are still uncomfortable talking about the nub of the question. Bloc Québécois MP Richard Marceau explained,

This was the whole dynamic of the debate: The people who were openly against gay marriage were deeply opposed and very mobilized, while those who were very much in favour were just as organized, but just as much of a minority. Most people said, "Let them get married and let them leave us alone!"

Some politicians who advanced the same-sex marriage file later confided that images of people kissing each other on the lips, repeatedly broadcast in the media, did not advance their cause. Many people were prepared to tolerate same-sex unions as long as they didn't have to see them.

Still, the couples who dragged governments before the courts never doubted that they would win some day. They just didn't imagine that, in the end, it would all happen so fast. As René LeBœuf of Montreal put it,

> From the moment when we took the first step, when we said, "Yes, we want to get married," it was already over — we knew that it would happen. It was like when Rosa Parks sat down in the front of the bus. That gesture, in itself, led to everything else that happened. When you challenge something, if you are determined enough, you will reach your goal.

Of course, the struggle required major sacrifices. Kevin Bourassa and Joe Varnell had to undergo extensive criticism, intimidation, even death threats. Bourassa remembered,

> If we could step back in time and you said, "Kevin, would you say yes to this? — you're going to have these and this and that," taking into account the positive and the negative, I would have kicked you out of my office! I would have said, "Go find someone else; you've got the wrong person." But having said this, I am so honoured and grateful we had this opportunity, and it changed our lives.

In March 2005, when he returned to the job market after three years devoted to advancing same-sex marriage, Bourassa had to settle for a lower-paying job, in addition to a loss of seniority.

Another participant who found the debate difficult at times was the cabinet minister Bill Graham. As he said himself, his personal life "was very complicated," and this left him open to all kinds of rumours about his sexuality, especially on the campaign trail and on the Internet. It was a delicate situation, for his wife and children as well as for Graham himself. But rather than shy away from controversy, he continued to express his convictions on same-sex marriage:

> Some of my supporters said to me, "Why don't you stay away from all that?" Colleagues in Parliament who had the same fears as me did very little [on the marriage issue] so that they wouldn't be exposed to controversy. But I'm in politics because I like it and because I want to do something for society. And if I run the risk of being defeated because of the positions I take, well, too bad.

Looking back later, he had no regrets:

> I'm very proud that Canada is a country where you can live your life, be in politics, serve your country, without people trying to drag you into territory that has nothing to do with what you do politically. We could have this debate in our Parliament and in our society without its ever becoming debased. At least the political class never debased itself, as would have probably happened if we had been in the United States. There, people would have been able to say whatever they wanted about other people's personal lives.

To be sure, the debate did have a whiff of intolerance and ignorance at times, as Richard Marceau indicated:

> I remember Liberal and Conservative MPs stopping me to say, "You're going to destroy Western society; the birthrate will drop if you legalize same-sex marriage." One Liberal even said

to me, "You'll turn the rest of Canada into what Quebec has
become — a society that doesn't have children any more, that
doesn't believe in marriage any more, that doesn't believe in
anything any more!"

One thing is clear: except for the vigorous intervention in the debate by
Quebec's Catholic bishops, the campaign against same-sex marriage
was carried out almost exclusively in English Canada. The weakness of
the campaign in Quebec can no doubt be explained by Quebecers' lack
of attachment to religion, and indeed to marriage itself, since the era
of the Quiet Revolution. In addition, the conservative political strain is
poorly represented in Quebec, and Quebec voters are split mainly by
the national question rather than along left-right lines.

* * * * *

Now that the dust has settled, where do things stand? For the moment,
same-sex couples can get married in almost every city, town and village
in the country, but there are few places where they are not liable to be
stared at if they hold hands. It's a curious contrast.

In an interview, Paul Martin made what may well be his most
thoughtful comment on the question. He expressed the wish that
same-sex marriage should bring lasting change to our society:
"Opening marriage to gays and lesbians should lead not only to greater
tolerance and greater acceptance of their reality, but to full recognition
of this community." He said he would be prepared, under the right circumstances, to attend a same-sex wedding.

Ottawa spent millions of dollars initially to block the redefinition
of marriage and then to promote it. But this saga has gained for
Canada some unaccustomed attention on the international scene. As
the first country to open same-sex marriage to foreign nationals,
Canada indirectly extended the debate to the four corners of the
world. Couples from the United States, Australia, Ireland, Hong
Kong and Israel, among other countries, have come to Canada to get
married in the hope that their status would be recognized by their

respective governments. As of the summer of 2005 this had not yet happened in any country, but it is clear that reflection on this issue on a global scale has only just begun.

For the same-sex couples that have exchanged vows since June 10, 2003, marriage is more than a symbol. "At the time we didn't imagine how much a piece of paper would change things — otherwise we might have wanted to fight much harder," Joe Varnell reflected. Before Joe married Kevin Bourassa, Kevin's mother saw him only as a "special friend." But, Kevin noted, "When we became married, he became the in-law." Joe commented, "The way I was perceived was very discernibly different. Now that we're married, we're the legal guardians of three children, because we're seen as the stable family union and the best atmosphere to raise children. That's quite a difference."

Joanna Radbord, the lawyer who represented same-sex couples in Ontario, also feels that her marriage to her partner has had concrete effects. "It really changed the relationship to make that kind of public commitment to each other," she said. "It changes the way other people look at your relationship; it changes the way you feel about it. Making that kind of promise to somebody is a different level of commitment." Above all, marriage has confirmed for Radbord that the life she shares with her partner as a couple is not fundamentally different from the lives of heterosexual couples: "I don't think my own part in marriage is particularly challenging. We have a child. We have a pretty stable lawyer life. Like, we're not some radical couple or anything."

Laurier LaPierre, the gay former senator, hopes that there will be many more such stories:

> Now we won't have to hide any more. This will push society to accept people as they are, and especially to love them as they are. But it will also help gays settle down. It will give them the opportunity to develop relationships that are acceptable and accepted. If gays used to chase 50 guys at the same time, it had a lot to do with the fact that they weren't accepted anywhere. That led to promiscuity. That was why marriage was created in the first place: to make men and women more settled. Hence

marriage will have a very positive impact on gays. They may continue to fool around, there will no doubt be adultery, but it will be the same as with heterosexuals. Adultery will be recognized as a sin by the gay tribe.

Of course, attitudes won't change overnight. Laurent McCutcheon of Gai Écoute recalled:

> Until very recently, society said to heterosexual couples, "You will get married and live together until death." To homosexual couples, it said, "You can't do that." They were two completely different messages. Gay marriage sends an unequivocal message, but that doesn't mean that everybody will accept it right away.

Egale lawyer Cynthia Petersen pointed to a very enlightening analogy:

> Even if it's not identical, recognition of same-sex marriage is a little like the United States Supreme Court's judgment in *Brown* v. *Board of Education* on racial segregation in 1954. That decision didn't eliminate racism. It didn't mean that black children who showed up in schools in the weeks that followed weren't harassed. And I'm sure, unfortunately, that there will continue to be homophobia, and obstacles for gays and lesbians. Of course, it will help a lot in reducing homophobia. But it won't happen overnight. Access to marriage has not ended the problems that gays and lesbians face.

Petersen would agree with me on this: if the legalization of same-sex marriage can help just one young lesbian to look to the future with hope, if it can allow one gay teenager to stop thinking about committing suicide, if it can persuade one thoughtless boy to stop making fun of "sissies," then it will have all been worth it.

EPILOGUE

While the same-sex marriage debate appeared to have been laid to rest with the passage of Bill C-38 in July 2005, it turned out to have a few more breaths in it after all. Indeed, as Stephen Harper's new Conservative government was sworn in on February 6, 2006, supporters of equal marriage saw their worst fear come true: Vic Toews took the oath as minister of justice.

Few MPs had attacked same-sex marriage more relentlessly than Toews, and now he was in the position that offered him the greatest opportunity to achieve the goal to which he had devoted years of struggle. It would be his responsibility to orchestrate the holding of a vote in the House of Commons on a motion to make marriage for gays and lesbians illegal once again.

However, the Conservatives had won only a narrow victory — demonstrating, perhaps, that not enough voters were horrified by same-sex marriage for Harper to win a majority. And so the marriage debate was reopened, but it appeared likely that this new round would be nothing more than a last gasp.

Harper had made the controversial promise to hold a free vote on the first day of the election campaign that would bring the Conservatives to power. Clearly, his objective was to make sure that the controversy died down well before election day. This objective was largely achieved, although the same-sex marriage issue did surface in the televised debates. In one of the early debates, a citizen's question forced the Conservative leader to declare that he would still love his children even if they were gay. Then, when the debates resumed after Christmas, Liberal leader Paul Martin, without referring directly to same-sex marriage, used the issue to go on the offensive against Harper. In the middle of the debate, Martin announced his intention to abolish federal use of the notwithstanding clause in the Charter of Rights. The proposal, which was not in the Liberal platform, was quickly ridiculed, but it showed how far the Liberals were prepared to go in exploiting gay and lesbian rights in their effort to stay in power.

But Martin, weighed down by the accumulation of scandals, no longer had the ear of the voters. Meanwhile, to make sure that the voters did not get sidetracked, the Conservatives had muzzled their more extremist candidates. The most striking incident in this regard involved Harold Albrecht, who would win the Ontario riding of Kitchener-Conestoga on election day. When the Conservative campaign caravan arrived in Kitchener a few days before the election, the reporters who were following Harper wanted to ask Albrecht some questions. "He's in a meeting," a Conservative official insisted, pushing a swing-door closed as Albrecht stood next to empty dish racks in a banquet-hall kitchen. The Conservative handlers' nervousness was understandable: in 2003, Harold Albrecht had said that same-sex marriage "would succeed in wiping out an entire society in just one generation."

* * * * *

Soon after taking power, Harper indicated that he would hold his free vote on marriage in the fall of 2006. But supporters of free choice in marriage could take heart in the fact that relatively few social conservative candidates had managed to get elected, and they had good reasons to be hopeful that the status quo would be maintained. Reflecting the population as a whole, a narrow majority in the new Parliament appeared to be against reopening the debate. Two surveys, one carried out by the Canadian Press and the other by the *Globe and Mail*, found 151 or 152 MPs in favour of same-sex marriage, with

between 136 and 144 opposed. Between 12 and 20 MPs were unde-
cided or wouldn't answer, so that the pendulum could swing either
way. However, since most of those MPs in the middle were moderates
in the Liberal and Bloc Québécois caucuses, chances for a majority in
favour of same-sex marriage were good.

In any case, Stephen Harper was clearly not counting on winning
this vote. He had absolutely no stomach for plunging his fragile minority government back into this divisive debate, which no longer had any
political value for his party. His promise to introduce a motion on marriage was directed at demonstrating to his supporters, once and for all,
that he was doing everything in his power to "defend traditional marriage." Moreover, even if the House of Commons reversed its previous
stand in favour of same-sex marriage, this initiative would never get
past the Senate, which in proportional terms passed Bill C-38 by a larger majority than the House. And, as a last resort, there were the courts.
Harper was both too clever a strategist and too ambitious to want to
get bogged down in this issue.

Of course, gay and lesbian activists need to remain vigilant. There
are still struggles to be won — and there is nothing in the Conservative
policy book to advance the rights of gay, lesbian and transidentified
Canadians. Even more than the previous Liberal government, Harper's
Conservatives will not agree to correct the remaining injustices until
the courts force them to do so. Minorities will always have to keep on
fighting for equality.

Montreal, February 2006

NOTES

Chapter 1

1 Hyde vs. Hyde provides the following definition: "Marriage as understood in Christendom is the voluntary union for life of one man and one woman, to the exclusion of all others."

2 For a brief description of the principal activists in the debate on same-sex marriage in Canada, see appendix 1. A chronology of key events can be found in appendix 2.

Chapter 2

1 In English Canada, as in most other Anglo-Saxon countries, the legal system is based on common law, i.e. on judicial decisions based in tradition, custom and precedent. This kind of jurisprudence complements legislation passed by elected representatives and carries the force of law. In Quebec and in many Latin countries, part of the law, particularly family law, is contained in a civil code adopted by the legislature. This creates a more limited role for judges. Canada is thus a bijuridical country where the two systems exist side by side. But since the adoption of the Canadian Charter of Rights and Freedoms, common law, the Quebec Civil Code and all other laws must conform to this constitutional document (and to provincial charters, regarded as semi-constitutional).

Chapter 3

1 The Supreme Court of British Columbia is the province's superior trial court. The highest court in British Columbia is the Court of Appeal.

2 Plato, *Symposium*, 182. Cited in John Boswell, *Same-Sex Unions in Premodern Europe* (New York: Villard Books, 1994), p. 61.

3 Martial, *Epigrams* 12:42. Cited in Boswell, *Same-Sex Unions*, p. 80.

4 Juvenal, *Satire* 2:132–35. Cited (in slightly different form) in Boswell, *Same-Sex Unions*, p. 81.

5 Theodosian Code, 9.7.3. Cited in Boswell, *Same-Sex Unions*, pp. 85–86.

6 Cited in Boswell, *Same-Sex Unions*, p. 229.

7 Cited in Boswell, *Same-Sex Unions*, p. 249.

8 Cited in Boswell, *Same-Sex Unions*, pp. 264–65.

9 Having taken the name Eleno to marry a woman, she too was burned at the stake.

10   Boswell, *Same-Sex Unions*, p. 113.

Chapter 5

1 McWhorter, Ladelle. *Bodies and Pleasures: Foucault and the Politics of Sexual Normalization*. Bloomington: Indiana University Press, 1999.

Chapter 11

1 Interestingly, in *Le Journal du Barreau*, a Quebec lawyers' publication, Justice Robert had expressed his disagreement with the immediate effect of the Ontario Court of Appeal judgment, saying that it "did not allow the Parliament of Canada any room to manoeuvre." Hendricks and LeBœuf wanted Robert to recuse himself from their case for that reason, a request Goldwater was hesitant to make. It was a further reason for the couple to dismiss Goldwater.

APPENDIX 1 — THE MAIN PLAYERS

Laurie Arron: A long-time activist in Egale, the national gay and lesbian advocacy organization, he was the first member of the organization to argue forcefully for the right to marriage for gays and lesbians. He and John Fisher were Egale's highest-profile spokespersons during the same-sex marriage debate.

Martin Cauchon: As federal minister of justice from January 2002 to December 2003, he convinced Jean Chrétien's government not to appeal the Ontario Court of Appeal's judgment, which took effect immediately. In July 2003, he introduced the draft bill to legalize same-sex marriage.

Douglas Elliott: A Toronto lawyer with Roy Elliott Kim O'Connor, he acted in numerous cases involving gay and lesbian rights. He represented the Metropolitan Community Church of Toronto in its challenge to the traditional definition of marriage in Ontario.

Michael Hendricks and René LeBœuf: They initiated the judicial proceedings that led to the legalization of same-sex marriage in Quebec in March 2004. They had lived as a couple since January 1, 1973.

Richard Marceau: A Bloc Québécois MP first elected in 1997, he was the party's justice critic. Using legal arguments, he was one of the leaders of the political struggle for same-sex marriage that followed in the wake of the court judgments. He lost his Charlesbourg–Haute-Saint-Charles seat to a Conservative in the election of January 23, 2006.

Martha McCarthy: A Toronto lawyer with Epstein Cole specializing in family law and constitutional law, she had only two years' professional experience when she began working on the *M. v. H.* case. The Supreme Court's 1999 judgment in that case opened the door to same-sex marriage. She later represented the couples challenging the traditional definition of marriage in Ontario.

Roy McMurtry: After practising law for 17 years, he entered politics in 1975 and was appointed attorney general in the Ontario government of Bill Davis, a position he held until 1985. He was appointed Associate Chief Justice of the Superior Court, Trial Division, in 1991; Chief Justice of that court in 1994; and then Chief Justice of Ontario in 1996. With his colleagues Eileen Gillese and James MacPherson, he wrote the historic judgment that legalized same-sex marriage in Ontario on June 10, 2003.

Réal Ménard: The only openly gay Bloc Québécois member of Parliament, he presented a motion to legally recognize same-sex unions in 1995. He was one of the most passionate advocates of same-sex marriage in Ottawa.

Cynthia Peterson: A Quebec-born Toronto lawyer, she has worked for the gay and lesbian advocacy organization Egale since the beginning of her career. She has acted in many cases of significance to gays and lesbians, including *Egan*, *M. v. H.*, *Vriend* and *Little Sisters*. She was one of the lawyers representing Egale in challenging the traditional definition of marriage in British Columbia.

Svend Robinson: First elected to the House of Commons in 1979, he became the first federal MP to come out as a homosexual in 1988. A tireless gay activist, he introduced the first same-sex marriage bill in March 1998. He did not run for reelection in 2004 and was defeated in his bid to return to the House in 2006.

Vic Toews: A Manitoba cabinet minister (labour and then justice) from 1995 to 1999, he was elected to the House of Commons in 2000. Justice critic for the Canadian Alliance and then for the Conservative Party while in opposition, he orchestrated the opposition to same-sex marriage in Ottawa. He was appointed minister of justice in February 2006.

APPENDIX 2 — CHRONOLOGY

February 11, 1974: In Canada's first same-sex wedding, Richard North and Chris Vogel are married in a Unitarian church in Winnipeg. Their marriage was never registered.

January 1992: Pierre Beaulne and Todd Layland claim the right to be married civilly. Their claim is rejected by the Ontario Divisional Court in 1993.

November 1993: Laval University professor Ann Robinson presents a brief to the Quebec Human Rights Commission advocating recognition of same-sex marriage.

Summer 1997: Michael Hendricks and René LeBœuf "test" the idea of same-sex marriage in Montreal's gay and lesbian pride parade.

November 4, 1997: Martin Dubé and Manuel Gambora are married in a religious service in Montreal. They subsequently try to have their marriage recognized civilly, but to no avail.

September 1998: Michael Hendricks and René LeBœuf begin court proceedings aimed at legalization of same-sex marriage in Quebec.

May 20, 1999: The Supreme Court's landmark ruling in the *M. v. H.* case broadens the definition of the word *spouse* in the Ontario Family Law Act.

May 2000: Michael Leshner and Michael Stark request a marriage licence at Toronto City Hall. City officials refer the matter to the courts. Cynthia Callahan and Judy Lightwater make a similar request in Vancouver.

May 3, 2001: The Supreme Court of British Columbia rules that exclusion of same-sex couples from marriage constitutes discrimination, but that this discrimination is justifiable in a free and democratic society.

July 12, 2002: The Divisional Court of Ontario rules that same-sex marriage must be allowed in the province before July 13, 2004.

November 2002: The House of Commons Standing Committee on Justice and Human Rights begins hearings on same-sex marriage.

May 1, 2003: The British Columbia Court of Appeal rules that same-sex marriage must be allowed in the province before July 13, 2004.

June 10, 2003: As a result of the Ontario Court of Appeal's historic judgment, marriage is immediately opened to same-sex couples in the province.

June 17, 2003: Prime Minister Jean Chrétien announces that the federal government will not appeal the decisions of the British Columbia and Ontario courts of appeal. Draft legislation expanding marriage to include same-sex couples will be referred to the Supreme Court of Canada.

September 16, 2003: By a vote of 137 to 132, the House of Commons rejects a Canadian Alliance motion to reaffirm the traditional definition of marriage.

January 28, 2004: Prime Minister Paul Martin's government announces that a fourth question is being added to the Supreme Court referral: does the exclusion of same-sex couples from marriage violate the Canadian Charter of Rights and Freedoms?

December 9, 2004: In its opinion on the federal government's referral, the Supreme Court confirms that same-sex marriage, "far from violating the Charter, flows from it."

February 1, 2005: Justice Minister Irwin Cotler introduces Bill C-38, stipulating that "marriage, for civil purposes, is the lawful union of two persons to the exclusion of all others."

June 28, 2005: By a 158-133 vote, the House of Commons passes Bill C-38 on third reading.

July 19, 2005: The Senate passes Bill C-38 by a vote of 47 to 21 with three abstentions. It receives royal assent the next day.

January 23, 2006: Canadians elect a Conservative minority government. The Conservative platform includes a promise to hold a free vote on the definition of marriage in the House of Commons and to introduce legislation restoring the traditional definition if a resolution to that effect is passed.

BIBLIOGRAPHY

Alderson, Kevin, and Kathleen Ann Lahey. *Same-Sex Marriage: The Personal and the Political*. Toronto: Insomniac Press, 2004.

Boswell, John. *Same-Sex Unions in Premodern Europe*. New York: Villard Books, 1994.

Bourassa, Kevin, and Joe Varnell. *Just Married: Gay Marriage and the Expansion of Human Rights*. Toronto: Doubleday Canada, 2002.

Chrétien, Jean. *Straight from the Heart*. Toronto: Key Porter, 1985.

Fisher, John, et al. *Outlaws & Inlaws: Your Guide to LGBT Rights, Same-Sex Relationships, and Canadian Law*. Ottawa: Egale Canada, 2004.

Juvenal. *The Sixteen Satires*. Translated by Peter Green. London: Penguin Classics, 1999.

Martial. *Epigrams*. Translated by D.R. Shackleton Bailey. 3 vols. Cambridge, MA: Harvard University Press, 1993.

Montaigne, Michel de. *Complete Works of Montaigne: Essays, Travel, Journal, Letters*. Translated by Donald M. Frame. Stanford, CA: Stanford

University Press, 1958.

Plato. *Complete Works.* Edited by John M. Cooper; Associate Editor D.S. Hutchinson. Cambridge, MA: Hackett Publishing, 1997.

Scott, Ian. *To Make a Difference: A Memoir.* With Neil McCormick. Toronto: Stoddart, 2001.

INDEX